If Only the Earth

Had Been Round

A life restored through faith, hope, love, forgiveness, and a wonderful sense of humor.

Ruth Thielke

By Bridget Harris Volden

As told to Ruth Thielke

All photographs are from Bridget Harris Volden's private collection, except for the picture of Bill Volden with his little dog Ginger and the picture of his mother and father's wedding. Those two pictures were donated by Bill's niece, Nancy Gilbertson, from the Volden family collection.

Cover Picture: Bridget and Nora leaving on the riverboat *Distributor* to spend nine months in the Indian residential boarding school at Fort Providence, 250 miles from their home.

ISBN   978-1-60458-477-6

Published by InstantPublisher.com

InstantPublisher.com
P.O. Box 340, 410 Highway 72 West
Collierville TN 38027

Email: questions@instantpublisher.com

Phone: 1-800-259-2592
1-901-853-7070

First Publication, 2009

Printed in the United States of America

Preface

Most of the stories in this book are from my memory of people, places, and events. No one experiences life in exactly the same way as another person. There will be stories my family and friends recognize, but their recollection may be different than mine, and that is okay. It is those variations that create delightful conversations when we see each other and share our stories. Please read the stories with an open mind as I invite you to look at the life I experienced through my eyes.

Another important differentiation should be made between my painful experiences in the Catholic residential school and the way those schools are today. Much has happened in Canada to make changes in the way children are treated in the indigenous schools, especially in recent years.

Also, the Catholic church is not the same today as it was when I was a child. I am thankful to those I learned to know in the Catholic church over the years who treated me with genuine love and kindness as they reflect the life they found in Jesus.

– Bridget Volden –

The University of Minnesota, Morris is mentioned in this book as a point of interest. In the late 1800's their campus was the grounds of an Indian residential school with some similarities to the school at Fort Providence that Bridget Harris Volden attended as a young girl. The University of Minnesota in compliance with Equal Opportunity places the same value on all religions and creeds.

Among our nation's many strengths, is the freedom of religion protected in our constitution's Bill of Rights. Each citizen has the freedom to choose and practice their religious faith. As an individual Bridget's description of her Christian faith which is rich and meaningful, has had a profound effect in her personal life. After the children of Israel came out of Egypt, as Joshua[1] was about to lead them across the Jordan River, he said, "Choose for yourselves this day whom you will serve . . .. As for me and my house, we will serve the Lord." Bridget and I have each chosen to serve the same Lord, who called his son Jesus.

– Ruth Thielke –

---

[1] Joshua 24:15, *NIV*

3

Acknowledgements

There are so many people who have worked together to make this book possible. Thanks to my nephew Gary Gilbertson for introducing me to Ruth and Neil Thielke. Thanks to Neil for encouraging me to write this book, and for allowing his wife Ruth to tape and transcribe our conversations, put our conversations into story form, and researched for documented information about my dad and other details in the book. Thanks for Gary's sister, Nancy Gilbertson, for hosting Ruth last summer when she attended the writer's conference. Thanks to Mary Lou Potts for going the extra mile beyond helping me with business affairs, to helping in so many other ways, including hosting Ruth on some of her visits to Helena, Montana as we continued to work on the book. Thanks to Mary Lou, Ruth's sister Jeannine Churchill and Ruth's friends Karla Klinger and Steve Granger who served as readers spotting so many details that needed attention in the book's early draft. Thank you, Kit and Debbie Elford, for hosting us as we were putting the final touches on the book. Thank you, Kit, for reading the book, and making so many helpful comments. Your experience in book publishing has been so valuable! Thank you to my sister Rose for visiting with us and supplying some delightful stories from growing up together and as adults. Thank you to Nora and her daughters for helping check some of the details about our family. I couldn't have written this without all of you.

There are also many people who have supported me throughout my lifetime, including employers who believed I could do more than I thought of myself. I am thankful to my family who provided me with such a good home to grow up in, and so much love and support throughout my lifetime. I am so thankful for my husband Bill, the best lifetime companion I could have ever imagined. Thank you to Rose Kostashen and her mother for providing me with family life and a place to live when I needed them most. In my churches in Minneapolis, Great Falls, and Helena I have had so many loving, supportive friends. Thank you to all who helped with The American Indian Bible Fellowship, especially the Macketys, Art Holmes, and John Bobolink, as well as those who served on the board of directors, and those who helped serve meals and with cleanup. Thank you to the pastors of Augustana Lutheran Church who allowed those meetings to be held in the church fellowship hall, especially Pastor William Berg and John Bohnsack. Special thanks to all of my friends in Alcoholics Anonymous who supported me through many struggles and have always *been there for me*. I couldn't have made it without all of you.

I am especially thankful to my Lord and Savior, Jesus Christ, who gave me new life when mine was broken, who gave me hope for a better tomorrow, and who filled my heart with love when I thought I was totally empty.

– Bridget Harris Volden

Map of North and Western Canada[2]

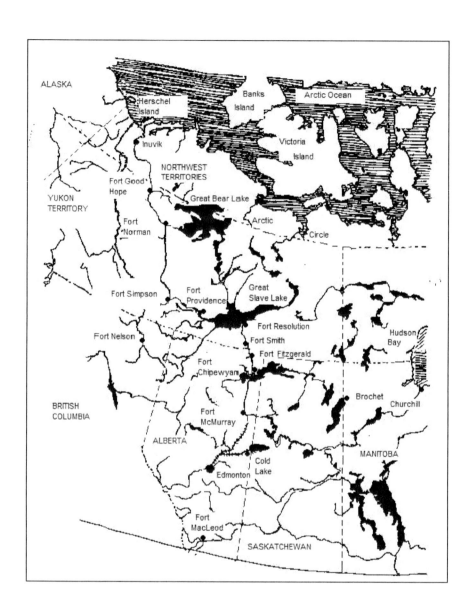

Foreword
by Ruth Thielke

Brisk gusts frothed the tips of the waves against the current on the Mackenzie as the riverboat *The Distributor*[3] was loaded for the last trip up river in the summer of 1927. The four-level stern wheeler had compartments for the passengers on the two lower decks with stairways from deck to deck. Life rafts hung over the sides on the second deck. Above the second deck was a smaller room where the crew and passengers could observe the country. Above the observation deck was the captain's deck. The engine was chugging in port ready to turn the paddles that would send the boat eastward toward the river's source at Great Slave Lake.

The most precious cargo were two frightened little Harris girls, Bridget age eight and her sister Nora age six, making their first voyage to the Fort Providence Indian Residential School (IRS). Their older brother Jim age ten was along on the trip, but he would be taken to the boys' side of the school once they arrived. The children were traveling over two hundred fifty miles away from their parents.

---

[3] Pencil drawing by Ruth Thielke from photograph.

Jim, Bridget, and Nora would be frozen in for nine long months where the sun barely creeps over the tree tops in the deep of winter.

Had the children been with their father on his summer visits to the villages along the 2,500 miles of the Mackenzie River, they would have been bursting with excitement. But their frightened hearts were breaking as they were separated from their protective father and their gentle loving mother. Josette Harris, the children's mother, was of the Chipewyan Tribe near Cold Lake, Alberta. Their father, T. W. (Flynn) Harris was of Irish descent, and served for twenty years as an Indian Agent in Fort Simpson, Northwest Territories where he became the Commissioner of Treaty 11.

Mr. Harris paid tuition for his children to attend the Catholic IRS in Fort Providence because there were no other schools along the Mackenzie River. Although many of the children were abused at the school, Bridget seemed to have been singled out for prolonged harsh treatment at the hands of the Grey Nuns. Bridget tells of the things she suffered between the ages of eight to thirteen at the residential school later in this book.

In 1957 a principal on a review board of Indian Residential Schools made the following observation of the Fort Providence IRS, "I would sooner have a child of mine in a reform school than in this dreadful institution[4]."

When Bridget appeared before the Indian Residential Schools Truth and Reconciliation Commission in 2006[5], the adjudicator's evaluation of Bridget's spoken testimony stated:

> Mrs. Volden claims that she was physically abused while in attendance at Fort Providence IRS. Further, that the physical injuries lasted more than six weeks and . . . should have led to hospitalization or serious medical treatment by a physician and permanent or demonstrated long-term physical injury. I find, on the balance of probability, that Mrs. Volden was physically assaulted while in attendance at Fort Providence IRS. I find . . . wrongful confinement and a physical assault resulting in long-term physical injury. Mrs. Volden is an elder of eighty-seven years. She gave her evidence in a straightforward and eloquent manner and responded

---

[4] 216. NAC RG85, volume 1224, file 630/110-3 (6), To R.G Robertson from..., 19 November 1957. Correspondent not identified for reasons of confidentiality.

[5] On June 29, 2006, at the age of 87 years, Bridget (Harris) Volden was invited by the Indian Residential Schools Truth and Reconciliation Commission in Lethbridge, Alberta, Canada, to testify of possible wrongful treatment at the Indian residential school in Fort Providence.

to all questions in a forthright and honest manner. This adjudicator was never, throughout the course of her evidence, led to believe that she embellished or exaggerated her evidence. I found her recollection of persons, places and events to be remarkable. I accept Mrs. Volden's evidence as trustworthy and credible. All parties present at the hearing were struck with the intensity of her recollection of particularly disturbing memories.

June 11, 2008 was an historic day in Canadian History as Prime Minister Stephen Harper issued a public statement of apology in the House of Commons of the Canadian Parliament for treatment of indigenous children and their separation from their families and villages in the IRS system. The prime minister's apology representing the Canadian government and the response of Phil Fontaine, National Chief of Canada, representing the people of the First Nations of Canada was an important step toward healing the wounds inflicted by the boarding schools.

Prime Minister Harper's apology marked a significant new beginning for Canada, but as National Chief Fontaine stated in his response to the apology, there is still much work to be done. The benefits of the apology can only be achieved as future generations continue to build bridges of appreciation, honor, respect, understanding and forgiveness between cultures. On that historic day in the House of Commons of the Canadian Parliament, several people from the First Nations bravely shared their stories of the abuse they had suffered while attending an IRS.

The full text of Prime Minister Harper's speech is provided in the appendix of this book by permission. Also in the appendix is the text of National Chief Fontaine's response given immediately following the Prime Minister's apology.

When Bridget at eighty-nine years of age heard of the Prime Minister's apology she burst into tears. Then she said, "This will help the healing begin for my people."

Bridget tells her story of the abuses she suffered at the Fort Providence IRS, the painful memories that led to her alcoholism, and of overcoming fears and bitterness as she allowed Jesus to heal her hurts. Healing from residual pain continues today as Bridget turns her memories over to the One who suffered for her on the cross so long ago, providing forgiveness not only for Bridget, but for her tormenters as well.

We Are Introduced to Bridget
By Ruth Thielke

I lift up my eyes to the hills —
   Where does my help come from?
My help comes from the Lord,
   the Maker of heaven and earth. Psalm 121:1-3 (*NIV*)

"You should write a book. I love your story. I think it is better than what people dream up and write in fiction books, because it is a true story and it's an incredible story! Not only that, it's a human interest story. People are interested in indigenous peoples and their assimilation into other cultures. It's like God is saying, 'Bridget, your life has meaning'!" my husband Neil exclaimed.

Bridget (Harris) Volden was sharing her experiences growing up in Fort Simpson in the Northwest Territories. Her life journey has taken her from Fort Simpson, to the Fort Providence IRS, and to Fort Good Hope, in the Northwest Territories; to Cold Lake and to Edmonton, in Alberta; to Brooklyn, New York; to Minneapolis, Minnesota; to Cedar Rapids, Iowa; back to Minneapolis; and then out to Great Falls and Helena, Montana

"I have thought of writing a book some day," Bridget said, "and I know what the title would be: *If Only the Rod Had Been Round.*"

"Why would you pick that title?" Neil asked.

"Because the rod the nuns beat me with in the boarding school when I was a little girl was square, and it hurt so badly when they hit me," Bridget explained hoisting her sleeve to expose her disfigured left wrist. "See that wrist?" Bridget asked. "One of the nuns beat me until my wrist broke because I was left-handed. She made sure I never used that hand again. The fracture was never set because we didn't have doctors at the school. It was like being in *prison.*

"Remember, in the beginning I didn't know Jesus. I knew a God of fear only. When I was in the Catholic boarding school I never knew that God really cared for me, forgave me – all that. I often say that if the white people had taken the time to really know the Indian people who lived on this land from the beginning of time, to learn their language, to understand how they lived, we could have all gotten along. Instead the whites had the attitude, 'I don't like your braids. You have to cut them off and put on this uniform!' They tried to take the *Indian-ness* out of the Indian people. Even the nuns, who were supposed to bring the love of Jesus, tried to change the Indian culture instead of just allowing Jesus to change our hearts with his love."

Neil suggested, "Let's open with prayer, and then we want to hear how your heart was changed as you came to know the Creator God who loves you." Neil prayed, "Lord, we thank you today for Bridget. Thank you for that little Indian gal from the Northwest Territories who went through indescribable pain. In the midst of all that, Jesus, you had a part to play in her life that goes beyond her. You have allowed her to tell other people that story, because it's important to you, Lord. We ask, Lord, that you will help us to be aware of your unseen hand. We pray that her story will be more than just her story, but also Your story of what You were doing in her life. We ask, Lord, that you will be here in the room with us as the story unfolds, bringing things to mind for Bridget to tell. We ask this in Jesus' name. Amen."

Bridget's life springs from the story of her mother's and father's marriage, which took place as their two cultures were being forged together to form the nation of Canada. Flynn and Josette Harris's children were born at the time when the Canadian government was enacting laws for the process of assimilation in the schools, empowering educators to take the *Indian-ness* out of the Indian children to turn them into Canadian citizens. It was through the children the Canadian government expected that change to occur. Indian children were to be separated from their parents and placed into boarding schools that would not only educate, but also *Christianize* the students. What the government meant by *Christianization* was unquestioning adherence to rules and forms of behavior, not the discovery of Jesus' love for them that would change hearts and set their spirits free from shame and condemnation. Bridget's parents were unwitting participants in that process until they discovered the damage that was occurring in Bridget's young life.

Bridget's story only begins with her boarding school experiences, however. The beatings Bridget suffered at the school played a large role in her ongoing struggle with alcoholism. In her young adult life, Bridget turned to alcohol to block the memories of the beatings at the boarding school.

But Bridget's story is also one of forgiveness and restoration. Bridget's life was restored and her marriage renewed when she and her husband Bill turned their lives over to Jesus. Bridget and Bill

11

Volden were able to forgive each other, to share their love for Jesus with each other, and to pray and read their Bibles together. Their relationship with God and with each other began to bring joy into their lives.

Neil and I were introduced to Bridget by her husband's nephew, Gary Gilbertson, a longtime friend of ours. Neil and Gary are fellow pastors in the True Bridge network of non-denominational churches out of Eden Prairie, Minnesota.[6] Neil and Gary became even closer friends teaching together in a school of ministry in central Siberia for five weeks in 1996.

Bridget's husband, Bill Volden grew up in Morris, Minnesota, across the street from our house. When Bill died in 2004, Bridget followed Bill's instructions and arranged for his burial next to his mother's grave in Summit Cemetery at Morris, Minnesota. When Bridget flew from Helena, Montana, to Minneapolis, Gary brought her to Morris. En route Gary called his friend Neil to request help in locating the grave site. Even in this, God was watching out for Bridget.

Neil and I knew how to find the cemetery, which is at the end of our block right next to the University of Minnesota, Morris campus. But we didn't have the foggiest idea where to begin to look for Bill's grave! As Gary parked his car, we noticed the caretaker of the cemetery working close by. The caretaker certainly noticed Gary, who drives a converted hearse for transporting young people to ministry functions. The caretaker had the map of the cemetery in his truck, and was able to walk us right to the place where Bill had been buried.

Bridget took time to remember Bill, talking to him as if he was present in spirit, and shedding her tears beside Bill's grave. Although Bridget didn't have much of an appetite, we accompanied Gary and Bridget for lunch at Don's Café in downtown Morris, famous for its gargantuan home-cooked meals. Over lunch, Bridget told of growing up along the Mackenzie River where her Irish father had been known as *The Famous Flynn Harris*. Bridget's mother was from the Chipewyan First Nations band on the Onion Lake Reserve near Cold Lake, Alberta.

---

[6] Neil Thielke is the founding pastor of Morris Community Church; Morris, Minnesota. Gary Gilbertson was the head pastor of New Covenant Church in Northfield, Minnesota, for many years before starting Prepare Campus Ministries, whose offices are at City Hill Church in Eden Prairie, Minnesota.

Bridget's father-in-law, Ed Volden, was Business Manager and Registrar of the University of Minnesota's West Central School and Experiment Station (fondly known as the *Ag School*) in Morris for forty years from 1915 to 1955.

Bridget's story intrigued me. Before my retirement in 2005, I had been Registrar at the four-year liberal arts campus of the University of Minnesota that replaced the Ag School. Until she met us that day, Bridget didn't know the campus of the University of Minnesota, Morris was originally the site of the Morris Indian School started by the Sisters of Mercy, a Catholic order, in 1887. Bridget attended a Catholic residential school as a child, but her school was very different.

In the early stages of providing education for Indian children to fulfill treaty obligations, as in Canada, the United States government welcomed help from churches. Most of the students in the Morris Indian School came from the Turtle Mountain Ojibwa tribe located near Pembina, ND. The Morris Indian School was run so well by the Sisters of Mercy there were no incidents of abuse or of the children running away. Corporal punishment of any kind was not allowed; the children were well fed and looked after. Parents willingly enrolled their students, even though they were far from home. The Sisters of Mercy were commended in 1895 by the Office of Indian Affairs for a job well done. Nonetheless, in 1896 in the midst of a nation-wide financial recession, the Sisters of Mercy had to sell the school for lack of funding.

The only available purchaser for the Morris Indian School was the Office of Indian Affairs (OIA) in the federal government. The school was not well administered under the OIA. As enrollment declined, students were not allowed to return home for holidays or vacations in an effort to retain them. This only angered parents who found other schools for their children to attend, causing enrollments to fall even further.

The OIA replaced their first superintendent with a man who rehired the Indian staff, and was able to make improvements in the administration of the school. Problems with low enrollment continued, however, as schools became available on reservations, and a school similar to the Morris Indian School was built at Wahpeton, North Dakota. The Wahpeton school was much closer to the students' homes.

The main reason for the Morris Indian School closing its doors was lack of finances that were ultimately enrollment related due to reasons stated above. On March 3, 1909,[7] the U.S. Congress deeded the Morris Indian School to the State of Minnesota on the condition "that Indian pupils shall at all times be admitted to school free of charge for tuition and on terms of equality with white students."[8]

In 1910 the West Central School of Agriculture (WCSA) began and continued until 1963. The college at the University of Minnesota, Morris campus started in the fall of 1960 and today is one of the leading four-year public liberal arts colleges in the nation. Many Native Americans from across the United States have completed their Bachelor of Arts degree at the University of Minnesota, Morris, utilizing the tuition waiver provided by the 1909 Congressional transfer of the Morris Indian School to the State of Minnesota.

Bridget's father-in-law Ed Volden never mentioned either the Morris Indian School that preceded the Ag School or the tuition waiver for Indian students. If he had, Bridget would have felt an immediate bond with her father-in-law. Perhaps Ed made no mention of the Indian school, because the tuition waiver was not widely publicized during the time of the Ag School. Although the Morris Indian School had once been the largest Indian residential school in Minnesota, only two Indian students attended the Ag School from 1910 to 1963.

After her husband died in 2004, Bridget came back to Morris to visit her Billy's grave each year. Each year Bridget joined us for lunch while we heard more of her story. When my husband Neil asked Bridget how her book was coming, the answer was always the same; she was having difficulty getting started. In May of 2007, Neil asked Bridget if I could help write her story. Bridget thought that might move things forward.

In one conversation, Bridget told us, "They called my papa *The Famous Flynn Harris*."

"What made him famous?" I asked.

"I don't know," Bridget said, "We just called him *Papa*."

Writers in the early 1900's were eager to capture the excitement of the vast unexplored regions of Canada. Bridget remembers her father, T. W. (Flynn) Harris, was approached by authors and

---

[7] While Ruth Thielke was Registrar, she was proactive in protecting the integrity of the tuition waiver. Ruth graduated from the campus in 1969, began working there in 1971, and served as Registrar from 1978-2005.

[8] History of the Morris Indian School is from Wilbert H. Ahern – "Indian Education and Bureaucracy: The School at Morris, 1887-1909," *Minnesota History*, 49 (1984), pp. 84-98.

journalists who wanted to write his story. Flynn turned them away by saying, "If my story is to be written, it will be written by one of my children someday." In the opening chapters of her book, Bridget fulfills that aspect of her Papa's desires.

This book contains Flynn's story as the backdrop for Bridget's life story. Flynn fought a war of diplomacy in Parliament alongside his friend Bishop Breynat defending the Indian people as the westward movement of European settlers threatened the Indian way of life. Bridget learned from her father's courage and leadership to overcome her fears in the face of life's challenges.

Bridget's story is also a story of salvation and healing as God rescued one of his beloved children from destruction. At a breaking point in her marriage, Bridget discovered God's love in her most desperate hour. As Bridget talked to the living Christ, Jesus delivered her from her addiction to alcohol. God turned evil into good in Bridget's life as she entrusted her life to Jesus. In gratitude, Bridget shared her new freedom in Jesus with as many people as she could. God inspired Bridget to help establish the American Indian Bible Fellowship in downtown Minneapolis which she led for ten years.

Now as Bridget has reached her ninetieth year, it is her hope that Indians and non-Indians alike will read her story and find freedom in Jesus, so that her story can be forever entwined not only in HIS story, but in yours as well.

Flynn Seeks Adventure

In his heart a man plans his course, but the Lord determines his steps. Proverbs 16:9 (*NIV*)

I didn't know much about my Harris ancestors or Papa's early years, but documents Ruth Thielke found on the internet provide the parts of his story I don't recall. Our Harris ancestry was not important to Papa, but knowing a little bit about them, helps me understand what type of life Papa left behind as he headed west. I will refer to Papa by his nickname *Flynn* in the parts of the story that are not from memory.

Loyalists and Revolutionaries

As revolutionary fever mounted in the American colonies, many English citizens remained loyal to the British Crown, living under growing pressure and fear from the colonists who wanted to break free from British dominion. About the same time across the border in Canada, an ongoing power struggle between the French and British displaced many French citizens. To solidify their presence, England offered land grants to the loyalists from the American colonies. The New England migration to Kings County, Nova Scotia in 1760-1761 brought a sudden influx of between 6,000 to 7,000 people.

The earliest person traced on my father's side was Lieutenant James Harris[9] of New London, Connecticut, who served in the British army when American colonies were under the British crown. In 1761, Lt. Harris's seventh child, Lebbeus Harris, was among the land owners from Connecticut who moved their families to Horton, Nova Scotia.[10]

The Harris Family in Nova Scotia[11]

The move to Nova Scotia proved economically beneficial to the Harris family. Lebbeus was given an officer's commission in a company of militia in Kings County upon his arrival in 1761 and served in many appointed government positions during his lifetime.

---

[9] See Appendices, "The Harris Family." Lt. Harris was born in Boston, Mass. April 4, 1673, and died in Feb. 1757.

[10] Horton was later named Kentville.

[11] Taken from *The History of Kings County*, by Arthur Wentworth Hamilton Eaton, M. A., D. C. L. (The Salem Press Co., Salem, Mass.: 1918) Facsimile edition printed by Mika Studio, ISBN 0-919302-49-1, Belleville, Ontario, 1972. Hereafter referred to as *History of King's County*. Also available on the web.

In addition to managing large tracts of highly productive farm land, Lebbeus owned one of the large mercantile stores in Horton.

Thaddeus Harris was the fifth child of Lebbeus and Alice Harris. When his father's mercantile burned, Thaddeus rebuilt the store which became one of the major stores in Kentville, remaining in the family for several generations.

Thaddeus's son, James Delap Harris and his wife Wilhelmina were for many years considered among the most important people not only in Kings County, but also in the province of Nova Scotia. James was one of the two early successful Kentville merchants and held several important government positions, including being appointed Judge of the Inferior Court of Common Pleas for Kings County in 1840.

Judge Harris and his family lived in one of the four most conspicuous houses in Kings County, built in the style of an Italian villa. His family attended St. John's, an Anglican Church in Cornwallis. Their second daughter, Rachel Ana, a gentle, cultivated, charitable woman, and a devoted, unselfish friend, was deeply loved by citizens of Kings County.

Harsh Discipline Scatters the Harris Children

> Better a dry crust with peace and quiet than a house full of feasting, with strife. Proverbs 17:1 (*NIV*)

Thomas William Harris, Barrister and Attorney, Q. C., the fourth child of the Hon. James Delap Harris and another respected leader in Kentville, was appointed Barrister in Kings County in 1860, 1867, and 1876. Thomas married Marie Sophia Fowler, and they raised their family in Kentville. Their eight children were John Inglis, Thaddeus, Frances, Wilhelmina Wemyss, James, Mary Owen, Thomas William, Jr., and a child who died young. Thomas William, Jr. was my papa.

Papa's life began on February 12, 1861 during the period of exploration of the western half of North America, as the United States and Canada extended their borders from ocean to ocean. Canada became a self-governing dominion in 1867. During Papa's teenage years the eastern seaboard of North America was buzzing with news of frontiers as Canada and the United States were opening new provinces and states for settlement.

Anything but "Country Cousins" at the time of Papa's birth, the United States and Canada were still ironing out protocol on how to respect each others' borders and work out a neighborly peace. Both settlers and Indians moved back and forth across the unmarked borders that stretched for almost 2,000 miles from the Great Lakes to the Pacific. In the early years of settlement the Canadian military peace keepers were the newly created North-West Mounted Police (NWMP)[12], who would soon find a willing recruit in Thomas William Harris, Jr. as he sought freedom and adventure.

Papa did not talk much about his family, but he did tell us that his father who followed strict Protestant beliefs was a powerful man of wealth and influence. Papa also told us that his father, Thomas Harris, Sr., was a harsh disciplinarian feared by his children. Even though they were raised as Protestants, two of Papa's sisters, Wilhelmina Wemyss Harris and Mary Owen Harris left home to become cloistered nuns.

Papa ran away from home at the young age of thirteen as a stowaway on a ship bound for Ireland. He planned to look up his uncle Charles in Ireland in the hope that his uncle would treat him well. However, Papa was soon discovered on board, and was treated badly by the sailors. They kicked him from one end of the ship to the other, but he said it made a man out of him. When another ship was sighted heading for Canada, Papa was sent back.[13]

After returning to Canada, Papa was sheltered by Jesuit monks in a Montreal monastery. Although his family was Protestant, Papa became a good Catholic while living with the Jesuits, and he was given a wonderful education. He learned to read, write and speak well in English, Latin, and French, studied the Bible, history, and classical literature, and prepared to become a priest. When Papa was near completion of his studies, the Archbishop told the candidates for the priesthood, "Go back home for a month and see if this is what you are called to do. At the end of the month, if you still want to be a priest, come back and you will be ordained." The Archbishop set their date for ordination and sent them on their way.

Papa had no home other than the monastery, so he did what many Irishmen of the area tended to do; he went on a long drunk. He woke one day thinking, "I'd better go become a priest." When he returned to the monastery *way* past ordination, the Archbishop met

---

[12] Northwest Mounted Police referred to as NWMP throughout remainder of book.
[13] Some stories Papa told come from a journal I wrote in 1971 while trying to capture those memories.

Papa at the top of the stairs, "Flynn, you don't belong here. Go back to the world with the rest of the devils."

Papa was *happy*! He didn't *want* to be a priest, so he headed west, following the path of adventure all the way to North Battleford in western Canada. He lost all contact with his family, but years later when he married, Papa honored his ancestors and siblings by selecting some of their names for his own children.

Enlisting as a Constable in the NWMP, 1886

At the age of twenty-five years and five months, on July 20, 1886, at Fort MacLeod, Flynn signed on as a constable with the NWMP.

In Flynn's military service file the medical examiner noted his light brown hair, light brown eyes, and circular scars on his left leg. What caused the scars? An accident perhaps as he traveled west? Had his cruel father whipped him? Was he put in leg irons when he was a stowaway on the ship? Whatever had happened, there were circular scars on his leg worth noting as identification marks. In 1886 Flynn skimmed past the height requirement of five feet six inches by a mere one and a half inches and only reached the chest requirement of thirty-five inches when he took a deep breath. At his discharge, his chest measured fifty-five inches. He may have been hungry traveling all the way across Canada from Nova Scotia to Fort MacLeod, he may have been well fed in the NWMP, and the military may have had an awesome body building regiment in their basic training. Whatever the cause, it is rather remarkable that his chest expanded by twenty inches in just under five years.

On the day of his enlistment, July 20th, 1886, Flynn signed the following Oath of Allegiance to the queen:

> I, Thomas William Harris, do sincerely promise and swear, that I will be faithful, and bear true allegiance to Her Majesty Queen Victoria, as lawful Sovereign of the United Kingdom of Great Britain and Ireland, and of this Dominion of Canada ... and all this I do swear, without any equivocation, mental evasion, or secret reservation. So help me God.[14]

Flynn also signed the NWMP Engagement form on July 20, 1886 at Fort MacLeod:

> I, Thomas William Harris, do hereby contract . . . to . . . serve in such Police Force for Five years from Twentieth day of July AD 1886

---

[14] NWMP - Personnel Records, 1873-1904. Hereafter referred to as NWMP Personnel Records.

. . . and that I will . . . take care of and protect all articles of public property . . . and make good all deficiencies and damages occurring to such property while in my care or possession . . .. And I do hereby decree and admit that by reason of such engagement no right accrues to me for any transfer of expenses returning from the North-West Territories of Canada on being discharged.[15]

Flynn's Engagement papers list his previous occupation as "student", and previous service with the "68th". There was a 68th King's County Regiment of Canadian Militia[16] in Kentville, Nova Scotia. Flynn may have trained there as a militia volunteer before heading west. On his enlistment papers for the NWMP his religion is listed as Roman Catholic.

Ah, what a handsome character Papa must have been in his bright red coat with shiny brass buttons, mandarin-style collar, black pants with a yellow stripe down the side, tall black shining boots to the knees, tall hat shaped to a point with a wide brim, long leather gauntlets, and riding a black horse!

Papa told us a story about a wild horse that needed to be tamed to ride, but no one had been able to get near the horse, let alone put a bridle or saddle on it. Papa was finally able to get close enough to climb on the horse's back. The horse started snorting and bucking with the fury of a wild stallion. Papa hung on to the horse's mane for all he was worth. They were on a high plateau, and the horse began racing toward the precipice which would mean certain death. The only thing Papa could think of doing was striking the horse as hard as he could just behind the ears. The horse fell to the ground just a few feet from the edge of the cliff, and Papa leaped to safety.

A year before Papa was in the Mounties, the Indian way of life was seriously being threatened by the encroachment of white settlers. Several treaties had been broken, the buffalo were beginning to disappear on the plains, and many Indians were nearing starvation. Louis Riel, an educated Indian who was half French, led the Indian people in a resistance movement called The Northwest Rebellion. One of the worst massacres of the resistance happened at nearby Frog Lake where two priests and several residents were brutally killed.

---

[15] Ibid.
[16] *History of King's County*, page 438.

Although the Indian resistance was put down in 1885, the Canadian government began to realize how serious the deprivation had become for the Indian people and began to take steps to improve their conditions. Papa's regiment was dispatched among a band of Chipewyan Indians to keep the peace on the Le Goff Reserve. The reserve was named after their priest, Father R. P. Le Goff.

Papa fell in love with the ways of the Indian. He saw how *vulnerable* they were, how *peace-loving* they were, and how they treated one another *so well*. The Chipewyan respected their elders, and they *shared* food with each other. Right then and there Papa decided to learn the Cree and Chipewyan languages. Papa's Indian scout J. B. (Jean Baptiste) Ennow, a Chipewyan Indian from Cold Lake, became one of Papa's lifelong friends. Whatever knowledge and education Papa possessed, J. B. Ennow could match in practical skill, wisdom, and understanding. Both men were extremely intelligent natural leaders, and they had a mutual love and respect for each other.

When we were children, Papa told us exciting stories about his life as a mountie. One day Papa and J. B. were completely surrounded by buffalo. J. B. told Papa to lie down to pretend they were dead. They held their breath so long, J. B. thought they might become dead, so they yelled at the top of their lungs and frightened the buffalo away.

Another time Papa had to rescue a mother whose child had died. The mother was mentally handicapped, and lived in a teepee by the creek on the reserve. Someone had taken advantage of her, and she bore a child. People in her tribe kept an eye on her to make sure she had food and supplies, because she lived alone. One day when someone checked on her, her child had died, and the woman had her dead baby in her arms. The people in her tribe tried to coax her to give them the child, but she would not let them take the baby from her. For two weeks her people tried to help the woman understand, but she hung on to the baby with even more determination.

The Indian people did not know how to remedy the situation, and asked the NWMP to help. Papa was chosen for the task. Papa brought the woman some food to cook in her pot outside her teepee. He suggested that she lay the baby down while she fetched water from the stream to cook her food. By this time the dead baby smelled so badly, Papa could hardly bear to be near it, but when the woman went to fetch water, Papa pickup up the baby, wrapped it in a blanket, and mounted his horse. To stay as far from the stench of death as possible, Papa held the baby at arm's length. Then Papa began walking his horse the eight miles back to the mission on the reserve. It took a long time, because the mother followed on foot. Papa's arm grew heavy until it ached too much to hold the baby away from himself. Then he moved the baby to the other arm until that arm got tired. When they got back, he was able to provide a proper burial for the child. Papa said that was his toughest assignment in his five years with the NWMP. The woman returned to her tribe where her relatives looked after her until she lived to an old age.

Mustering Out of the NWMP, 1891

While Flynn was protecting the Indian people as a Mountie near the Le Goff reserve, the teacher at one of the Indian schools left in the middle of the year. Father Le Goff knew that Flynn had the proper credentials to be a teacher in a Catholic school. Father Le Goff sent a letter[17] requesting that Flynn fill out the teaching year at the Beaver River school with the following conditions:

January 25, 1891
Thos. William Harris, Constable, Battleford

My dear Sir,

The following are the conditions which I offer you, besides the government pay which is yours solely, you would receive from me, on condition that you keep me in board, and do all in your power for me, such as, putting up my hay, or at least helping me to put it up, hauling it, hauling my wood, and water also, taking care of my horses, (which Mr. Todd does, and Lake d'Orgny for the Reverend Father Dauphin), for the sum of $250, (two hundred and fifty piashes, not in cash, but payable at my small shop.)

If you arrive before sowing time, we shall try to enlarge my little garden for you, and to sow in it potatoes, some cabbages, carrots, onions, etc., which will be of great use to you in the kitchen. Of course you will get a nice little woman, who will both cook for us and make our beds.

Awaiting your answer I remain, my dear sir,
Your devoted servant,
R. P. Le Goff[18]

---

[17] NWMP Personnel Records
[18] Ibid.

Flynn was willing to set aside his remaining months of promised service to the Queen. He lost no time in requesting permission to purchase an *early out* from his military duties from the NWMP. Flynn did not have long to wait for the reply which was dated February 2, 1891.

Things are not always as easy as they seem, however. Separation from the force seems to have bogged down a bit at this point. It may have taken the administration a little time to determine what to charge Flynn to purchase his early release. Flynn mustered out his remaining pay of twenty dollars and fifteen cents for thirty-one days in the month of March, and on April 1, 1891 he became a teacher at the Beaver River school for the Chipewyan people at the Onion Lake Agency in the province of Alberta, Canada.

Flynn's term of service went on record as approximately three and a half months short of the five contracted years of engagement. The purchase of his release at fifty dollars was rather expensive for Flynn, considering what a dollar was worth in 1891 and just how little a soldier was paid. In addition Flynn's discharge was stamped with the words: "This discharge does not entitle the person named therein to a Free Grant of Land."

Papa had been rejected from the priesthood as a young man, and now he was denied the free grant of land given the NWMP upon completion of their full term of service. Nevertheless he received benefits that could never be taken from him. The tasks Papa had been assigned in the NWMP would be the very duties Papa would carry out years later as an Indian agent providing a foundation for his life's journey. Although mistreated by his parents, Papa had a loving Father in Heaven who was looking out for him. Papa hungered for a home where people cared about him and where he could also love and care for others. He was soon to find that acceptance and sense of *home* among the Indian people.

At the time of his discharge, Flynn returned the following items to Her Majesty the Queen[19], via the NWMP in Fort MacLeod:

---

[19] Ibid.

1 pair boots, long
1 pair cloth breeches
3 pair blankets
1 blanket strap
1 burnisher
1 bridle
1 cloth belt
1 cloth cloak
1 cloth cape
1 forage cap
1 fur cap

1 buckskin gauntlet
1 helmet
1 haversack
1 kit bag
1 pair mitts
1 pillow case
1 rug
1 waterproof sheet
1 pair jack spurs
1 cloth tunic
1 surge tunic

A Place to Call Home

God sets the lonely in families . ... Psalm 68:6a, (NIV)

At the La Goff Reserve near Onion Lake my mother's people were becoming good farmers, especially in the care of livestock. They were harvesting enough grain to supplement their food supplies, and therefore didn't need to be given as much flour from Indian Affairs.

Agent George G. Mann noted in his 1891 report to Indian Affairs, "The Indians no longer use blankets for clothing. Both men and women make it an object to dress as respectably as their limited means allow." With one of the first saw mills in western Canada, my people enthusiastically cut 1,700 trees in the first year of production to improve their buildings on the reserve, even replacing thatched roofs with wooden shingles. [20]

According to Agent Mann the Beaver River band of Indians where Flynn was teaching, *lived by the chase*, tending cattle, raising horses, and growing garden produce like turnips and potatoes.[21] While teaching at Beaver River, Flynn improved his use of the Chipewyan and Cree languages. Flynn was greatly loved by his students who were extremely attentive and anxious to learn.[22] Flynn's teaching was praised in Inspector Albert Bourtenay's 1892 report on Roman Catholic Industrial Schools:

Beaver Reserve
Mr. T.W. Harris teaches here; he has a Bachelor of Arts from the University of Acadia. The school has been in operation for a little more than a year, and the pupils have prospered greatly during that short period.[23]

Flynn settled into the rigorous life of the young teacher, organizing lessons for the Indian children at various age levels, and working hard for his room and board. In addition to his teaching duties, T. W. (Flynn) Harris was appointed Justice of the Peace in

---

[20] DOMINION OF CANADA. ANNUAL REPORT OF THE DEPARTMENT OF INDIAN AFFAIRS FOR THE YEAR ENDED 31st DECEMBER, 1891. (Page 115) Hereafter these reports will be referred to as *Indian Affairs Report*.
[21] Ibid.
[22] Ibid.
[23] 1892 Indian Affairs Report, Reports of Superintendents and Agents, pp 195-196.

1892.[24] Flynn soon became an integral part of Indian life on the reserve.

Papa had not forgotten the suggestion from Father Le Goff, "Of course you will get a nice little woman, who will both cook for us and make our beds." Papa might also have wanted help with the long list of daily chores he was expected to complete in addition to teaching, but he wanted more than a hired maid. Ever since running away from his parents, Papa had longed for a home of his own.

Papa soon found a *nice little woman* among the Indian people. On April 18, 1892, near the end of his first full year of teaching at the Beaver River school, Papa married Judith Scani, a Chipewyan Indian. Their marriage ceremony was performed by Father Le Goff at Le Goff, Alberta. Judith, daughter of Jean and Charlotte Scani, was only fourteen. Although it was not unusual in those early days on the frontier for brides to be in their mid-teens, Papa at thirty-one was over twice her age.

Papa treated Judith with respect. He patiently waited three years allowing Judith's relationship with him to grow before they became parents. Their first daughter, Francoise Sara Harris was born on September 18, 1895. Their second daughter, Wilhelmina Weams Campbell Harris was born February 18, 1901. Life seemed good, but without warning, tragedy struck.

Judith developed a cough that wouldn't go away. She lost her appetite, lost weight, and kept getting weaker and weaker. Judith had contracted tuberculosis[25] (TB), the number one deadly disease in Canada at the time.[26] Judith died on Jan 18, 1902 at the age of twenty-four as Papa watched helplessly. After a marriage of nearly ten years, he was left with his two small daughters to raise alone. Frances at only six years was too small to provide the type of full-time care her one-year-old sister Wilhelmina required. With the demands of life in the Canadian wilderness, Papa needed help to care for his two little daughters.

My mother Josette Watchapeze Janvier was then a young Chipewyan woman attending Papa's school. Papa noticed that Josette loved to care for the younger school children. She was a good

---

[24] Sessional Papers of the Dominion of Canada – 1892, No. 13, Part III, Page 6.
[25] http://www.lung.ca/tb/tbhistory/diagnosis
[26] TB had no known cure until the mid-1900's.

student with artistic skill who was always neat and clean, kind-hearted, and attractive.

Mama's father, Noah, was intelligent and wise. He had lots of cattle on one of the best spreads on the reserve. In the summer he cut hay for his cattle and grew wheat and barley. In the winter he hired someone to take care of his cattle while he went north with others to hunt game and trap furbearing animals. They dried moose meat to last a year and then came home with the meat and animal hides. In the summer Mama's people went fishing on the lakes in birch bark canoes they had made. Gum from spruce trees was used to seal canoes. They also made their own dog sleds with hand tools, and fishing nets from woven string. In the summer the extra fish was dried.

All summer while the men fished, my grandma Anzalee (Angela), Mama and her sisters tanned hides and made moccasins, gloves, and mittens. They decorated them with silk work, which is colorful artistic embroidery. They also trimmed beautiful clothing articles with fox or beaver fur, and sometimes the white fur of an ermine. They made their own silk blouses, buttoned high with standup collars, and long sleeves. Their handmade long skirts with full pleats were usually decorated on the bottom with braid or silk. All the women wore bright plaid shawls with long fringes and embroidery imported from England or Scotland.

Mama's people made pemmican out of dried meat pounded with tallow and sometimes sugar. Berries that were dried could be kept indefinitely. There was always work to do that gave the people a sense of purpose, achievement and stability as the rhythm of life ebbed and flowed with the changing of the seasons.

When Mama turned sixteen, Papa rode his horse to visit Noah Watchapeze, Mama's father. Noah greeted Papa and invited him to stay awhile. Papa stayed about two weeks with Noah. Every evening Papa and Noah smoked their pipes and talked into the night, as Noah was checking Papa out. Papa tried to be unhurried as he began his conversations with Noah about ordinary affairs, but finally Papa could wait no longer, and told Noah that he was interested in marrying one of Noah's daughters.

Noah asked, "Well, is it Marie you want to marry?" Marie was the oldest. Papa said, "No."

"How about Catherine?" Noah asked. Catherine was the youngest. "No, it isn't Catherine," Papa replied, trying to be patient as he waited for Noah to get to the point.

Noah may have noticed that Papa had already shown an interest in Mama, so Noah waited with her name. "Josette?" Noah asked at last.

"That's the one I want to marry," Papa said. Noah fell silent and thought a long time, and after what seemed an eternity to Papa, Noah finally said, "She's awfully young."

Papa promised that he would take *very* good care of her. He pointed out that he was a *well-educated* man, and he said that he would *respect* her. So, Noah excused himself saying that he would need to talk it over with Josette and her mother Anzalee.

Mama was not pleased with the idea of marrying a man who was twenty-five years her senior—old enough to be her own father. Mama had begun to develop feelings for a young Indian fellow who was also interested in her. Noah and Anzalee carefully explained the benefits of having a husband who was able to provide a good home, food, and clothing for her family, who wouldn't be getting drunk all the time, beating her and her children, or using harsh words with them. *Reluctantly*, Mama agreed to marry Papa, not only because her mom and dad said that she *should* marry this man, but also because Papa really did need help with his two little daughters.

Please don't think that Mama was forced to marry Papa, however. Our Chipewyan culture is matriarchal where the women let the men know what needs to be done. If Mama had said, "No," her parents would have honored her decision, and that would have been the end of it. Mama loved her father Noah, honored his counsel, and trusted that he really did know what was best for her. I am so thankful that Mama agreed to marry Papa, because she was the best mother any child could ever know!

T. W. Harris and Josette Watchapeze Janvier were married on September 27, 1902 when he was forty-one and she was sixteen. At first Mama was rather shy and naïve about marriage. Although she was a capable helper, it took time for Mama to adjust to the idea that her teacher was now her husband. It was a tall order to become the wife of a much older man. Papa was always kind, but had a rather commanding presence from his time in the military. Papa was also an Irishman who wanted things *just so* around his house.

In addition to her other duties as Papa's wife and homemaker, Mama had the immediate responsibility of caring for Frances and Wilhelmina. Even though she was still an infant, baby Wilhelmina had bonded with Papa and her mother Judith. Something in little Wilhelmina's infant heart broke when her own mother Judith died, and it seemed she was never able to allow Josette to be her mama. Wilhelmina attached herself to Papa after Judith's death, and remained close to him all of her life.

As time passed, Mama adjusted well to marriage. Papa, true to his word, was *wonderful* to her. Although he was a very aggressive man in business, and a strict man with his children, Papa honored Mama, treating her with patience, gentleness, kindness, love and respect. Papa encouraged Mama to invite her family to visit us in the north, and let Mama visit her family in the south when she was lonely. Mama for her part raised Frances and Wilhelmina as if they were her own, took care of Papa, and was a wonderful mother to us all.

Agent Harris on the Mackenzie

As it is written "He has scattered abroad his gifts to the poor; his righteousness endures forever." 2 Corinthians 9:9, (NIV)

After Papa and Mama were married, Papa needed to support Mama, Frances, and Wilhelmina, and that required a higher salary than he earned as a teacher. Reports of the Hudson's Bay Company needing a qualified manager who was not afraid of living in isolation intrigued Papa, who had a family to keep him company. My family stayed in Fort Chipewyan until 1913. Four of Papa and Mama's eleven children were born at Fort Chipewyan: Mary Owen Harris, born April 12, 1905; Rachel Fowler Harris, born May 31, 1907; Charlotte Tremain Harris, born Aug 18, 1909; and Thaddeus Richmond Harris, born July 11, 1912.[27]

Fort Chipewyan located in northeastern Alberta, was established by Sir Alexander Mackenzie in 1789.[28] It soon became the main collection point for furs west of the Great Lakes, and therefore a major trading center for the Indians and white trappers. The furs were transported by cart and canoe to Grand Portage on the northwestern shore of Lake Superior, then loaded on ships for passage through the Great Lakes, and then on to sailing vessels to cross the Atlantic Ocean to England where the furs were made into expensive beaver hats and fur coats.

The Hudson's Bay Company's inventory included blankets, clothes, canned goods, dry goods, tea, flour, boots, shoes and other supplies. The Northern Traders (NT) carried the same line of goods, but unable to compete with the Hudson's Bay Company's selection, they provided better service. In place of cash, Indians used food and handmade items in addition to furs to barter for products in the stores.

Papa's concern for the Indians soon outweighed his loyalty to The Hudson's Bay Company which had been offering unreasonably low compensation in trade for the Indians' valuable furs. For example, the Hudson's Bay Company traders would take a hundred pounds of flour, stand the bag up, and *press* the furs down until the pile of furs reached the top of the flour sack. Although they knew

---

[27] Canadian census records.
[28] *North-West Mounted Police, Sessional Papers by Canadian Parliament 1899.* Page 161.

each fur in the bale was worth a lot more than the bag of flour, they gave the Indians only one sack of flour, worth almost nothing, for the whole bale of furs. *That* was how the company made their high profits. Papa decided to begin giving the Indians a fair trade.

After a few years the Hudson's Bay Company realized that Fort Chipewyan showed much less profit under Papa's management. Papa was soon out of a job, but not out of a future. While Papa was managing the Hudson's Bay Company Store, he met Bishop Breynat who shared Papa's disdain for the unfair practices of the fur traders. The two men soon became friends. In Bishop Breynat's book published just before his death in the 1950's he wrote of the fur traders' unbalanced concern for the value of furs at the expense of the Indians' well-being:

> If all fur traders put as much energy and perseverance into the business of saving their souls as they do into the pursuit of furs they would all be saints. Bishop Grandin often remarked, in appealing for recruits to the missions: "Not a wolf's tail is ever lost in the whole of our Far North, but how many souls are, for want of apostles to win them to our dear Savior!"[29]

Bishop Breynat had been making appeals to Parliament to establish Indian agencies along the Mackenzie River. An agency was established in Fort Simpson, but when the first agent left, the government in Ottawa asked Bishop Breynat if he could recommend a qualified replacement. Appreciating Papa's credentials, his knowledge of Indian languages, and his love for the people, Bishop Breynat recommended Papa.

In 1913 at the age of fifty-two, Papa moved his growing family to the banks of the Mackenzie River in the Northwest Territories, four hundred miles northwest of Fort Chipewyan to assume his new job. Fort Simpson was just a little Indian village with very few white men when our family arrived in 1913. In addition to Papa, there was a Hudson's Bay Company store manager, the manager of the NT, the policeman, the manager of a smaller store called Hyslop and Nagle, the Protestant minister, and the brothers and priests in the Catholic Church.

The Fort Simpson Agency provided another opportunity for adventure, as well as the promise of a career that would put to use

---

[29] Gabriel Breynat, *Bishop of the Winds: Fifty Years in the Arctic Regions* (New York, New York: P. J. Kennedy & Sons, 1955). Page 82. Hereafter noted as "Breynat".

all of Papa's acquired knowledge, including statistical skill developed while serving with the NWMP. Before 1913, Indian Affairs' population reports for villages on the Mackenzie were only rough estimates. Papa's report for the 1913-1914 fiscal year shows exact counts painstakingly tallied from each village as he made his annual visits. He gathered notebooks full of precise data on bushels grown and acres under tillage for various crops, including garden produce for each Indian reservation. Livestock reports charted the various types of animals, as well as the quantity of meat, milk, eggs, and other animal products on hand and amounts sold each year.

Not much is known of Papa's early years, but he recorded several years of indigenous history in the early 1900's in his Indian Affairs journals he kept for the Canadian government. The annual reports for Indian Affairs published in England contained wonderful descriptions of life in the far regions of Canada, which must have been of great interest to members of British Parliament. The narrative portions were informative and descriptive, providing fascinating reading material.

In addition to monitoring agricultural production, Papa visited schools reviewing maintenance of buildings, administration, quality of teaching, and the students' progress. Education reports listed staff and the numbers of students in each school. Religious schools as well as public schools were all reported with the attendance from various races and tribes. There was information for each Indian reserve listing types of businesses and industry, health care facilities, numbers of births, deaths, and reported diseases. The gathering of data was extensive and time consuming. I have never been interested in all those details. Numbers mean nothing to me, but the data must have helped people in government make decisions.

Many of the Indian Agents and administrators within Indian Affairs were well educated. Their reports often contained a spirit of adventure. Articles in Canadian newspapers and popular novels were written about the exciting life on the frontier. Some of the members of Parliament became interested enough to tour western Canada, allowing the agents to show them firsthand the most urgent needs for funding. The agents also noted ways the Indian people were adapting to European civilization, which paved the way for settlement of the provinces.

Papa's extended Indian family offered cultural sensitivity and accelerated his language acquisition. Papa learned the ways of the Indians from Mama and her relatives, and he conversed freely with

Indians or white men in his travels. Papa was soon busy visiting the villages along the Mackenzie learning the Indian dialects of the various tribes, providing much needed services for the Indian people, getting the sick to hospitals, making sure children were attending school, and gathering data for his annual reports.

The region began enjoying many benefits of having an Indian Agent. From age thirteen, Papa's disciplined life at the monastery, the rigor and discipline of the NWMP, and the long list of chores added to his teaching duties had turned Papa into a highly efficient *take charge, get the job done* kind of a man. In addition to Papa's booming voice and commanding presence, he was extremely intelligent, well-educated, skilled, resourceful, and respected. His directions and careful instruction helped people understand how to improve their villages.

The Fort Simpson sawmill built under Agent Gerald Card's oversight in 1911 was put to good use under Papa's supervision. In addition to new buildings in Fort Simpson and repairs to government buildings, the lumber for our home was sawn in the new mill. Papa hired an agricultural instructor to teach the Indian people farming skills to find out for Indian Affairs if crops could be grown that far north. Inspector Conroy praised Papa's work in his annual report of 1915:

> At Simpson, where Mr. D. Von der Osten is farm instructor at the agency, I found that everything looked very promising under the management of Agent Harris.
>
> Two additional acres of land had been reclaimed and put under cultivation, and were producing a splendid crop of oats. In addition to this, the other crops of wheat, barley and roots, although not in such an advanced state as might have been expected, owing to the early drought and late seeding, were coming along very well.
>
> At the sawmill the grade of lumber cut is very good, and both the Royal Northwest Mounted Police and the missions have been supplied from time to time. The mill itself is in good running order and is a considerable boon to this district.[30]

As an Indian Agent Papa reported to Parliament his disapproval of falling fur prices in 1915 which no longer provided a living for the Indians.

---

[30]1915 *Indian Affairs Report.* 127-128.

This agency comprises all the Mackenzie River basin, and includes nine posts of the Hudson's Bay Company. The Indians are thus divided into nine bands as to their habitat, and into four tribes as to their origin. These four tribes – Slaveys, Hareskins, Loucheux[31] and Siccannies – form part of the Chipewyan or Chipewyan nation, each speaking a dialect of the Chipewyan language. With the exception of the Indians who frequent Fort Nelson, the native population of this agency has not yet entered into treaty, and gain their living as in former times by hunting and trapping.

Health and Sanitation. – Lack of sufficient pure air in their houses probably accounts in a large measure for their weak lungs, while the practice of intermarriage, which is common to the whole Chipewyan nation, has gradually made them all more or less scrofulous. They are much addicted to the use of medicine whenever they can procure it, believing that they strengthen themselves by loading their systems with any medicaments on which they can lay their hands, and this propensity certainly does not tend to ameliorate their general health.

Occupations. - All the Indians of this agency are hunters and trappers, sometimes in the midst of plenty, and at other times in actual want. The Indians who frequent the posts of Wrigley, Norman, and Good Hope, usually have access to the large herds of barren land caribou, which are not difficult to approach and are very easily hunted. In the other parts moose are fairly numerous, although their numbers are greatly diminished according to the records of the trading companies, and are getting less every year. A few Indians from Liard, Simpson, and Norman, hunt mountain sheep in the Nahannis, a branch of the foothills of the Rocky mountain range; but, as the country is very rugged, these animals are hunted only by men in full vigor. Fish are found in small lakes all over the country. In Great Bear Lake the fish are plentiful and nutritious, and are of excellent flavor.

The fur-bearing animals are fairly well distributed throughout the agency and include bear, beaver, ermine, red fox, cross fox, silver fox, white fox, lynx, mink, marten, musk ox, otter, skunk, wolf and wolverine. Before the outbreak of the present European war (WWI), the Indians were able to make enough from their fur

---

[31] Also known as Kutchin, but not part of the Athabascan language group. Chipewyan is a long version of all the words. All the other subgroups are shortened versions of Chipewyan. Someone who can speak Hare or Slavey would have an easy time understanding Chipewyan, but someone who is Chipewyan would have a more difficult time with the other dialects, because parts of the words are missing, according to Kit Elford of Northern Canada Evangelical Missions.

hunts to supply themselves; but at present, the price of all fur has gone so low that only the best hunters can gain enough to furnish tea and tobacco for their families.

Buildings. - Nearly all the Indians build themselves small huts or shacks around their respective forts, and also at their winter hunting ground. These shacks are built of logs, with roofs of poles covered with earth or bark, the windows of cotton. These shacks are small and low, and do not give sufficient fresh air for the number who live in them. They are heated with a chimney of stones covered with clay or a stove providing good protection against the severity of the northern winter, and are very acceptable shelter to travelers during stormy weather. Since the establishment of a government sawmill at Fort Simpson, several of the Indians there are building new houses, with the intention of roofing them with shingles, which will be an improvement on the old style.

Stock. - The only stock owned or kept by the Indians in the north, are the train dogs, which they use in winter for hauling their sledges, and in summer for packing their household effects when obliged to make portages. These dogs are fed when their masters are in plenty and have to shift for themselves at other times. When rabbits are numerous the dogs are in good condition, but when there are no rabbits the dogs sometimes go for days without food of any kind.

Farm Implements. - No farm implements are owned by these Indians, except, perhaps, an occasional spade, which a few use to plant potatoes.

Characteristics and Progress. - Generally speaking, the Indians of this agency are peaceable, law-abiding, and are amenable to reason, in so far as reason does not conflict with their superstitions. They are wanting in energy and foresight, and this is caused, by their hand-to-mouth style of providing for their needs. Their intelligence seems to be about equal to that of the other tribes whom I have been among, and their receptive faculties are good. When engaged in any regular occupation, they appear to give satisfaction, and do not show discontent with their work. Having obtained employment, they keep it as long as they are wanted. They do not seem to be as emotional as some of the other tribes of Indians, nor to feel so deeply such afflictions as the sickness and death of their relatives, but to be more stoical than the tribes that inhabit the plains. They are making a certain amount of progress as they are adopting the whites' mode of life more and more each succeeding year. When they can obtain the seed, those who have houses put in a small quantity of potatoes each spring, and in some cases garden seeds are also sown.

Temperance and Morality. - There are some isolated cases of intoxication occurring among the Indians when the opportunity presents itself, but on the whole drunkenness is unknown. Their morals are comparatively good. Theft is practically unheard of; conjugal infidelity is rare; exaggeration is more common than fundamental untruth; and fighting is confined to the women, and is generally conducted with the tongue rather than with the fists. They are more reasonable in their demands for commodities for which they have to barter than the tribes who have acquired greater business instincts from contact with the whites. They are accepting the fall in the prices of fur in a good spirit, and look forward with eagerness to the time when fur shall go up higher than ever before. They are giving more attention during the present winter to hunting meat than fur, and in this I think they are wise, as a few years respite would give the fur-bearing animals a chance to increase.

Papa contended that the disappearance of fur-bearing animals was due to an increase in white trappers. The Klondike gold *rush* in Yukon Territory in 1897 became a gold *bust* by 1900. Most of the gold miners went broke. Many died in snow and ice-packed mountain passes or while trying to traverse perilous rapids. Those who made their fortunes during the Klondike gold rush were the merchants who sold materials, food, and other supplies to the miners who came in droves. Some disillusioned, disgruntled, and disenfranchised miners stayed to become trouble-makers in the north. When the gold didn't *pan out*, they began looking for other sources of income which they discovered in the valuable fur trade. Trying to obtain wealth from furs, white trappers began wantonly killing animals that the Indian people had carefully harvested for centuries. The white trappers also had no respect for the Indians' property, sometimes stealing furs from the Indians.

In the fall, the Indians loaded up their dog teams with their food and went into the wilds for the winter, hunting and trapping until spring. If anybody stole any furs, the offended Indian appeared in Papa's office to report, "So-and-so stole stuff out of my traps." As Justice of the Peace and Indian Agent, Papa investigated crimes with the police, and threw the trouble-makers into jail. Papa would tell them, "Next spring, back home you go. We don't need any thieves like you in the north."

In his 1916 report, Papa again reminded Parliament of the disastrous impact of falling fur prices on the Indian economy, especially in light of the disappearance of the game and fish that had been their food supply.[32] In 1918 the Superintendent of Indian Affairs wrote, "The higher prices paid for raw furs this year have greatly relieved the situation of the hunting Indians."[33] Perhaps Papa's letters, reports, and speeches began to make an impact in Ottawa.

Papa needed what he had learned as Hudson's Bay Company store manager to order supplies for our family and for the Indians in his agency. For our use, Papa stocked our basement in much the same way as he used to stock the shelves when he managed the Hudson's Bay Company store in Fort Chipewyan. For winter distribution to Indians who came on hard times during the long winter months, provisions were kept in an agency storage building.

In winter there was no capacity to haul freight on the dog sleds used by the postal service. In addition to the mail sacks, the sleds were needed to carry provisions for the dogs and their mushers. Every necessary supply that couldn't be produced from the land was mail-ordered in the winter and delivered during the brief summer shipping season. Extra charges for freight were tacked on every time the loads had to shift from one route to another, making products much more expensive than in the south. Although bananas and other soft fruit would have been crushed in shipment, the riverboats and barges brought fresh oranges and apples, and a lot of dried fruit. The Mackenzie was only open to river traffic for approximately two and a half months a year. By the end of August, all of the supplies that had been brought on the river had to last until the next June. The ice started to form on the river in September or October ending the shipping season.

In 1922 my papa, T. W. Harris, was appointed Treaty 11 Commissioner of the Northwest Territories for all the tribes along the Mackenzie River to the Herschel Islands in the Arctic Ocean. This meant that Papa had to spend more time away from our family. It was safer to travel on the riverboats in the summer than on dog sleds in the winter when the temperature in the north could dip to minus eighty degrees Fahrenheit.

---

[32] Ibid. 56-58
[33] 1918 *Indian Affairs Report.* 13.

In June after the river opened, Papa boarded the steamboat to spend the summer going north on the river to each village along the Mackenzie. After Treaty 11 was signed in 1922, Papa paid treaty of five dollars per person at different forts, in addition to looking after the needs of the people.

Papa often traveled on Bishop Breynat's mission boat with Bishop Breynat and the priests, and the doctor from the Catholic mission hospital in Fort Simpson. The boat stopped in each village only long enough to unload and load cargo and passengers, but when Papa, the doctor, and Bishop Breynat were on board, they had to wait for up to two days for treaty work, missionary visits, and annual physical checkups to be completed. Papa also gave out rations of staples such as flour, baking powder, bacon, sugar, tea, and other food stuffs to the older inhabitants who could no longer trap or hunt.

Eating and drinking as they traveled north, other passengers tried to tempt Papa by making him smell their liquor bottles. People admired Papa for abstaining from whiskey until his books were closed at Aklavik. After his treaty payments and other work had been completed, Papa opened his own bottles of Scotch on his return trip. When he arrived home our house became the party place again. When the last of the whiskey was gone, that was it until the following year. Mama must have breathed a sigh of relief, because she did not approve of drinking.

Papa remained a *staunch* Roman Catholic throughout his lifetime. Although Papa was never allowed to minister within the church, he was truly among the "priesthood of believers", as the Bible describes all of us who follow Jesus Christ from the heart. Papa was fashioned by God to be a *caregiver*, one of the key ingredients in pastoral ministry. Papa went about doing good with humble dignity, fully aware of his own foibles and human frailties. Papa was outspoken, and did like whiskey now and then, but his ever-widening responsibilities over the passing years molded and shaped Papa into a powerful and well respected spokesman for Indian Affairs in Canada's Parliament.

Our Home Life in Fort Simpson

For you created my inmost being;
    you knit me together in my mother's womb.
I praise you because I am fearfully and wonderfully made;
    your works are wonderful, I know that full well.
My frame was not hidden from you
    when I was made in the secret place.
When I was woven together in the depths of the earth,
    your eyes saw my unformed body.
All the days ordained for me
    were written in your book
    before one of them came to be. Psalm 139:13-16 (*NIV*)

The Harris family home in Fort Simpson

At Fort Simpson we lived among the Slavey (Slay-vee) people. Our family quickly learned to speak the Slavey language, because Slavey and Mama's Chipewyan were both from the Athabascan language group.

There were so few educated residents for government appointments in the far north, that Papa carried several titles. In addition to serving as Indian Agent, T. W. (Flynn) Harris was Justice of the Peace in the Northwest Territories from 1914 to 1933, a fire ranger from 1914-1931, sub-mining recorder from 1920 to 1934, and coroner in Fort Good Hope from 1931 to 1933. As Indian Agent, Papa represented the Canadian government. Every morning without fail Papa raised the Canadian flag and lowered it at night on the pole beside our house. Winter nights were long and days were very short. Papa kept busy typing all the statistics and events of the year for the Indian Affairs annual reports.

Three Harris children were born in Fort Simpson. My older brother James De Lapp Harris, named after Papa's grandfather, was born Dec 21, 1916. I was born April 16, 1919 and named Bridget Angela Harris. My younger sister Nora Harris was born May 31, 1921. Our little sister Rose was born in Grandma and Grandpa Watchapese' home in Le Goff, Alberta on December 28, 1924. Three and a half years after Rose, a set of twin boys arrived in our home in Fort Simpson: John (Jack) Patrick Harris and Thomas William Harris born June 10, 1928. Thomas William was named after Papa, but we *never* called him T. W. Harris, III. We always called him Bill. My youngest brother Ned was born in Cold Lake after Papa retired.

Papa's first child, Frances, married and had a few children, but Frances died young. Her death may have brought back memories of losing Judith for Papa, but I was too young to know how deeply Frances' death may have grieved him. I'm sure Mama also mourned for Frances, because Frances had accepted and loved Mama. When Papa made a comment in one of his annual reports that the Indian people in the Mackenzie valley were stoic and did not seem to express grief as deeply over the deaths of family members as the tribal people on the plains, he was writing from his own family experience.

In 1916 Wilhelmina married Harry McGurran in Fort Simpson. Wilhelmina and Harry moved to Fort Rae, a few hundred miles away on Great Slave Lake. Harry and Wilhelmina had several children. When Wilhelmina was married, Mama's responsibility to care for Judith's daughters ended. Mama had treated Frances and Wilhelmina as her oldest girls, but now for the first time Mama could give her own children her undivided attention. Wilhelmina had been married for three years when I was born, so I never knew her as well as my other siblings.

The first agency house in Fort Simpson burned down, so a new house was built just before our family arrived. Because Papa worked for the government we had a *beautiful* two-story home with linoleum-covered floors and a lot of woodwork. We had four bedrooms upstairs. Downstairs was a dining room, a big office for Papa, a living room, a nice bedroom for Papa and Mama, and a nice big kitchen.

The many plaques on Papa's office wall included degrees he had earned and official appointments. A big desk in one corner was flanked by an old fashioned leather chair that made into a bed for Papa's afternoon naps.

I was the middle child – number six of eleven children. By the time I arrived, Papa was a robust Irishman, and Mama was a beautiful Chipewyan lady. Papa was an exceptional linguist speaking many languages fluently. Other Indian Agents who used translators suffered through miscommunication both of their words and cultural miscues. Papa represented all the natives in his work, from Fort Simpson to Aklavik on the great Mackenzie River. Papa also represented the Eskimo of the Hershel Islands at the mouth of the Mackenzie where it empties into the Arctic Ocean. Although I didn't speak as many languages as Papa, I grew up speaking English, French, and Chipewyan in our home; I learned to speak Slavey and Hare well; and I understood Cree.

To help Mama overcome homesickness, Papa was generous in accommodating her wishes. Whenever Mama was having a baby, Papa sent word nearly a thousand miles back to Le Goff, Alberta for Grandma and Grandpa Watchapese to come. Mama's parents enjoyed trips to Fort Chipewyan and later to Fort Simpson by steamboat. In addition to serving as midwife on the Le Goff reserve for both Indian and white women, Grandma Anzalee delivered Mama's babies in the north as well. If Mama was going to have a baby in the winter, Grandma Anzalee came in the fall and stayed through the winter until the boats were traveling the river again in spring. The only Harris babies Grandma Anzalee did *not* deliver were the twins. Papa, took extra precaution when Jack and Bill were born, summoning the doctor in lieu of complications.

When I was old enough to care about my looks, I complained to Grandma Anzalee that she pulled my hair too far back when she delivered me, moving my hairline way up on my head.

Mama's family were no burden when they visited, because they hunted, trapped, and fished adding richly to our food supply with moose and rabbit meat, and they provided hides for material for Mama to make clothing for our large family. Uncle Jean Marie also left fur pelts for Mama to trim our clothing. Mama's brother, Jean Marie Watchapeze, was one of the best fur trappers in the north country. Mama said if there was only one martin in the whole Northwest Territories, Jean Marie was sure to find it.

41

Grandma Anzalee was an herbalist among the Indian people. She cured lots of people with all sorts of herbs. My sister Nora still has the recipe for boiling a whole bunch of wild plants to make a tea for certain ailments. They had one plant we called rat root. When times were tough and there wasn't much to eat, the Indian people brought Seneca roots into the store to trade them for food and supplies. The white people sold the Seneca roots to pharmacies in North America and Europe for cold medicines[34] and other ailments.

Our home environment was very nurturing. Though Papa was strict he rarely spanked us. We were happy that most discipline was left to our patient gentle and loving Mama.

Our beautiful mother dressed in the fashion of the times for the native woman. She wore long-sleeve hand-embroidered blouses with a big brooch at the neck, long skirts trimmed with braid or fancy silk work, as well as beautiful shawls with long fringes. As we walked to church we all clung to Mama hiding shyly behind her skirt and fringes.

Although Papa was Irish, he was the best-dressed *Indian* in the Northwest Territories. Mama tanned hides and was an artist at making beautiful moccasins, mukluks, mittens, and gloves for her family. Papa practically sat on top of Mama's sewing machine as she fitted him for his new wardrobe. To keep Papa warm, Mama always trimmed the hood with beautiful beaver or fox fur. Papa became excited like a little boy again when he had something new to wear. He loved showing off Mama's skillful handiwork after she had trimmed his gloves or moccasins with colorful silk work and fur. When he was wearing his parka, you could hardly see his face as the rich fur protected him from the elements.

Mama made sure the Harris family stayed warm in bitterly cold winters. She lined mukluks, gloves, and parkas with Hudson Bay duffel—a heavy wool blanket material. Papa's gloves were made out of smoked and tanned caribou hides with very fancy embroidery. Sometimes Mama made nice warm mittens out of beaver with fur and leather on the outside for Papa. Mama's children all wore her big handmade beaver mittens, and luxurious leather parkas trimmed with fox fur.

---

[34] The Native American herbal cures formed the basis for many of our modern medicines and are now being studied in medical schools as part of homeopathic medicine. According to the World Health Organization, approximately twenty-five per cent of modern drugs used in the United States have been derived from plants.

The heavier beaver mittens were often worn over the thinner caribou gloves by the hunters. They threaded a long rawhide strap from one mitten to the other that they carried over their neck. The straps allowed them to slip off the outer moose hide mittens when they were ready to shoot without dropping their mittens into the snow. They kept their caribou gloves on that were thin and flexible to protect their hands while shooting.

Babies were kept in a U-shaped moss bag for the first year of their life, which took the place of diapers. The outside of the moss bag was usually velvet with fancy embroidery. The inside of the bag was lined with a flannel blanket to keep it soft. Moss picked by Indian women from muskegs[35] and dried in the sun was tucked around the baby's legs and wrapped around from back to front, much like we use diapers today. Another flannel blanket was wrapped around the baby, the baby was placed into the bag, and the bag was laced up to be carried on its mother's back. When the baby cried, it was usually trying to tell its Mama, "I want dry moss!" The wet moss was thrown away, and dry moss was tucked around the baby's bottom again. The moss was completely biodegradable, not like modern diapers that build up as debris in landfills.

Joe Villeneuve was Papa's handyman. Joe lived close to our house. In those days he filled our water barrels with drinking water right out of the river. When our barrels were full, Joe split wood for our furnace and kitchen stove and fed our cows.

When my oldest sister Mary grew up, she married Joe Villeneuve's son. They remained in Fort Simpson where they raised their children. Like our mother, Mary sewed all the clothes and moccasins for her family and did a lot of beautiful silk work. Mary was very strict like Papa, and kept her house very clean and neat like Mama. No one dared come into her house without taking off their shoes.

Old Josephine, a Slavey woman, helped Mama with the laundry, scrubbed floors, ironed clothing, mended moccasins, and was a great help all the way around. We loved her like our own family. We soon learned her Athabascan dialect which was similar to Mama's Chipewyan language. Old Josephine lived right across the Mackenzie from us, and paddled her little canoe to our house every week. She usually came early on Friday, and worked all day. Mama

---

[35] Northern Canadian word for bog lands.

made a bed for Josephine to stay with us Friday night. Old Josephine was as happy to stay with us as we were to have her. She brought a gunnysack with her that Mama filled with flour, bacon, tea, sugar, and anything else she needed. She worked part of Saturday to allow time to get home before dark, but before she left she went to Papa's office squatted on the floor, and said, "Tsamba l'on se ganitcho," which in Slavey meant something like, "Pay me my money."

Papa got quite a chuckle out of Josephine, because she was not a bit afraid of him. She always managed to get a little more money out of Papa than he expected to pay her.

When she left, I went upstairs to our bedroom to watch her paddle across the river until she was just a small dot on the far shore. Then I would holler to the family, "She made it!"

Treaty Day in Fort Simpson was busy at our house. Papa got up early as usual, put kindling in the stove to get the fire going to boil water in the big kettle for coffee. Then he went out to hoist the Union Jack[36] on the flag pole. Returning to the house Papa made breakfast. Daylight came early in the North in the middle of June. Papa rousted Thad and Jim from their slumber to milk our cows. Then they helped him set up his tent for treaty payments. They hauled out a desk and chairs for Papa, the constable, and the doctor. Papa recorded all the proceedings carefully in his account book.

The first man in line was Nakkekon, the wonderful Slavey Chief. He was the spokesman for his people bringing their complaints to Papa. The chief received twenty-five dollars in treaty payment. Next came about four headmen who served as leaders with the chief. They each received fifteen dollars. Then all of the other people who received their five dollar annual treaty payment at Fort Simpson would come past the table. They had been squatting on our lawn since the first light of day, waiting for the treaty formalities to begin. The constable was there to witness the payments, and also to record any complaints that needed the attention of the NWMP. Doc Truesdell examined all the Indians and either gave them a clean bill of health, or recommended they be hospitalized.

As Josephine came up to the table, she told Papa that she expected a little more than her normal five dollar treaty payment. Papa asked, "Josephine, why do you think you are entitled to more money? You are alone and have no children."

---

[36] The Canadian Flag.

Josephine answered, "There is one on the road," as she pointed to her fat tummy. She was about sixty years old at the time and was just joking with Papa. Everyone laughed heartily!

Mama was up very early on treaty day making bannock with raisins for the lunch she served all day until the last Indian was paid. Mary and Wilhelmina came to help Mama with the lunch, while all of us children were hustled to Mary's house to stay out of the way.

We always had a good time at Mary's house. She had everything placed in boxes that we were not supposed to get into. Then she hid the boxes under the bed and way up on top of the kitchen cupboard for safe keeping.

One time we managed to peek into almost everything Mary had tucked away. Most of the boxes held Christmas presents, and there was a lot of her silk work for gloves, mittens and slippers on moose hide. Mary also had lots of nice perfumes in her dresser. It was when we sampled the perfumes that our sin found us out. Toward evening we heard Mary coming home, and just like Adam and Eve tried to hide from God in the Garden of Eden, we hid upstairs knowing what was coming.

Mary called to us, "Biddy[37]! Nora! Mavis! Where are you? I have a nice surprise for you."

We decided we had better face the music. Mary's spicy temper was much like Papa's. When we showed ourselves, Mary scolded, "Who told you to open all these boxes? I suppose you started it, Biddy!" She paddled us all, and sent Nora and me home with sore behinds and a deep sense of humility.

When we got home we found a very tired Mama, and we decided not to tell her our troubles. She would not have taken pity on us regardless of how well we told our side of the story. Mama trusted Mary to take the proper action if we had misbehaved, and maybe the lingering fragrance of Mary's perfume told the story well enough. Mama's kindness left the incident unmentioned at home as she fed us, washed us really well, and sent us to bed. After so much excitement, we fell into an exhausted sleep.

Each year after treaty day, Papa got the boys up early again the next day. After breakfast and chores Thad and Jim helped Papa fill a couple of wheel barrows with his books to read while on the steamer, and all his luggage and account books. They made their

---

[37] Biddy was my family nickname.

way with Papa to help him get settled into his cabin on *The Distributor*. Papa also brought along a case of his favorite scotch, but he left it untouched until his treaty business was completed at his final stop, the Herschel Islands.

In his youth, Papa had enjoyed live theatre and musical performances in concert halls, but his entertainment options in the north were rather limited. Papa developed a great library in his office from books he ordered and had sent on the barges each summer to satisfy his love for reading. Papa was always reading in his spare time. Even when we were eating he had a book in front of him at the table. Somehow he managed to look right through the book, though, if we did not eat our bread crusts.

Although his office was off limits for us children, I often sneaked a good book and read a lot of Sir Henry Rider Haggard's books. My favorite was *Nada the Lily*. We were always telling stories from our vivid imaginations. Papa chided us, "Ah, the devil you say. The devil you say." He meant, "Oh, you're just making that up."

Papa was well versed in prose and poetry. He loved to recite Shakespeare, but our favorite story was the *Wizard of Oz*. When Papa told the story, he acted out all the characters, screwing up his face trying to look like them. We sure laughed!

Our family's favorite treat when celebrating a birthday or holiday was a big bowl of red Jell-O. Oh, we thought that was *so wonderful!* On special occasions we also made ice cream. We all took turns cranking the ice cream maker. We turned, and turned, and turned, and turned, until the paddle wouldn't budge and the creamy mixture had frozen ready to eat!

My brother Jim loved to play tricks on us. He made dummies from hat to boots out of Papa's clothing, and laid them on our beds. When we came to bed and screamed, just about dying from fright, we could hear Jim laughing in his room.

In 1913, as far as I know, there were no horses in Fort Simpson. Later on cows were shipped on barges in the summertime. Papa gave our cows Irish names: *Daisy*, *Shamrock*, and *Rosebud*. When the boys got up – *when they got up* – they went to milk the cows in the morning.

I remember waking to the smell of bacon, eggs, and coffee. True to his promise to take good care of Mama, Papa let her rest. An early riser Papa had the coffee perking on the stove, and the bacon sizzling in the pan at five o' clock. Oh, it smelled so good! Then Papa called up the stairs to his older boys, "Thad, Jim, get up! Time to milk the cows!"

Papa went back to the kitchen to turn the bacon and pour himself a cup of hot steaming coffee. The boys didn't move in their beds. Papa came up the stairs a few steps, and hollered, "I'm coming up the steps. Get out of bed now. Get up and milk the cows."

Thrusting arms out from under the warm covers, Thad and Jim clomped their boots around a little on the floor to make Papa think they were getting dressed. Again there was silence. The third time, Papa's heavy boots on the stairs almost drowned out his booming voice as he bellowed, "By the gods of war, I'm coming to get you!"

That did it! Thad and Jim threw back the covers, leapt out of bed, dressed in a flash, and burst out of their room falling over each other on the stairs buttoning their shirts and lacing their boots on the run. They bundled up in warm outer clothing, and trudged through the snow to the barn, bracing temperatures of minus fifty, sixty, and even seventy degrees below zero Fahrenheit.

If they didn't come back in what seemed a reasonable time, Papa went to the barn to check on them. There they were hanging on to the cows teats with their heads nestled against the cows' flanks sound asleep, exhausted from being up all night! Papa kicked their stools out from under them as they fell crashing to the barn floor. What a rude awakening! Thad and Jim quickly finished their chores and hurried in for breakfast.

In the wintertime after Papa had breakfast he attended morning mass and visited the priests and brothers at the mission. Papa wanted Mama to sleep as long in the morning as she wanted, but as soon as the door closed behind him, all of us little children *bounded* down the stairs and *jumped* into bed with Mama. Oh, that was the *best* time in the whole world! We snuggled close and then we all fell back to sleep.

After returning home from morning mass Papa sat watching the road finishing his morning coffee and smoking his little clay pipe. From our kitchen there was a clear view down the road to the mission. Pretty soon Father Mosian came walking toward our house. Papa's speech was a bit spicy as he started muttering under his breath, "What the heck does that son-of-a-gun want from me today? He's probably going to borrow my typewriter, grr, grr, grr –son-of-a-gun!"

Mama cautioned, "Flynn, don't talk like that!"

Ignoring Mama, Papa kept grumbling. Pretty soon Father Mosian arrived. Knock, knock, knock, knock, knock. "Come in Father*rr*. Come in Father*rr*. What can I do for you, Father*rr*," Papa crooned sweetly to the priest in his Irish burr.

Father Mosian explained, "Well, Flynn, I've come to borrow your typewriter."

Papa offered, "Ah, Father*rr*, whatever I have is yours. Whatever I have is yours. Come in. Sit down. Have a cup of coffee with me."

Father Mosian sat down as Mama poured a cup of steaming coffee. The priest warmed his hands on the cup and settled back into his chair for a comfortable chat with Papa that stretched into a couple of hours. After the coffee pot was empty and lunch had been served, Father Mosian roused himself. Picking up Papa's typewriter, Father Mosian took his leave.

As the priest made his way down the road struggling under his new burden, Papa resumed his complaining, "I figured that so-an-so was just coming to borrow my typewriter."

Mama had the final word. Referring to Papa's grumbling she said, "There goes Papa saying the rosary again."

Papa ate only a bowl of warm milk and bread for his evening meal during Lent. All of his life he remained faithful to his Lenten fast. He seldom broke a lifetime vow once he made one.

As an Irishman, Papa loved Saint Patrick's Day. In the morning Papa got up very early, put on his hand-knit green V-necked sweater and green beret with the beautifully embroidered Saint Patrick's Day emblem Mama made for him. The emblem was a harp and shamrock embroidered in silk work on white deerskin, and backed by emerald green ribbon. It was a sort of pendant he pinned over his Irish heart. She made a new emblem each year. After he was all dressed in green, Papa went to the mission to help serve Mass as an altar boy. When he sang, however, Papa had trouble finding the melody, until the priest finally asked him to be quiet.

The rest of the day was spent with the priest. After mass they had breakfast together, and then went to the beer parlor for a few beers. Mama made a huge feast at dinnertime with the greenest iced cake you ever saw! Papa often forgot the time, so one of us had to fetch him. All the way home he would belt out *The Wearing O' The Green* so off-key we were embarrassed for him. After he had plenty to eat and we had told him how well he sang, it was easy to tap him for spending money.

The Catholic mission and the Harris family each had a garden. The priest had us Harris kids help the brothers at the mission plant the garden, weed, and take care of their potatoes. We raised a lot of good food from our garden. The growing season was short, but the days were *so long* in the land of the midnight sun. We grew potatoes, *huge* cabbages, onions, carrots, beets, and other cool weather vegetables. Everything grew so fast and so big you wouldn't *believe* it. It is amazing that gardens produced vegetables so far north, but in the short summers for about forty-five days the sun was in the sky almost around the clock. You could practically watch plants grow.

In Fort Simpson Mama canned all kinds of wild strawberries, blueberries, raspberries, and cranberries for our annual fruit supply. I didn't *dare* go out into the woods to pick the berries alone, but my sister Rose wasn't afraid and loved to explore as long as she was within earshot of Mama's voice to call her back home. Mama often waited for the Indians to bring fruit into town. Instead of using money the Indians traded wild berries, fish, moose meat, and deer meat with our family for store goods. We also caught our own fish in the river. The Irish are known for their potatoes, but in this one instance Papa abandoned his heritage with a strong preference for macaroni and cheese.

Refrigerators weren't necessary so far north. To keep things cool, we dug a pit in the permafrost, put things into a bag, and lowered the bags on ropes into the pit. When the pit was covered the bags of food stayed icy cold. If we needed something from the pit we hauled the bag up by its rope. We *never* had running water. We carried all our water from the Mackenzie River. When we wanted a bath we warmed water on the stove.

Papa had to order our Christmas presents along with all of the other supplies for the year. Each year Papa asked me, "What would you like for Christmas this year, Bridget?" Every year I responded, "A harmonica." I must have worn them out, so each year I needed a new one for Christmas. I grew up playing the harmonica, and I can still play it today.

When Christmas came there was so much excitement! Papa kept his office locked up tight from children for a whole month while Mama and Papa wrapped and hid all the gifts. We were so curious, we stared at the door hoping it would melt so we could see what they were doing, but not a chance! We never even saw when they brought in the spruce tree, but we could smell the fresh pine needles.

49

Mama decorated the tree with strings of cranberries, all kinds of tinsel, and bright shiny balls. We had no lights on our tree. Fort Simpson didn't have electricity yet for tree lights, and Mama didn't dare burn real candles on the tree. With so many of us little Indians running around, she thought we might set the house on fire and burn to death.

For Christmas Mama dressed us in pretty handmade silk dresses with little lace collars, fancy moccasins and mukluks. Christmas Eve Papa read some stories, and recited 'Twas the Night Before Christmas in his usual elegant way with all the facial expressions that kept us spellbound. At nine o' clock Mama fed us a bowl of warm oatmeal we called porridge. When she brought us upstairs she told us, "Now, remember, don't fall asleep. Santa Claus will be here at midnight with lots of toys and dolls."

That was Mama's homespun psychology. Children will often do exactly what they are told not to do. She fed us this warm stuff with milk and then told us not to sleep. No matter how hard we tried to stay awake, the first thing we knew we were soon in the Land of Nod. We slept all night until the next morning. When we woke up we thought, "Aw, we missed Santa Claus!" Christmas morning we couldn't wait to rush down the long stairway, and run into the office to see all the packages under the tree.

Papa was always making breakfast having left the office door wide open to greet us. What a sight to behold! Presents were gaily wrapped with lots of bows. Bright tinsel sparkled on the tree. Papa pretended to be Santa calling our names one by one as he handed us presents.

There would be a new pair of handmade moccasins or a new pair of handmade mittens wrapped up pretty for each of us girls. We had dolls – so many dolls! They were beautiful china dolls with china faces all fixed up with curly hair and beautiful dresses! My interest was only in the harmonica, the best Christmas gift I could ever have! I searched through all the gifts for my little harmonica and there it was under the tree!

I didn't learn to play any Christian songs when I was a child. I played Western songs and nursery rhymes. I played little ditties like, Jack and Jill Went Up the Hill, or Hickory Dickory Dock. Papa had Irish songs for the gramophone like What Do We Do On a Dewy, Dewy Day, When Irish Eyes Are Smiling, and Turaluralay. I cranked the gramophone to listen until I was able to play some of those songs, too.

50

Although my favorite pastime was playing the harmonica I also loved to play with the dolls. I put my dolls to bed, and after awhile I ran upstairs to check on them to see if they wet the bed. They were dry, so I poured a little water on the doll bed to make believe they needed their diapers changed. My brothers weren't as kind to my beautiful dolls. They hitched them up to pretend they were a dog team. I guess they didn't care what happened to the dolls, because they were *white porcelain*, not Indian.

The two-mile walk from our house to the church at the mission seemed longest in winter. Papa bundled us up, carrying one small child on this back and another in his arms. Our brother-in-law Joe Villenueve picked up Mama and the rest of the small children with his dog team, the only available winter transportation, and delivered us to the church.

After the ice floated away in spring, the greatest excitement for Mama was the arrival of all the children coming back home from the boarding school in Fort Providence! When we saw the smoke coming around the bend of the river, we all dressed up in our Sunday clothes and stood on the bank until the boat landed. Mama was so happy to greet her children: Mary, Rachel, Charlotte, and Thad. Undoubtedly, they were very happy to be home as well.

After our enthusiastic welcome the people proceeded to their destinations. Papa was the first to meet and shake hands with all the famous passengers. Government representatives came to our home for lunch and a visit with Papa, the nuns or priests went to the mission, the fur trade inspectors went to the Hudson's Bay Company on the bay, and the Mounties would go to the NWMP barracks.

Many Canadian dignitaries and famous people visited in our home. When airplanes began carrying freight to the north, we even made friends with Wilfred *Wop* May[38] the famous WWI pilot ace instrumental in the early days of Canadian aviation. Papa discovered that *Wop* May could fix watches and clocks. Papa always took out his old time pieces for *Wop* to work on to pass the time while he visited us. The clocks and watches always ran well after *Wop* landed.

It took the men all day to unload supplies for the mission, the bay, the police, and for our agency warehouse which held the

---

[38] During WWII in the 1940's Wop May was commander of the No.2 Air Observer School in Edmonton, as well as supervisor of all the western Canadian air force aviation schools.
http://en.wikipedia.org/wiki/Wilfrid_R._%22Wop%22_May

government supplies and rations for the Indians. Supplies from Edmonton were also unloaded for our house. Our large basement storage room was restocked with our year's supply of food stuffs. We had ordered all our canned goods, clothes, dishes and other household goods from the Eaton's department store in Edmonton. Timothy Eaton, from Ireland, opened his first store in Toronto in 1869. In 1884 Timothy Eaton Company, Ltd. published their first mail-order catalog making it possible for Papa to have the goods of the largest Canadian cities brought to our door. [39]

It may be hard to believe, but there were no bars selling beer or liquor stores in the whole Northwest Territories! It was unlawful to sell liquor of any kind to Indians when I was a child. The law was based on the belief that Indians could not handle liquor and became too wild and disorderly. Indian people noticed that liquor also made white people rather wild and disorderly.

Liquor was carefully distributed to white people through a permit system allowing them a quota they might purchase each year for their household use. The first boat coming down the river in the spring brought the liquor to fill the annual liquor permits for the white people. They could get cases of Scotch, wine, and hard liquor. The white people in the village would party from house to house until their annual supply of liquor was all gone.

Our home in Fort Simpson was the center, the hub-bub of the little village. On a Saturday night, the Hudson Bay man, the Northern Traders man, the policeman, and Papa would play poker at our home. Papa loved to play poker, and so did my brothers. In all there would be about five or six men playing poker around the table. In those days there was a lot of fur. Oh, boy, the stakes were high, like maybe a thousand dollars a game.

We younger Harris children didn't want to miss out on the excitement. We lay on the floor around a heat grate in a bedroom upstairs to watch and listen to everything that was going on just below us around the dining room table downstairs. The saying, "more things are caught than taught," is often true in family life. Children learn by example, whether good or bad. I developed a special love for poker long before I ever played the game, because Papa seemed to be having such a good time. I thought to myself, "Someday I'm going to play that game, too."

---

[39] http://en.wikipedia.org/wiki/Timothy_Eaton

After it got late, Mama came upstairs to find us all asleep around the heat register. She sang to us in Chipewyan, "Se bebee yaze wah te" ("my baby go to sleep"), over and over in a lovely chant. We liked our mother's singing, but we would be sound asleep. In the morning we woke in our own beds without knowing how we got there.

Educational options were limited in Fort Simpson. Nora and I attended the little Catholic pre-school in Fort Simpson taught by the Grey Nuns at the mission. They often asked Papa to fill in as a teacher for them if they needed a substitute. After kindergarten, Papa paid tuition for his children to be sent away to the only school in the entire Mackenzie River valley. The Harris home in Fort Simpson had been a warm cocoon of happiness, love and peace that would soon be torn away as we headed two hundred fifty miles eastward toward the Fort Providence Catholic residential school near Great Slave Lake, the headwaters of the Mackenzie.

The "Little Praying Man"

May God be gracious to us and bless us
  and make his face shine upon us,
that your ways may be known on earth,
  your salvation among all nations. Psalm 67:1-2 (NIV)

When Papa met Bishop Breynat at Fort Chipewyan, they became lifelong friends. Bishop Breynat and Papa were about the same age, and had both been trained to become priests by the Jesuits, who were a French order. Papa was trained at a monastery in Montreal, but Bishop Breynat was from France. Bishop Breynat was a source of encouragement to both Papa and Mama bringing hope and cheer wherever he traveled, even when his own strength was low. He came to our house on visits when he was in Fort Simpson, and he and Papa traveled together during the summer on the Catholic mission steamer.

This is how Bishop Breynat ended up in northwestern Canada. In the 1880's Bishop Grouard of Edmonton, Alberta, traveled to France to call priests to work on the Canadian Frontier. Through his love for the Indians' quiet ways and his appreciation for their practical skill and intelligence, Bishop Grouard was able to inspire a group of young priests from France to join him in Alberta, Canada, to be sent to the vast regions of the Northwest Territories and beyond.[40] He was looking for priests who would be willing to sacrifice the European comforts in exchange for the privilege of bringing the good news of Christ's salvation to the native people. Faced with many hardships and challenges, the new priests would need to trust God for their daily needs and safety.

Father Gabriel Breynat was among the new priests. Father Breynat was sent first to Fond du Lac on Lake Athabasca on the north central border of the Province of Saskatchewan where he served among people called the Caribou Eaters. They accepted Father Breynat quickly, calling him their "Little Praying Man." This tiny indomitable French priest faced many challenges in the wilderness, not the least of which was gathering food for himself and his dogs. He soon began to adopt the Indian customs, learning their method of fishing as a means of survival. The Caribou Eaters

---

[40] Breynat, Page 1.

showed Father Breynat how to thread his weighted nets with poles fed from one hole to the next under the ice. Whenever he pulled the nets through one of the holes, there would be a variety of good fish to eat.

The Indian people were attracted by Bishop Grouard's and Father Breynat's acceptance of them and their adaptation to the Indian way of life. When the Indian people felt Father Breynat's love for them, they were willing to listen to him and learn about God from the Bible.

The indigenous people were very superstitious before they met Father Breynat. In order to believe in *Him Who Made the Earth*, the Caribou Eaters needed to lay aside their superstitions and begin to accept the teachings of the Bible.

Several years later on a visit in our home, Bishop Breynat told us the story of the first caribou he shot. The big animal didn't die right away, so he hit it over the head with a large piece of wood to put it out of its misery. Well, did he ever get in trouble with the Caribou Eaters for that!

The superstitions of the Caribou Eaters prevented them from killing an animal by hitting it over the head with a stick. They were certain the spirit of the caribou would punish the people and there would be no caribou for their hunting. But that year there were more caribou than ever before! Thousands of Caribou just kept coming and coming and coming for days. The miraculous gathering of the vast caribou herd helped the Caribou Eaters overcome their superstitions and put their trust in Jesus not only as the God who *made* the earth, but also as the God who *saved the world*.

Yet, it was their ability to see life as spiritual that helped the Indian people accept what the priests were teaching about God from the Bible. The Indian tribes in the northwest had an awareness of a God of creation before the priests arrived, but they didn't know about Jesus' life and how his death on the cross opened a way of salvation for all mankind.[41]

When the elderly Bishop Grouard realized his time as Bishop was coming to a close, he wanted the man who would take his place as the next bishop to shepherd the Indian people with Jesus' love. Bishop Grouard noticed that Father Breynat did not treat Indians as savages to be exploited, but instead considered them created by God

---

[41] Ibid. 29.

as fellow citizens of earth. Just like Papa, Gabriel Breynat's faithful dedicated service demonstrated the *special something* that Bishop Grouard expected. In 1901 Father Breynat received word from the Archbishop of St. Boniface that the Pope had named Father Breynat the Vicar Apostolic of Mackenzie, and Bishop of Adrementum. Gabriel Breynat was then thirty-four years old.

Both Papa and Bishop Breynat knew that if they were to be effective in serving among the Indians, they needed to speak indigenous languages fluently. The Indians, to their credit, were also adept at language acquisition. They didn't study language development. They used the abilities that God gave them to figure out new words as they were needed. The Indians soon learned to speak both English and French in order to trade their furs, and showed a keen ability to acquire words in their own languages for merchandise used by the white settlers.

I still remember some of the Indian dialects I learned as a child. The word for God meant, *He who made the world*. Their word for powder used in the gun meant, *the little lead for gun ground up*. They could make up new words right away, because their words were formed from other words that were familiar and carried meanings that were similar to the new things they were seeing. When they saw the first wagon, they called it a *sled on wheels*. When they saw fire coming out of the smoke stack on the engine of the train, their word for train meant *the sled moved by fire*. They called the first car they saw *a canoe moved by oil*. They referred to the first airplane they saw as *the flying canoe*.

One of the greatest challenges Bishop Grouard had faced was changing opinion popularized in Europe that Indians were savages. Breynat quoted Bishop Grouard's account of the war of ideas at the 1875 Congress at Nancy in France as follows:

> This Asiatic origin of the Tinnehs, and of other American peoples, was for some time doubted by scholars interested in the history of America before its discovery by Christopher Columbus.
>
> They argued from written remains and from the ethnography of the native races of the New World. The scholars of various nations who belonged to this school were known as Americanists. At a congress held at Nancy, from the 19th to the 22nd of July, 1875, a definitive conclusion was reached.
>
> I can hardly do better than quote Bishop Grouard, who as a simple Oblate priest was present at various sessions of the congress, along with another Oblate, Father Petitot.

Several speakers had their say, and in view of the direction in which their ideas tended, it became clear to us that what they desired to establish was the autochthonous character of the American peoples and so contest the unity of the human race. M. de Rosny stood out prominently as the champion of this godless theory. He boldly proclaimed his anti-Christian doctrine and took a lofty stand on the authority of Voltaire, "whom," as he held, "one can always safely quote anywhere."

What Voltaire said was: "Once God could create flies in America, why could he not have created men also?"

Hence he wanted to establish on principle that the American peoples derived from America and nowhere else.

M. de Rosny made his peroration with all the aplomb of a Paris professor, and concluded to the satisfaction of all who wished to establish a fact which seemed opposed to the truth of Christianity.

Father Petitot then sought leave to speak. He urged the Bureau not to conclude too hurriedly that the Americans were autochthonous: "Because we do not have in Europe any document that can throw light on their origin, we should not conclude, without further discussion, that they could not have come from Asia. I am not prepared at the moment to enter into the debate, but if anyone cares to listen to me tomorrow, I will bring my proofs."

There was some applause at this. "So the Father wants war," M. de Rosny exclaimed; "very well, he shall have it."

At the next session, Father Petitot soon captured the audience's attention. When it was learned that he had spent thirteen years on the barren lands in the Arctic, among natives whose languages he knew so well as to publish dictionaries of them, when he promised to say nothing he had not seen with his own eyes or heard with his own ears, "At last," said one of my neighbors, "here is something positive, not fantastic fiction or unsupported hypotheses!"

The Reverend Father adduced cogent proofs, from the traditions and manners, beliefs, language and weapons of the Eskimos, that these people have a common origin with the Asiatics and are therefore not autochthonous.

Next day he resumed his notes on the analogies between the language of the Tinnehs and those of the peoples of Asia and Oceania, on the similarity of their observances to those of the Israelites, and on the conformity of their customs and traditions with those narrated in the Bible.

Finally, at the fourth and final session, he confined himself to treating the question of Indian weapons, specimens of which he had brought with him to France. These he compared with the stone weapons preserved in the national museum at Saint-Germain-en-Laye[42]. In the perfect resemblance to be found, both in material and shape, between the weapons and implements of different nations, he found new proof of the common origin of the human race.

His conclusion was, "the Americans are not an autochthonous race, but belong to the one human family of which all the peoples on earth are members."

It was the conclusion approved by the prolonged applause of the whole assembly.

Thus the Voltarians "had to witness the triumph of a poor missionary from Mackenzie."[43]

Bishop Breynat carried on the battle that Indians were part of the human race and not savages, standing against the tide of popular opinion of his day. Bishop Breynat attributed the ability of the Indian people to understand God as they studied the Bible as one demonstration of their intelligence:

I am often asked if the Indians are intelligent. A distinction should be made here between speculative and practical intelligence. We should hardly expect them, entirely uneducated as they are, to be versed in the subtleties of metaphysics. Yet are they lacking in speculative intelligence?

One of them said to me one day (and he was not the only one to confide in me this way):

When I walk in the woods in search of game, I often wonder at the great trees, the plants of all kinds, the flowers, the fruits and the different animals, each with a life of its own; and when I see the rivers and lakes full of fish, when I watch the sun rise and set, and behold the moon and the stars, do you know what I say to myself? I say: all these could never move and grow by themselves. There is someone very mighty who has made them all and takes care of all things on the earth.

So when Father Grollier came and told us of Him who is called *Ni'oltsi-ni*, 'he who made the earth,' I believed at once.

---

[42] Located in one of the wealthiest suburbs in western Paris, France.
[43] Breynat. 63-64.

There are plenty of philosophers and scientists who are unable to reason as well as this. Here is another example, a remark of my old friend Deaf Laurence:

> Before Father Grollier came we were medicine makers (sorcerers). We treated women just like toys, or else as beasts of burden; when our parents grew old, we abandoned them in the forest; we were afraid of death. When someone we loved died, there was crying and weeping for days on end.
>
> The first Praying Man came among us 'with empty hands'. He had, like you, his cross on his breast. A number of Praying Men came after him. They spoke to us of *Him-who-made-the-earth*, who created us out of love, and loved us so much that he sent his Son to show us the way to Heaven. It was he who died on a cross to gain pardon for our sins and save us. We accepted the words of the Praying Man and also the commandments of *Him-who-made-the-earth*, our Master and Father. And we had no more fear of death. It was hard for us to change our life and obey the Praying Man. But it was not just his words that changed us. If there had not been someone all-powerful to speak through his mouth, enlighten our minds and make our hearts strong, we would never have been able to do it, or be happy and at peace as we are now.

Further proof of this reasoning power came from my friend Porcupine-Tooth. Originally he had belonged to that band of Indians who live on the borders of the Great Plains and are noted for their *caribou mentality*. Today, most of them know how to read and write in syllabic characters, and thanks to religious instruction their mentality has gradually improved.

Entering my room on one occasion Porcupine-Tooth caught sight of a summary of Sacred Scripture on the table.

"That's a grand book," he declared with conviction, "it tells a lot of interesting stories."

It happened to be open at the passage about the meeting of Nicodemus with Our Lord.

"It took me a long time," he admitted, "to understand what Our Lord said to Nicodemus, but I got it in the end."

"Good," I said, "let me hear you explain it."

Thereupon my Caribou Eater gave a perfect explanation of how a man must be born again spiritually in order to have eternal life.[44]

---

[44] Ibid. 68-70.

Bishop Breynat underscored the practical intelligence of the Indians as further proof the Indian people were equal members of the human race:

> As for their practical intelligence, it is astonishing to see how ingenious they can be. I have already described to what good purposes they turn the caribou of the plains. And look at the little portable engines they now attach to their canoes. How quickly they learned the mechanism, and how skillfully they can make any necessary repairs with string, bits of rubber or leather thongs! Properly instructed they would soon be able, just as were our Eskimos, to pass on the lesson to many a white man.
>
> If some of the braggarts who boast of civilization and modern inventions, as if these things were due solely to their own personal genius, were to be transported to the great plains and left in the middle of herds of caribou to fend for themselves with nothing but their intelligence and two hands, they would be only too glad, I fancy, to be rescued by a family of those savages they so loftily despise.[45]

However, the most overwhelming challenge Bishop Breynat faced was the immensity of his vicariate. Bishop Breynat was notified that the two districts of the Mackenzie and Yukon were joined, and that he was responsible for both. He objected to Bishop Grouard that one man could not adequately care for the needs of the people in such a vast region. In his book Bishop Breynat described how huge his vicariate had become, "The boundaries fixed by the Holy See extended from the 60th parallel to the North Pole, and from 102 degrees longitude in the east to the borders of Alaska in the west. On the mainland alone this meant an area of about 889,000 square miles."[46] To have an idea just how large the area was, the combined area of the two largest states in the U. S. A., Texas and Alaska, would need Iowa thrown in to come close in size.

It was the promise of funding from the Klondike gold rush in the Yukon that prompted the decision. Bishop Grouard told Bishop Breynat, "Our Mackenzie missions are very poor . . . . The Klondike mines will provide us with plenty of funds."[47] Unfortunately, this hope quickly disintegrated as the gold fizzled out.

---

[45] Ibid. 70.
[46] Ibid. 95.
[47] Ibid. 115.

The shortage of funds made it difficult for staff already in the Northwest Territories who were stretched to the breaking point. These shortages began to affect morale among the priests, nuns, and brothers. Bishop Breynat's energies were spent raising funds and overseeing the construction of the churches, schools, and hospitals within his realm of responsibility. He often overextended himself until he was near death at times. His overseers eventually sent him back to France for a sabbatical to regain his health.

The Indian Act of Canada passed in 1876 gave the Canadian government responsibility for health care and education of Indian children.[48] The Canadian government entered into agreements with the churches to share expenses for the schools. However, the government at first would only fund schools within lands that had been turned over to the Canadian government through treaties. The Fort Providence IRS was begun by the church in 1867, but the Fort Simpson agency did not enter into treaty until 1922. The government provided a token stipend expecting the church to fund the school until a treaty was made.

Bishop Breynat wrote of the difficulties in providing the needs of the children at the mission schools:

> Funds came from the societies of the Propagation of the Faith and the Holy Childhood. The Ottawa government made an annual contribution of four hundred dollars to help us feed and clothe the forty children in the boarding school at Fort Providence, or ten dollars per child per year, less than a dollar a month.
>
> Every mission, with the exception of the Arctic Red River post, cultivated a small garden which provided potatoes, turnips, cabbages, carrots, and other vegetables. The Providence mission school had a farm and a few head of cattle to furnish milk, butter and a little meat. The farm, in addition to potatoes and the usual vegetables, also grew barley for soup and a kind of coffee.[49]

When reports indicated the gold rush had ended and no funds were coming from that direction, near the end of 1902 Bishop Breynat decided to make an appeal to the Canadian government to increase their portion of support for the parochial schools:

---

[48] http://encarta.msn.com/encyclopedia_461510992/Indian_Act_of_Canada.html
[49] Breynat. 97-98.

At Ottawa I stopped to see Sir Wilfrid Laurier, Prime Minister of Canada, and called his attention to the fact that the monthly contribution of a dollar each to our forty children at Providence was far from enough to cover the cost of their feeding, clothing, and lodging. Bishop Grouard had told me of the friendly reception he had received from Sir Wilfrid and the encouraging promises he had brought away. Like Bishop Grouard I was very well received. The Prime Minister listened to what I had to say with much interest and apparent sympathy. I too carried away . . . encouraging promises!

It was my first experience with politicians. I had to wait till January 30, 1907, before I could announce to our Sisters at Providence the success of my mission. Then the Department of Indian Affairs made me a grant of seventy-two dollars a year per child, but only for twenty-five children, whereas at that time we had nearly fifty. Moreover, it was to be regarded as a favor and it was carefully pointed out to me that "the Mackenzie, being a missionary field, is the Church's responsibility."[50]

In 1903 when he realized he had been placated by the Canadian Prime Minister, Bishop Breynat brought his appeal for funds to his homeland. But in France "the anti-clerical movement was at its height"[51] and all was in an uproar. There would be no funds coming from the church in France. Breynat's final appeal was to Pope Leo XIII in Rome:

My words were effective and I was privileged to kneel at the feet of Leo XIII, while several cardinals were waiting to come in, apparently for some important deliberation. Finally I reached Rome. Leo XIII, then ninety years of age, had virtually ceased giving audiences. I had to be insistent with the majordomo, telling him that my Indians would never understand how I could set out from the Arctic Ocean to see the Pope and not have audience with the "Great Praying Chief." A few moments were all I required and I promised not to tire the Holy Father.

Like all who had this privilege of meeting Leo XIII, I was struck by the beauty of his face which had an ascetic and almost transparent quality. He showered me with blessings for my missionaries, their flocks and my own humble person. He was to die soon after, on July 20, 1903.

I had an interview with Cardinal Simeoni, Prefect of Propaganda, who gave me all the directives I needed,

---

[50] Ibid. 116.
[51] Ibid. 116.

understanding readily enough that in countries so remote and difficult of access, missionaries and vicar apostolic alike must be entrusted with the most extensive powers. I remember submitting to him three cases of conscience in the matter of canon law. Each time he threw up his hands, explaining: "*Eh! Eh! Ad impossible, nemo tenetur!*" (No one is bound to do the impossible.)

"Thank you, Your Eminence," I said, "I know the principle and shall apply it when the occasion arises!"[52]

Bishop Breynat left Rome with blessings, but not so much as a promise of funds. The Roman Catholic Church established missions in the far reaches of the globe, and the resources of the Holy See, although vast, were stretched thin by the time they reached the Canadian Northwest. He described his voyage on the ship bound for North America:

> On board there were some sixty religious, male and female: Dominicans, Franciscans and others expelled from France by the anticlerical laws. Also aboard were the members of a commission which the French government was sending to the Olympic Games at Los Angeles or New Orleans. This commission was presided over by a M. Michel who, if I remember rightly, had distinguished himself in the liquidation of the Carthusians' property. Naturally the presence of sixty religious was visibly embarrassing to the representatives of the government that was sending us into exile. However, we had no complaint to make of them; their attitude throughout the voyage was perfectly correct.
>
> When we were a day out from New York there was the customary banquet, with champagne. There was also to have been a great ball and the ladies had donned appropriate costumes. However, the religious had arranged among themselves to leave the salon before the champagne made its appearance. They all went up to the gallery overlooking the salon and assembled there around a piano which was at the passengers' disposal. Then, at the top of their voices, they sang the famous hymn composed by Gounod for the departure of missionaries. A deep silence fell among the guests, and there was no ball that evening. Later a member of the commission came and knocked at my cabin door. Without saying a word — though he was visibly moved — he handed me a thousand-franc note. . . . From the representatives of their homeland who had

---

[52] Ibid. 116-117.

just banished their priests, God provided the funds for the children in the parochial schools of the Canadian northwest.[53]

Bishop Breynat now had money for the schools in northwestern Canada. All of his energy for the schools was spent in providing the buildings, securing the staff, and providing their food and other practical needs.

Regardless of all his efforts, Bishop Breynat could not be everywhere at once. There was a deep seated problem within the schools themselves that he did not have sufficient time and energy to solve. In the Catholic boarding schools, not all of the nuns, monks and priests shared Bishop Breynat's love for Indian culture and language. Some nuns and brothers who were teachers in the Fort Providence Catholic residential school still considered the children *savages* and treated us cruelly. Although they had taken vows of service, learning *about* Jesus and repeating *prescribed* vows does not guarantee that the Holy Spirit will live in someone's heart. Those who had recited their vows without a heart commitment were soon unable in their own strength to cope with the harsh conditions of the Arctic region and the increasing numbers of children placed under their care. Add to that the prejudices that some harbored in their hearts against Indians, and the schools became more like detention centers than halls of learning.

---

[53] Ibid. 117-118.

If Only the Rod Had Been Round

He called a little child and had him stand among them. And he said: "I tell you the truth, unless you change and become like little children, you will never enter the kingdom of heaven. Therefore whoever humbles himself like this child is the greatest in the kingdom of heaven. And whoever welcomes a little child like this in my name welcomes me." Matthew 18:2-5, (*NIV*)

After Papa's first year as Indian Agent, his 1914 report to Indian Affairs was comprised of praise of the Fort Providence school:

FORT SIMPSON AGENCY.
Mr. T.W. Harris, Indian agent, reports as follows:[54]

The Roman Catholic boarding school at Fort Providence on the Mackenzie River is the only educational institution in this agency. The building is sufficiently large, having two commodious classrooms and three dormitories. All the rooms are kept scrupulously clean. There is also ample fire protection. A bountiful supply of water is secured from the Mackenzie River.

In their scholastic work the pupils are divided into four standards, and I am pleased to say that the curriculum prescribed for Indian schools is faithfully carried out. All the children assist according to their capacity in the work of the farm and garden, while the girls are specially instructed in sewing and cooking. The older girls make gloves, moccasins, etc., out of moose or deerskins and work in silk. These are readily sold to tourists passing through Fort Providence in summer. I had the pleasure of being present at the annual entertainment, and, while all the drills and recitations were well executed, special mention must be made of the vocal music. During recreation English and French are spoken, preference being given the former.

It is impossible to praise too highly the care and devotion practiced by the reverend sisters and missionaries, who have charge of the educational work in this territory.

When, at the age of eighty-nine, I saw his 1914 report to Indian Affairs for the first time I wept, "Oh, Papa, *you never knew*. You didn't understand what we *went* through."

---

[54] 1914 *Indian Affairs Report*. 169.

The harsh life of the children in the boarding school under the direction of the Grey Nuns was kept well hidden. When Papa made his annual visit to the school, the children were on display, carefully prepared for presentations staged and polished by the nuns. Papa had never been allowed to see the deprivation, the beatings, the poor food, the absence of loving care, or the children's forced labor. The nuns tried to create an aura of quality education and loving care for their annual review, and Papa had been duly impressed.

Without knowing the real situation at the school, Papa faithfully recorded the census, including numbers of school age children who were or were not attending school. Indian children considered truants were rounded up by the NWMP, the monks, and the priests. It is very likely that parents, law enforcement officials, and clergy brought children to the school in good faith trusting the children would be well looked after.

The nuns might understandably have become stir-crazy in the remote Arctic wilderness cut off from family, friends, and almost all communication. However, the harsh climate and isolation could not justify their extreme cruelty toward the children entrusted to their care. The nuns' lives dedicated to represent Christ were intended to portray Jesus' willingness to go to the cross to spare us the punishment our sins deserved. Jesus had such a great longing for us to live with him in heaven forever that he had allowed his own body to be whipped, beaten, and pierced in our place. In sharp contrast, many of the Grey Nuns portrayed God as a harsh judge with a big stick in his hand waiting for the least infraction of the rules so the *children* could be severely beaten. They must not have known what Jesus taught about children: "See that you do not look down on one of these little ones. For I tell you that their angels in heaven always see the face of my Father in heaven."[55]

Mary, Rachel, Charlotte, and Thad Harris all went to the Catholic boarding school in Fort Providence before James, Nora and me. My older sister Rachel suffered torture similar to what I later experienced. When Rachel was caught talking during a time of silence, one of the nuns decided to sew Rachel's mouth shut with a great big needle used for sewing leather. Rachel came home that year with scars on her mouth that she bore the rest of her life.

---

[55] Matthew 18:10-11

In 1927 when Jim was ten, I was eight, and Nora was six years old, our trusting parents purchased our passage and made sure we were settled into our stateroom on board *The Distributor*. Nora and I tried to be brave as Mama and Papa had us pose for a picture in our new school dresses with large white bows in our hair before giving us hugs and kisses. The worst was watching them turn and walk away from us back to shore. We were leaving everything that felt safe and familiar without our parents to watch over us. As the steamer's paddlewheel churned *goodbye* to Fort Simpson, we were two little homesick sisters making our first voyage *up* the river to Fort Providence with our older brother Jim.

On deck the bitter winds swept the cold spray from the paddles and waves, penetrating even the thickest coats. Thankfully, the stateroom Papa reserved for us protected us from the weather. We were heading in an easterly direction toward Great Slave Lake, named for the Slavey Indians[56]. After several days, our rough two hundred fifty mile voyage to Fort Providence ended, but we had to endure nine cold months of total separation from our parents.

Great Slave Lake is the ninth largest fresh water lake in the world. The lake is just under three hundred miles long and almost seventy miles wide. The southwestern point of the lake tapers to an inlet where the Mackenzie begins flowing. Fort Providence is several miles further west of the river's source, protected somewhat by heavy forest, but close enough to the lake to hear the howling winds. Buildings in the little Indian village are buried in winter from the heavy lake-effect snowfalls.

Like adjusting the wick on an Aladdin lamp, Autumn's slender fingers turned down the summer's midnight sun, changing Fort Providence into a land of increasing darkness. For a few weeks during the depth of the winter, the sun appeared only briefly above the tall treetops on the river's southern shore. We wondered if the river ice would ever thaw to free us from our prison.

---

[56] Great Slave Lake is the deepest lake in North America, but not the largest lake in the Northwest Territories in terms of surface area. Great Bear Lake is larger, but not as large as Lake Superior. Lake Superior has the largest surface area of any fresh water lake in the world. The maximum depth for Great Slave Lake is 614 meters (2,010 feet) compared to Lake Superior's depth of 406 meters (1,332 feet). http://en.wikipedia.org/wiki/Great_Slave_Lake

Fort Providence Residential School

All the children were so *very, very* lonely for our folks. Very *few* of the nuns demonstrated any love for us; they seemed prejudiced against Indians. I cried for Mama the first year I was in school. We never saw our parents until the *next spring* when the ice on the river began to break up. When the first boat came down, we could go home. To discourage us from trying to run away, the nuns terrorized us with stories that demons were right outside the door. Where did they think we would run when we were in the middle of a barren wilderness? We would soon have frozen to death, starved, or been eaten by wild animals.

When Nora and I arrived, we were in the first wooden school[57] that dated back to 1867, but a couple of years later a newer more modern school took its place. Throughout the year children were told repeatedly, "Remember you're no better than a dog. You have no soul." We were called *des sauvages*, or the savages. The nuns said they were sent by God to change us – to make something of us.

After school hours we all had assigned chores. At first I worked in the dining room for the fathers, but one of the girls helped herself

---

[57] Sketch by Ruth Thielke from a photograph of the old wooden school.

to a small piece of pie. I was blamed, and reassigned to peeling potatoes in *the pit*, a dark damp little room. Students also carded wool and spun yarn to knit socks and mittens. I had an awful time, because I was left-handed, and everything seemed backwards for me. I don't believe I ever finished a knitting project, because I had to keep ripping up my attempts. In the spring we helped plant the school gardens and scrubbed down all the walls.

In the midst of so many difficulties, there were a few enjoyable times at the school. One thing I enjoyed was singing in the choir. My voice was weak and a little off-key, but no one noticed when we all sang together. The hymns were in either French or Latin which helped me become more familiar with those languages. Another thing I loved was performing in a skit or play, or reciting some piece I had learned by heart. Papa's dramatic faces, animated voice, and gestures must have carried over to me. I was usually in a play for our Christmas programs, and often given the longest part.

Life at the school was almost unbearable. We had to wear itchy wool clothing and sleep on old straw mattresses. My sister Nora and I suffered mental abuse from the nuns' threats and promises of being beaten if we tried to talk to our brother Jim at mealtimes, or anywhere throughout the whole school where we might see him.

We got up at seven o' clock, straightened our beds, did our toiletries, and made it to chapel by seven-thirty. After eight o' clock breakfast, we walked to the school building about a block away. No one was allowed to speak their native language. Some children had never heard English or French, so I felt compelled to help them understand. I was beaten many times for speaking native languages. Sister Leduc struck me on the head hard enough that I would see stars and experienced headaches as a result. Sometimes I lost consciousness momentarily when she back-handed me, sending me flying to the floor like a little rag doll.

Sister Leduc was always threatening, and the one who gave the severest beatings. She was a tall skinny French woman with a very twisted mean temperament. I can still *see* her. She had psoriases on her face which she picked at and then touched us on the face.

One of the forms of punishment was being denied washroom privileges; we soiled our clothing, and sat in our filth the rest of the day. That may have led to bladder infections and increased the incidents of bedwetting. Bedwetting can be related to fear or severe damage to the kidneys. I never wet the bed when I was in my family

Bridget's Nightmares of the Grey Nuns

home, but at the school I was filled with fear and wet the bed every night.

I had nightmares[58] when I tried to sleep always *waiting* for that stick to come down. Rather than getting me up during the night *before* I wet the bed, Sister Leduc[59] stood by my bed with a big stick to listen until she heard me *do* it. Then she beat me until I had welts and black and blue bruises that never had a chance to heal on my mid to lower back, especially around the kidneys. After beating me, Sister Leduc made me wash my sheet and hang it out in the freezing weather. I *barely* had a good night's sleep *ever* at the school; this was repeated every night the entire five years I was in attendance. I believe the severe beatings on my back resulted in my infertility.

Sister Metivier twisted our ears every time she walked past us in the schoolroom. My ears were pulled and twisted until they cracked and bled with continuous oozing and scabbing. The sores on my ears were always painful and never allowed to heal. Sister Leduc and Sister Sylvain locked us outside in the subzero weather *to play* for hours where we had no way to warm ourselves. We huddled together near the building freezing until we were finally allowed to come inside. Despite warm clothing, our frostbitten feet, hands, and

---

[58] Ruth Thielke's sketch from picture with fisheye special effect.
[59] NOTE from Truth and Reconciliation Commission: We found documents on a "Sister Beatrice Leduc" who was at Fort Providence SR IRS during the Claimant's dates of attendance. *"Information Relating to Alleged Abusers", Indian Residential Schools Resolution Canada, Alternative Dispute Resolution* (File #E5442-V-0106, Bridget Angela Volden, 11 April 2006)

70

faces were often numb with cold, and very painful as we thawed out indoors.

Even as small children, we had to do heavy physical labor scrubbing floors and washing all the dishes including huge pots and pans. The nuns made the young boys cut up trees, sawing and chopping all the wood. Wood was burned in large furnaces to keep the massive school building warm.

If there was an outing planned, the nuns often singled me out for punishment ordering me, "You go in the closet." They threw me into a closet with no windows where the dirty clothes were kept. There I remained all day while the rest of the school was on their adventure. The closet had a wooden door fastened with a little hook on the outside. I don't know why I didn't just bust the door open, but I was probably too afraid of more beatings. I believe the claustrophobia I suffered all my life started in that closet; to this day I don't like to ride elevators or to be in confined places.

The coping mechanism I developed as I sat in that dark little room, so sad, scared and all alone, was to store up really funny memories to keep myself from going all to pieces. For example, our dormitory was one large room with curtains on either end where the nuns slept. The nuns had to have their heads almost shaved in order to wear the head coverings that went with their garb. One evening the nuns were sitting on their beds behind the curtains giving each other a haircut when suddenly the heavy curtains, rods and all, fell crashing down. We stared at the nuns' bald heads for a moment in shock and amazement, and then we all burst out laughing.

Another funny memory was of heavyset Sister Laplante standing at the end of a bench as she reached for the coal oil lamp that was growing dim. Sister Laplante was a large overweight French nun with a bad odor and a terrible disposition. She told us to put our hands on the bench so it wouldn't tip over. *But* when she got up on the end of the bench and started pumping the lamp we all just let go. She shouted, "WHAAAAY," as with arms flailing and skirts flapping she and the bench flipped over backwards. That was a memory that made me laugh out loud while I was sitting in the dark. While the others were on their excursion I could laugh as loudly as I liked, because there was no one to hear me in that part of the building.

The abuses weren't only done to Nora and me; there was a really sad thing that happened to two little girls. The Catholic brothers from Fort Providence had gone to chop wood. As they were working in the forest, they passed a house off by itself when they heard little whimperings. Nobody answered their knock on the door. As the monks went inside and their eyes adjusted to the dim light, they discovered two cold, sad, hungry, pitiful little girls. The girls' parents lay dead and frozen in their bed, maybe from influenza or starvation, and the little girls were left all alone with no one to care for them. The fire had been out for awhile, it was very cold in the winter time, and the little girls were just shivering and freezing.

The monks buried the mom and dad right there in the woods before they brought the little girls back to the Convent where the Grey Nuns could care for them. Of course the girls' soiled clothing and dirty matted hair was filled with lice and bugs. The nuns didn't want anything to do with the filthy little girls, so it became our job to scrub them, de-louse them, and make sure they were dressed in clean warm clothes. They were so hungry; we found them something to eat. The tiny girls were maybe two and four years old. They were very lonely, very sad, very scared, and they couldn't speak either English or French.

The nuns gave the girls Rosaries: one bright red and the other bright blue. The little girls had never seen Rosaries before; naturally they thought the beads were toys and played with them in church. After church on our way to the dining room, surly old Sister Sylvain said, "We have to teach these little girls right now that they can't play in church with their Rosaries like that."

Sister Sylvain threw a rope over the big hot water pipes near the tall ceiling, and she tied the older girl's hands with one end of the rope. When she told the rest of us to pull the other end of the rope, Nora and I screamed. We didn't want to obey, but from fear of the nuns beating *us*, eventually everybody hoisted the four-year-old right off the floor. Sister Sylvain made us hold on tight keeping the little girl suspended in the air. When she passed out, the nuns let her down, and put the rope on the toddler. Then they tied her tiny hands and we had to hold her up off the floor until she also fainted. We felt worse for them than anything else! Those were some of the atrocities the nuns did that haunted us the rest of our lives.

The school administrators finally decided that Sister Leduc was so cruel; they were going to ship her to Fort Resolution.[60] The day the

---

[60] Fort Resolution is on the southeastern shore of Great Slave Lake at the mouth of the Slave River.

boat came for her, she came to our refectory[61] to give us the news. We started to cry – for joy! We cried for joy! You couldn't stop us. We were crying, and crying, and crying at the top of our voices. Everybody was crying! She thought we were crying because we were sad she was leaving, but we were so happy to be relieved of that monster. When the boat got around the bend we burst into cheers and laughter!

Another dreadful aspect of the school was the *terrible* food. In the morning they would mix up oatmeal porridge, but it was thick *lumpy stuff* not even *cooked*. They *slapped* that on our plates and we had to eat it that way. We *seldom ever* got sugar to put on it and never any milk. We had homemade bread, but instead of butter they used some sort of rancid *tallow* from animal fat for a spread. That's *all* we ate for breakfast. If there was fruit at that school way up in the Arctic, the *nuns* ate it. Sometimes we had potatoes. A lot of the fish we were given was not *even cleaned*. They just *shoved* the whole fish in the oven all filled with *guts* and everything. By spring the stored fish had begun to spoil, but we had to eat it. A big chunk *of rotten fish complete with the scales* would be slapped on our plates and we had to eat all of it. They almost made us eat the fish skin; the food we ate was not fit for a dog. I could not *stomach* the uncooked baked beans with a little bacon on top. The beans were *hard* as a *rock*, we couldn't even chew them, but we had to swallow them whole. If the beans had soaked all night and then baked all morning, they would have been tasty, but, no, our food was just *awful*. We got sick quite often from the food. It's a wonder we're *alive*!

The nuns did not allow us to pour out our hearts in our letters. We had to lie to our parents that we were happy and treated wonderfully. The nuns *dictated* on the blackboard what to write:

Dear Mother & Father, We are so happy here. *Blah, blah, blah . . ..*
Your loving daughter, Bridget.

Our parents had no idea how we lived, because we were so far away from our homes! There was no way to get to our parents or for our parents to get to us. There were two or four men who drove their dog teams for winter mail delivery dressed warmly in fur-lined parkas and fur-lined mukluks handmade by the natives. It took a *long* time for the dog teams to pick up the mail, and then to get back

---

[61] dining hall or gathering place

to Fort Providence. Our mail was always old by the time it got to us. One dog team musher was our brother-in-law, Mary's husband Joseph Villenueve, but we were not permitted to speak to him.

Nora was on the other side of the big dormitory in a bed far away from mine. One night when we were so lonely, I woke up in the middle of the night, went over, and crawled in with Nora. It felt so good to be close to her; we hugged each other and fell asleep. The next thing I knew, there came that big stick on top of me again. One of the nuns beat me for sleeping with my sister and sent me back to my bed.

After the long and bitterly cold winter months, we couldn't wait for the river to break up in the spring. We watched and listened with great anticipation for the river to begin flowing again. Then some April night we would hear thunderous crunching and grinding of ice and we knew that the great Mackenzie was yawning and stretching as it wakened to spring.

We rushed out to the bank to watch the river. The noise of the river breaking up was so loud, we thought it could be heard throughout the whole Northwest Territories! Like a giant kaleidoscope the chunks of ice unfolded from one masterpiece to another as the ice moved a little and then stopped. Every time the ice moved in the coming days we looked for the different images it created. We imagined all kinds of faces, fairies, or animal formations in the ice. Sometimes the ice wouldn't move for a week or so. Then it moved again and stopped. As each day passed we saw more open water. It usually took all of May and into June before the last of the ice floated away.

To add to the excitement of spring, the hunters and trappers began returning with their dog sleds to spend summer with their families in the village. As the river began to flow freely, some villagers returned from their winter hunting in birch bark canoes that were full of furs, and their belongings.

We were so happy to be sent home to Fort Simpson to spend the summer with our family. How excited we were to see Mama and Papa waiting on the shore! We rushed into Mama's arms and never wanted her to let go. We wanted summer to last forever, but as fall approached an increasing dread fell on me at the thought of returning to school.

In 1928, my second year of school, Mama wanted to spend the winter with her mother in Cold Lake. Rose was only three-and-a-half at the time which was too young to be separated from Mama. Papa sent Mama and Rose with us when we left for Fort Providence. At Fort Providence we got off the boat to go to school, and Mama continued on her way with baby Rose.

Papa got too lonely after Mama left, however, so he sent word on a steamer for Jim to come back home to help him. Jim made it aboard the last boat going to Fort Simpson. Even though we hadn't been allowed to have contact with Jim in school, it had been a comfort just to know he was there. Now Nora and I had to face a whole year with just the two of us in school.

As Christmas approached Papa missed Mama so much that he decided to fly to Edmonton on the only plane that came down north on its routine run making Christmas deliveries. Without a place to land at Fort Providence, that plane circled above the mission a couple of times as it flew lower and lower until it finally dropped a bag of mail into a field of snow for the school boys to retrieve.

In the mail bag Papa sent a note to us that he was aboard the plane, but for us not to get too lonesome. He promised to come back with Mama on the boat for us in the spring. Papa must certainly have missed Mama, because he was petrified of flying, especially in such a tiny plane! Papa had also dropped a Christmas package for us that Mama had helped prepare during the summer before she left Fort Simpson.

When the nuns retrieved our package, they called us into the front parlor. The box was full of beautiful warm moccasins and mittens that Mama had made for us, hand decorated with her artistic silk work. There were also colorful boxes of delicious chocolates from our parents, chocolate covered cherries, gum and hard candy – everything that any child would dream of for Christmas!

Just seeing all those delightful gifts brought our parents' love close to us. It was the only contact of any kind that we had with them. Many of the gifts had been made by our own mother's kind gentle hands. She must have thought of us with each loving stitch, but they did not let us keep any of it. The nuns coaxed us, "The Sister Superior likes these things. Is it okay for you to bring the box to her? Would you like to give them to her for Christmas?"

We knew the nuns wanted to divide our gifts among themselves, but what could we do? If we said we wanted to keep the gifts, the nuns would have beaten us. The thought of never enjoying those beautiful presents made all the life drain out of us. With big lumps in our throats and tears stinging our eyes, we hung our heads staring at the floor not daring to disclose our broken hearts. We whispered that we guessed it would be okay to give our gifts to the Mother Superior.

However, now the nuns had a problem. The other children had seen the airplane drop a package for us. The nuns couldn't send us back to our dormitories empty-handed, or the other children would know our gifts had been confiscated. In exchange for our wonderful presents, they brought a horrible box of prunes and lump sugar. That was the final blow. We could contain our sorrow *no more!* The dam in our wounded spirits burst. Oh how we cried! Our parents never knew that their wonderful presents expressing so beautifully their love and tender care had been *stolen*.

My will to rise above my troubles had also been stolen that day. Somehow I made it through the daily routines as one day wasted into the next. I have no memory of the following months at school, only of a growing desire for summer to come so I could see my parents again.

The whole village watched and waited for the first steamboat of the season to arrive. The first person to spot its arrival would shout, "The boat is coming!" The nuns could not contain our excitement on that wonderful day! We all ran to the windows to look. What a sight to behold, to see the smoke from *The Distributor* coming around the bend in the river! We were so excited! Once again we had contact with the outside world! Soon one of the sisters had Nora and I dressed in our coats and hats with our valise all packed and ready to go to the river bank as the steamer docked at Fort Providence.

Straining our eyes we soon recognized Mama and Papa holding our little sister Rose. We began screaming and jumping up and down for delight! We could hardly wait for the gang plank to be laid in place so we could run aboard! We felt a little sad to say goodbye to some of our friends. As we looked around at them, we noticed that the sisters who were kindly had tears in their eyes. We liked to think they would miss us, but maybe they were relieved that their long winter was also coming to and end. Soon we rushed into Mama's waiting arms as Papa stoically shook our hands in welcome. Mama's tummy was really huge. She was soon to have twins.

There was a bustle of activity at the boat landing. Supplies for Fort Providence were unloaded from the barges while old friends greeted one another. They excitedly exchanged news from their trip through Edmonton and along their journey north. Papa shook hands with the priests, brothers, and sisters from the mission and school.

Mama brought Nora and I to the cabin so we could tell Mama our news, and kiss Rose. We were so happy to see Mama and get to hold little Rose, that we were oblivious to what was taking place outside our cabin. Finally, *The Distributor* was pulling away from port and heading toward our home at last!

There were three bunks in our cabin. Nora and I were given the top bunk. What excitement! We could hardly wait for dinner to taste the wonderful food! What a joy to hear the tinkling of the glasses filled with ice water atop spotless linens set with beautiful silver and real chinaware. What a contrast from the chipped granite dishes in the school. At that first meal our eyes were much bigger than our starved tummies. Not knowing any better, we ate *way* too much, especially mashed potatoes, gravy, and dessert. Needless to say, we got horribly sick as soon as we left the table.

Mama took us to the bathroom to help us in our distress. The nice Purser brought us a little baking soda to help settle and soothe our stomachs. Mama put us to bed early. Listening to the gentle throbbing of the ship's engine, we soon were fast asleep.

By six o' clock, Nora and I woke up too excited to sleep any longer. We lay awake whispering in our upper bunk until we heard Papa getting up. After breakfast, Papa went to the club room where other passengers were enjoying conversation over a drink, and some were playing poker. Mama took us back to the cabin to pack our things.

Immediately I began helping with Rose. After Mama finished packing, she joined Papa to say goodbye to the friends they made on board. She found Papa holding everyone's attention in a recitation of Shakespeare. I stayed behind in the cabin to watch Rose and the twins, while Nora stood by the rail to watch for the first glimpse of Fort Simpson. After awhile Nora came yelling at the top of her lungs, "I see the Fort!"

Everyone ran to the deck to see, and sure enough, there was good old Fort Simpson! First were the Indians' teepees down by the flats, then the Hudson Bay Company and the mission came into view. Finally way down beyond the fort, we spied our house, the doctor's house, and our sister Mary's house. As we approached the fort, *everyone* was there to meet us!

First I saw Jim by the river's edge, then Mary and Joe and their daughter Mavis. By that time Nora, Rose, and I were yelling, "Mary! Jim!" We were so loud, Mama told us to hush up. As soon as the gang plank was down, Jim came bouncing up with a hug and squeeze for each of us! Papa greeted him, "Hello, son. I hope you didn't burn the house down while I was gone. Where is Thad? When you bring this to the house, get him to help you. We have enough stuff to keep us busy unloading all day!"

Then turning to Mama, he directed, "Josette, you get the children home, and I'll take care of our things."

Mama added, "Mary is here, too. She can help you with the baby things. I'll take the children, and we will see you at home."

I enjoyed my summer at home, but once again dreaded going back to the school for the next year. Yet in spite of the severity of my situation, other Indian children fared far worse. The way children were treated was *terrible*. Several children died from poor food, lack of medical care, and beatings. A lot of young boys were molested by some priests, and grew up to become alcoholics with nothing to live for. Even though the boys were the victims, they were so ashamed of being used as sex objects, that several of them committed suicide. I cry for the boys who were misused, and understand Jesus' stern teaching against child abuse:

> "But if anyone causes one of these little ones who believe in me to sin, it would be better for him to have a large millstone hung around his neck and to be drowned in the depths of the sea.
>
> "Woe to the world because of the things that cause people to sin! Such things must come, but woe to the man through whom they come! If your hand or your foot causes you to sin, cut it off and throw it away. It is better for you to enter life maimed or crippled than to have two hands or two feet and be thrown into eternal fire. And if your eye causes you to sin, gouge it out and throw it away. It is better for you to enter life with one eye than to have two eyes and be thrown into the fire of hell." Matthew 18:6-9, (NIV)

You might wonder why the atrocities were allowed to continue. Things were so different in the early 1900's. Sadly, without a change of heart yielding ownership of their lives to Jesus, many of the nuns and priests were still being ruled by their own thoughts and desires. Children were afraid of further punishment if we spoke out against the nuns and priests. We believed that even God would punish us. We had been beaten physically so often, we were also defeated in spirit.

Certainly not all of the nuns and priests were bad. Even in the darkest corners God sent a ray of sunshine in the form of Sister St. Claire, a nun with a tender heart who noticed my suffering. Sister St.

Claire saved little treats from her table, like a piece of bread with honey on it. She wrapped it and tucked it away discretely in her pocket. Then she found me and slipped the little treat into my hand when no one else was watching.

Bishop Breynat was also like a beacon in that dismal place, although we rarely saw him because of all of his other responsibilities. Bishop Breynat was different from the rest, because he had Jesus' love for the people. When he walked into a church, or into our home, I felt like something wonderful was happening from God. It was the Holy Spirit alive in his heart, but I didn't know anything about the Holy Spirit at that time.

In our world at Fort Providence, I was powerless and isolated from my parents who would have protected me, but God noticed my suffering and remembered me. He saw in me a little girl who was willing to suffer for doing what I knew was right. In my desperate hours throughout my lifetime God always provided for my care.

Fort Good Hope

When the Lord brought back the captives to Zion, we were like men who dreamed. Our mouths were filled with laughter, our tongues with songs of joy. Psalm 126:1-2 (*NIV*)

Papa could have retired in 1930, but he wanted to work longer to support his young family. To help Papa phase into retirement, the Canadian Department of Indian Affairs split his territory in half. Another agent was brought to Fort Simpson to cover the southern half of the Mackenzie River, while our family moved *down north* to Fort Good Hope. The river runs north, therefore the locals say *down north* meaning down river, but further north. Our new home at Fort Good Hope was roughly midway between Fort Simpson and the Arctic Ocean.

The Mackenzie drops gradually enough to allow riverboat traffic from Great Slave Lake all the way to the Arctic Ocean. Traveling as a family in the opposite direction from the Fort Providence school to a new home made the trip by steamboat exciting. The riverboat made scheduled stops at the few Hudson's Bay Forts located along the Mackenzie. While supplies from the boat were being unloaded and passengers were boarding, Papa got off the boat to greet people he knew from his work. Now and then at the longer stops we could all get off the boat to stretch our legs, but Mama worried about losing track of us.

For us children this trip was a grand adventure! We enjoyed the luxurious dining room on board, and Papa had booked our passage in a stateroom where we children had bunks, and Mama and Papa slept in a bed. As we were nearing Fort Good Hope we stood on deck in awe of the breathtaking white cliffs called *The Ramparts* that drew tourists from other parts of the world even in the early 1900's. Our trip ended with thrilling excitement as the captain shouted orders to the crew, applied skillful maneuvers to avoid a dangerous stretch of rapids, and piloted us safely to the landing. When we arrived in the summer of 1930, Fort Good Hope was just a little village. The Canadian government provided us with a brand new three-bedroom house with beautiful wooden floors and a large office for Papa.

The house was very well-built, lacking only the modern conveniences of an indoor bathroom, running water, electricity, and telephone. In our bedrooms we used older-fashioned kerosene lamps, but the main floor of the house was lighted by Aladdin lamps. Papa put coal oil in those lamps, pumped them, lit the little sack-like mesh mantels, and then adjusted the flame until the mantels glowed with a bright white light. I cleaned the Aladdin chimneys for Papa, while he watched closely to make sure I didn't drop them. The one time I broke one, Papa hollered so loudly I almost died. We would almost rather have had Papa spank us than yell.

Old newspapers were used for insulation in the walls in those days with tarpaper as a moisture barrier under the clapboard siding, but the house was built so tight, it stayed warm all winter. Papa stuffed the big furnace in the basement with wood, got a good fire going, and turned the damper down. Soon the Arctic chill was chased away as heat rose from the vents in each room making the whole house cozy. Most often the family huddled together warm and snug in the kitchen, the center of family activity while Mama did all of her cooking and baking on a large wrought iron wood burning cook stove. Papa was often in his office working at his books, keeping records for all the tribes and writing reports for Indian Affairs.

Fort Good Hope was a *good chapter* in the life of our family. Located in the Arctic the sun never fully sets for about six weeks in the summer in the land of the midnight sun. In contrast in the long winter nights for about six weeks sunlight breaks the horizon for only about two hours a day. We didn't see the northern lights in the summer, but in the winter they are especially dazzling, much more brilliant than in the south and sometimes in rainbow colors. The amazing thing about the long days in the summer is that people didn't need much sleep. If we got three or four hours of sleep in the summer we felt rested, but in the wintertime, we could sleep a long time each night.

In Fort Good Hope we lived among the Hare, or Rabbitskin Indians as some called them. What wonderful people! Our whole family just loved them, and we quickly learned to speak their Rabbitskin language with its beautiful lyrical sing-song sound, derived from the same Athabascan language group as Mama's Chipewyan tongue. There were only three white people in addition to Papa with about fifty Indians: the store keeper at the Hudson's Bay Company, another store keeper at the Northern Traders, and the priest at the mission.

The tribe was called Rabbitskins, because their livelihood was from the abundance of rabbits in their region. People lived on rabbit meat, which was very tasty. All bundled up in homemade white rabbit fur parkas and pants the children[62] looked like big fluffy rabbits. Even their blankets were made out of rabbit fur cut in strips and woven together. It could be one hundred degrees below zero, and they would stay warm in their tents.

Most of the Indians lived in the woods in the winter, their hunting and trapping season. In the nine to ten months of winter, only the old folks among the Indians were left in the encampment. The bush was thick with lots of pine trees, and a large variety of deciduous trees. There were red willows along the river with the Mackenzie Mountains for a backdrop. Children didn't dare venture into the bush alone. Bear and other wild game roamed the bush and mountains, but weren't seen in the village.

One spring day I was outside playing my harmonica when a flock of grouse came out of the woods to dig through a pile of excelsior behind our house. Excelsior is the wood shavings used to pack breakable things like new dishes that were shipped in on the barges. As I played my harmonica the grouse were listening and were all lined up on top of the pile doing their little dance. I called to my brothers and Papa, "One of you had better get your gun! If you hit them just right, you could get a whole bunch in a row!"

Thad, Jim, and Papa each grabbed a gun – 410, double-barreled shotgun – I don't know what they were, but they each had their own gun.

My brother Thad said, "I'll get 'em.' "
Jim said, "I'll get 'em.' "
Papa said, "Oh, let me get them."
"Well," the boys figured, "let Papa do it then."

---

[62]Pencil drawing by Ruth Thielke from picture.

Papa picked up his shotgun, took aim with his one good eye that was a little bit crooked, and shot as the grouse scurried for cover. "Doggonit. I missed them all!" he shouted.

Oh we laughed! My brothers thought, "You wanted to do it, and there you are."

Papa was strict. His punishment for the little children was to stand them in a corner. When my youngest sister Rose was in the corner, her lower lip would start to droop. Papa teased her, "Rose Pout. She stands in the corner all day and pouts." The more he teased, the more Rose put her head down. At the time Rose was scared of Papa. She disliked him, too, because he was the only one who punished her.

Rose was kind of mischievous and would get herself into trouble. When Rose was small, she would stand under the table and say all the bad things she could remember about Papa under her breath. One day Papa laid her across his lap and spanked her little behind. Whatever she had done to deserve the spanking, she must have learned her lesson, because Papa never spanked her again. Once was enough for Rose.

Rose was very inquisitive, and she loved to do whatever Mama was doing especially if it involved the sewing machine. As soon as Mama left the machine, Rose would sit down and start sewing. When she heard Mama returning, Rose jumped back out of the way, but by then the threads were all knotted. As Mama fixed the mess she scolded Rose, "You've been at it again, haven't you?"

One day when Mama got up from her sewing machine, Rose sat down and began sewing, but her thumb got in the way. The needle went right through her thumb and just stuck there. The pain was incredible, but Rose wasn't sure if that was any worse than the punishment she was sure to receive. It was dark in the house by then, and her thumb really hurt, but Rose knew she was in trouble and didn't cry out. Mama found her in a sorry state. It took Mama and Papa a long time to get the needle out of her thumb. They didn't scold or reprimand Rose that time, because she had already suffered enough.

One day, when Mama put Rose down for her afternoon nap, Rose pleaded, "Tell me a story."

Mama asked her, "What do you want to hear?"

"Cinderella," Rose said.

"Okay," Mama said and began telling the story. Rose lay with her eyes closed. Pretty soon Mama changed a word here or there.

Rose piped up, "No. That isn't right!" Mama corrected herself, and continued.

Before Rose fell asleep she said "Mama, of *alllll* the children you have, who do you like best?"

Mama said, "Well, I love you all the same. I love all my children."

"But isn't there one you like just a *little* better than all the others?" Rose asked. Rose bugged Mama until she finally said, "Oh, I guess I like you the best." Then Rose fell fast asleep.

Rose really liked Fort Good Hope, even though the only playmate her age was one cousin. Most often Rose played alone. She wasn't afraid of the great outdoors, and she loved walking alone in the woods near enough to the house to hear if Mama called.

We children loved the old people in Fort Good Hope. When Rose was little she adopted Old Azanie, who seemed about one hundred years old. She was like Grandma Anzalee in some ways, and Rose was entertained by her. Nora and I called Azanie the witch because she smoked a crooked little pipe with her lip curled over it. Old Azanie lived in a teepee along the river and quietly did her sewing and other household tasks. When Rose came to visit her granddaughter they would sit cross-legged on the floor when they played, and Old Azanie fed the girls.

If Rose disappeared from our house, Mama asked, "Where is Rose?"

Nora and I answered, "Oh, I suppose she's down at old Azanie's place." We went there with Mama, and sure enough, the old lady was talking to Rose in her Indian language, and Rose was just loving it.

Animals and other things in nature fascinated Rose. The red ants made great big ant hills, but they never bit Rose. As she lay close by their hills watching them, Rose sang them her little made up songs and talked to them. Looking back on it now, Rose thinks a guardian angel must have been busy keeping her from harm.

One springtime day Rose found a robin's nest just off the ground in a fur tree. The little blue-green eggs really fascinated her. Rose petted the eggs and then put them back into the nest. The next day she visited all her special places. When she came to the nest, all those eggs were on the ground broken open with tiny dead birds in them. Rose ran into the house crying. Mama said, "Well, Rose, you learned something today. Never touch eggs, because birds don't want someone else's scent on them."

Another day when it was raining really hard, Rose came upon an old cook stove that had been thrown away. There was a little yellow bird that had found its way under the cook stove to be sheltered from the rain. Rose grabbed the bird and took it into the house. Mama helped her clean out a basket to make a nest for the little bird. They gave it water and food and hung the basket in the middle of the dining room. Rose was so excited! The next morning Rose ran into the dining room to check on her yellow bird, but the poor little thing had died. Mama told her, "Rose, you have learned another important lesson. Wild things are not to be kept in the house."

Although she was learning so many things, Rose was too young to go away to school with Nora and me when we first lived at Fort Good Hope. Nora and I attended the school together two more years at Fort Providence. I do not remember being in the school at all after we moved to Fort Good Hope, but my name shows up in the school's attendance records. My school experiences were so terrible, that those two years are blocked from my memory.

One incident was too painful to forget, however. Our teacher Sister Metivier[63] who was large and buxom insisted that I was not going to write with my left hand; she beat my left hand constantly at school with a square rod for writing left-handed. I tried writing with my right hand, but it didn't work well, because I was left-handed. One day she struck me two or three times sharply on my left wrist. *How I wished the rod had been round,* the sharp edges hurt so badly! As she whacked me hard again, I felt a sudden intense pain; my left wrist was broken, and became swollen and bruised, hurting terribly. I couldn't rotate my left wrist or lift anything, and I lost the use of my left hand for a long time. The swelling and pain lasted three or four months. Although there was a nun on staff who was a nurse, I never received medical attention. As a result I have always had very poor handwriting.

From all the beatings for being left-handed, I can no longer tell my left from my right, and hence cannot tell east from west, or north from south. The countless beatings got me all confused; directions get all mixed up in my brain. I never drove a car, because I don't know my way around and can't read maps. Even now, when I get off the elevator, I will turn the wrong way, *always*!

---

[63] NOTE from Truth and Reconciliation Commission: We found documents on a "Sister Valerie Metivier" who was at Fort Providence SR IRS during the Claimant's dates of attendance.

When I returned from school in May of 1932, Papa and Mama couldn't make any sense of what I was saying. I was so *petrified*, I stuttered and shook uncontrollably. I quaked in fear if any adult came near me, even my gentle loving Mama. Mama wondered what was *wrong* with me until she examined my bruises and my disfigured left wrist. With her gentle love and encouragement, Mama was able to calm me down, until a few weeks later I finally told her everything that had happened to me at the school. Papa had been so blinded by his allegiance to Catholicism that he could not believe the nuns at Fort Providence would treat his children badly. Mama finally convinced him that I had suffered extreme abuse.

When summer was over and it was time for us to return, Mama put her foot down and said, "Flynn, I don't want you sending Bridget to that school! She has been treated *very, very* badly, and I *don't* want her to go back there anymore." She added, "You are a *well-educated* man. You *buy* the books, and *you* teach Bridget at *home*." So that's what he did. In the fall of 1932, I stayed home. Nora attended with Rose the last year we lived in Fort Good Hope, and neither of them were mistreated at the school.

I was especially thrilled to be allowed to remain at home that year. Mama's *love* and *kindness* helped me heal from some of the things I had suffered. But the atrocities had gone on for so long, they affected me my whole life. I was always nervous and afraid of everything, even my own shadow. My fear of the dark never left me.

I enjoyed being taught by Papa who was an excellent experienced teacher. Although Papa was very strict, he never laid a hand on me. I learned to focus on the twinkle in his eye that reassured me of his love. When I studied my books and did the lessons Papa assigned, I did pretty well. Papa taught me the basics including English literature and grammar, spelling, arithmetic, and history. Papa made sure I learned how to speak English properly. Mama made sure I did my homework.

It wasn't long before I began to blossom under Papa's instruction. I loved spelling and grammar, and I loved to read. However, with my poorly mended left wrist, I had trouble with my handwriting. In one of my first penmanship lessons from Papa, he went to the board and wrote "A", "B", "C". Then he turned to me, handed me the chalk and said, "Print it just like that, okay?"

I looked up at the board, but for the "A" I made just single lines without connecting them. The "B" was backwards, and the "C" went another direction. Papa looked at what I had written and said, "Oh, my God! I'm raising an Oriental!" My printing must have looked like Chinese characters. Eventually with hard work and lots of practice, I learned to make my letters understandable.

Papa tried to share his love for classical literature with his children. Sometimes Papa lined us all up so he had an audience for his recitation of Shakespeare. He made sweeping dramatic gestures as he recited:

> To-morrow, and to-morrow, and to-morrow,
> Creeps in this petty pace from day to day,
> To the last syllable of recorded time;
> And all our yesterdays have lighted fools
> The way to dusty death. Out, out, brief candle!
> Life's but a walking shadow, a poor player
> That struts and frets his hour upon the stage
> And then is heard no more. It is a tale
> Told by an idiot, full of sound and fury
> Signifying nothing."[64]

Papa put his best effort into his performance for us, and he looked and sounded like an actor on a stage, but instead of applauding, we would giggle because we were too young to appreciate Shakespeare.

In Fort Good Hope, the winters were long, the days were short, and it was very cold. We were cooped up inside for the winter, but Mama knew how to make the best of every situation. Papa took care of the smaller children while the two of us went rabbit hunting. Bundled up against the cold with her little 22 rifle slung over her shoulder and her bag in hand to collect the rabbits, Mama and I set out to check her rabbit snares in the woods. Hunting with Mama passed the time and added fresh meat to the table. That was the nicest, nicest time in my life!

The Snowshoe Rabbit with long ears and gangly hind legs was larger than the cute little Cottontail bunnies commonly seen further south. Snowshoe rabbits taste much like chicken and are so good in stew or soup.

On Mondays Mama set half a dozen snares by pulling a little branch down to tie a loop for the rabbit, and covering the loop with snow so the rabbit wouldn't see or smell it. Later when a rabbit came hopping along, the rabbit tripped the snare, the loop tightened

---

[64] Shakespeare's *Macbeth* (Act 5, Scene 5, lines 17-28).

around one of its legs, and the rabbit was pulled up in the air as the branch released. Mama was not only good at setting snares; she knew the best places in the woods to catch the rabbits. On Wednesdays when Mama and I came back through the woods there was always a rabbit hanging from each of the snares, and that was wonderful! Our family ate lots of rabbits in Fort Good Hope. In those days there were no chemicals or rabbit diseases that harmed humans.

We also ate wild blueberries, strawberries, gooseberries, and raspberries that Mama had canned. In the swamp we found yellow berries like a raspberry that in English are called butter berries. There weren't many of them, so they were special treats. They tasted almost like apple butter when made into jam. Mama shared her cooking skill with me letting me help even when I was little. We ate a lot of bannock, an Indian biscuit made from flour, water, lard, and baking powder, that was kneaded really flat and then baked until it came out nice and crispy – the crispier, the better. Even though we flattened it, the baking powder made it rise just a little. My mother made other kinds of homemade breads as well.

In May on Mama's birthday the whole family went into the woods for a picnic on top of a very big hill behind Fort Good Hope. We sisters brought food for the picnic and our brothers made the bonfire. From the top of the hill we looked around at all the Mackenzie Mountains. It was so beautiful! We cooked pieces of rabbit meat on the bonfire and toasted some bannock. Those picnics on Mama's birthday were some of my fondest memories.

Mama took us to midnight mass every night in the summertime. My mother was a very religious, spiritual person, and she loved to go to church, but I thought repeating the liturgy over, and over, and over, and over would get me to heaven. Later in life when I gave my life to Jesus I discovered that the liturgy had never given me the peace of knowing I belonged to Jesus. It was his death on the cross that made the way to heaven available to everyone who gives their life to him.

Our Lady of Good Hope Catholic Church is a masterpiece. Father Emile Petitot arrived as priest in Fort Good Hope in 1865. He was a famous artist who painted beautiful scenes on the inside walls and the altar of the church. We had to be careful when we went inside the church they said, because it was so old and in need of repair that it might fall down. It wasn't strong enough for a bell.

One of the events related to that church stayed with me all my life. Some time prior to our arrival, the priest at Fort Good Hope was preaching that marriage was between one man and his one wife until death parts the couple. He finally found one example in Mr. Chinnah and his woman who had remained faithful to each other. The priest asked if they wanted to be married, and they agreed to seal their union in the church. Apparently after a little time passed, they weren't getting along very well, so Mrs. Chinnah decided to go down to the priest and ask him if she and her husband could be unmarried. The priest said, "All right, but I'm kind of tired now. I've been listening to confessions all day. Come back tonight, and we'll take care of that."

Sure enough after supper when they came back the priest was waiting for them with holy water and the song book. When Mr. and Mrs. Chinnah came and knelt down the priest started to pray and sing, and pray and sing. Then he sprinkled them both with holy water from his aspergillum. On and on he prayed and sang over them. Finally he hit them with his aspergillum a little on each side. Then as time went by, he hit them a little harder until they were rubbing their heads from the pain. Finally the old lady said, "How long is this going to take?"

"Well," the priest said, "when you were married, you said you would be married as long as you both will live. So I'm trying to see if one of you will die, but neither of you has died yet."

They decided they had taken enough head thumping! They went back home and stayed together, but they never got along very well. The old man was away fishing or hunting as much as possible.

In June of 1932, Mr. Chinnah took his grandson down the river moose hunting, but in the night the old man had a heart attack and died. The grandson came back paddling his grandfather's canoe. Paddling and paddling, coming up the river. All the people who saw the canoe thought it was Mr. Chinnah and his grandson coming back with the moose. Most of the people in the village followed Mrs. Chinnah to the shore with their meat bags to be filled with moose meat. But when the boat arrived, it was just the grandson hollering and screaming, "Grandpa's dead! Grandpa's dead!"

Old Mrs. Chinnah was the first one right there by the river to welcome them home. She started to cry. "*Ene tu se de ne! Ene tu se de ne! Ene tu se de ne!*" It meant something like, "My wonderful husband." She kept saying that over and over, rocking back and forth, and flailing the rocks with her arms outstretched.

I can still see her. She was down at the end of the beach by the rocks. Pretty soon the priest came along and went down to console Mrs. Chinnah, but she wouldn't be comforted. The marriage bond when it was finally severed in death hurt too much. She kept crying and crying. She mourned bitterly for her husband for two weeks.

Everyone loved it when summer began. The days got longer, and the sky never got completely dark at night for about a month and a half. Papa was away from home on the river all summer doing his work visiting the villages. Sometimes Mama and all of us children stayed up all night watching, listening, and singing along with the people. All night long we could play outside in daylight, even though it was night time. As soon as supper was over, the fellows went down by the river to build a fire. They warmed their drums by the fire to tighten the skins. As they pounded the drums they began to chant. The women sang high, and the men sang low in a chant of syllables that didn't use words for meaning, but was just beautiful singing. *Haya ay he ay, haya ay he ay-ay-e-a, ay-e he ay, haya ay he ay ah, heya ay he ay.* I can still play that melody on my harmonica really well.

Our family was in Fort Good Hope for three years, and then Papa retired. Papa let Mama decide where they would live out their retirement. Mama chose her childhood home, Cold Lake, Alberta, to be near her large extended family and my sisters Rachel and Charlotte who married there and were already living in Cold Lake. By this time my sisters Mary and Wilhelmina were both married and living in Fort Simpson and stayed in the north. Mama had been in the north with Papa for nearly thirty years, and looked forward to returning home to her family on the Le Goff Reserve near Cold Lake, Alberta. She wanted to spend time with her parents and her brothers while they were still alive.

Papa Retires

O Lord, what is man that you care for him,
    the son of man that you think of him?
Man is like a breath;
    his days are like a fleeting shadow. Psalm 144:3-4 (*NIV*)

When we left Fort Good Hope, it was so sad. The Indians bought some of our furniture, and the rest we gave away. Papa donated his whole library filled with all the books he had collected over the years to the mission for the priests to share.

Papa may have prepared himself for what he was going to say to Thad and Jim, but he hadn't prepared our family, not even Mama. Just before we left Fort Good Hope, in a father-son talk with Thad and Jim Papa said, "I made it in the world at thirteen, and you can do it too."

Thad at twenty-one was ready to be on his own and make his own decisions, but it was a great shock to us that Papa intended to leave sixteen-year-old Jim behind as well. Papa thought both Thad and Jim were ready to leave home, but it had been so different for Papa. Papa was escaping his parents' harsh treatment, and may have plotted what to do after he actually ran away. Furthermore, the Irish are more independent and do fairly well on their own. In the Indian culture a person's base of support are family and community.

Papa's children had his Irish side, but we also had Mama's gentle nurturing Chipewyan side. Jim had grown up in a loving, supporting home environment. Papa didn't understand how much it meant for our brother Jim at sixteen to remain close to his family for a few more years. After we left, Jim was so lost and so lonely; he felt like he was being abandoned. I don't blame him.

We never got over leaving Jim behind. Mama was heartbroken when she said goodbye to Jim; it was the last time she saw him. Mama cried many years whenever she thought of Jim, and I cried, too. At fourteen years of age, I was the next child after Jim and loved him enough to feel his hurt, confusion, and pain. I longed for Jim and didn't know if any of us would ever see him again.

Rather than stay at Fort Good Hope, Thad paid his own passage on the steamboat. Thad started out with us, and bade us farewell in Fort Norman where there were plenty of jobs.

As our boat rounded the bend at Fort Simpson, everyone in town was lined up on the shore. The big event in Fort Simpson had always been meeting the boats when they arrived. It was so difficult for us, because this time we no longer were part of that welcoming crowd on shore. This time the people knew Flynn Harris and his family were on board, and they all knew Papa was leaving the north. Papa's friends Bishop Breynat and the priests, and all the Indians were there to greet us.

When we stepped ashore, all the people were hugging us and crying. There was one little old lady who was missing – Mama's helper Old Josephine. All of a sudden someone gave up a shout, "Here she comes!" We looked across the river, and there came Old Josephine, paddling her little canoe. She just fell to her knees on the ground by my mother, and they hugged each other and cried. That was the last time they saw each other. It was really sad when all the people cried at Fort Simpson!

When we got to Fort Providence, Rose and Nora were waiting at the boarding school to join us. Papa got off the boat to greet people at the mission and to pick up the girls at the school. I didn't even want to get off the boat; I had too many bad memories there.

When Rose and Nora came on board I wondered how they had been treated by the nuns. Apparently things had improved at the school. The nuns hadn't picked on Nora and Rose like they had singled me out for punishment, but Rose did tell about the children only being allowed to use the bathrooms when the nuns released them.

That rule had caused an embarrassing incident for little Rose. Once at Benediction, Rose was sitting in the front of the chapel getting desperate to use the bathroom. She couldn't hold it any longer, and pretty soon there was a little stream going up to the altar. Rose didn't know what to do, because it was at the end of the service and the kids were filing out of the church, so she just knelt down right there near the front. One of the sisters who took care of the chapel came to her and asked, "What's the matter?"

Rose showed her what had happened, and the nun said, "Oh, that's all right. Instead of punishing Rose, the nun brought Rose a pail of water and a rag to clean it up. I wondered if the nun had been kindly Sister St. Claire.

Rose said that once in awhile to punish a child, the nuns kept the child back from an excursion to sit in a room and pull rags. They had the child pull squares of wool apart to be used for stuffing in some of the blankets they made. I thought that wasn't nearly as bad as being left in that little smelly dark laundry closet with no windows and nothing to do all day.

After leaving Fort Providence the boat headed into Great Slave Lake. We stopped to visit a few of Papa's friends on the southeastern shore at Fort Resolution where the Slave River empties into the lake. Then we got back on board to ride the boat up the Slave River to Fort Smith. Like the Mackenzie, the Slave River runs north, so going *up river* means going *south*.

Fort Smith was the last port of call for riverboat passengers on that leg of the journey. Near Fort Smith are dangerous rapids which make the Slave River impassable to riverboats. At Fort Smith we had to be shuttled over the portage in a big old Model T van by an old Irish lady. After the portage we continued to Fort McMurray.

From Fort McMurray to Edmonton we rode on the Alberta and Great Waterways Railroad[65], a steam powered freight and passenger train, a subsidiary to the Canadian National Railways. Papa had money to reserve a suite for us on the train. Because we were a big family, we had the biggest room on board. The train was beautiful; everything looked brand new. There was a dining car with fine china, crystal, silverware, and tablecloths. The railroad grade was pretty steep in one place where the train couldn't make it up the hill, so all the passengers got out and helped push the train. Finally we were underway again. At Lac La Biche we stayed overnight while we waited for another train to take us to Edmonton.

We arrived in Edmonton in July. Edmonton was larger than any city we had seen in the north. There were so many new sights and sounds we had never experienced. There were three-story brick buildings that looked so tall to us. We stared *up, up, up* as we walked with Mama holding hands so we wouldn't get lost in what seemed to be a very large city. Cars and buses were just beginning to be used in the town. There were cars honking their horns and streetcars dinging their bells. They seemed to go *so fast*, and their engines and horns made *so much noise*. Ooh we did not *like* it!

Papa got a great big suite in a hotel for the six of us kids to stay together with him and Mama. After a night in the hotel, Papa and Mama went out into the city to buy furniture. We didn't have a house yet, but they ordered all the furniture we would need to make a home in Cold Lake.

---

[65]www.royalalbertamuseum.ca/vexhibit/thennow/english/timferburs_cap.htm

Papa brought us a great big bag of fruit to keep us entertained while they were out furniture shopping. We had seen apples, so we knew how to eat those. We had seen oranges, so we peeled the oranges and ate them nicely. At first we scattered the peelings all over the floor, but I was always neat, so I made sure we put the peelings in the bag before Mama and Papa returned.

Then we came across some bananas. We had never seen a banana in our lives, because they couldn't bring them into the north. They were kind of brown. We didn't know how to eat them, so we bit into them. The peelings were bitter, and the over-ripened fruit squished out the side. Ooh, we didn't *like* them, so we threw them into the bag. When Papa and Mama came back from shopping, Papa looked in the bag and saw that it was full of bananas that had been squished out. I said, "Papa, we didn't like the bananas."

Papa asked, "Didn't you even peel them?" We didn't know we were supposed to. He thought that was so funny, he told the story in town. We made the headlines in the paper, because people thought we were so primitive.

Once again we boarded a train to Beaver Crossing where all my people lived. The whole Indian reservation was lined up to greet us. My grandma, my grandpa, my aunts, my uncles, my cousins, everybody was standing there! My sisters Rachel and Charlotte were among our relatives. They had visited on one of the trips our parents made to Cold Lake while our family was still living in the north. On that trip Rachel and Charlotte met their future husbands, got married, and settled down in Cold Lake. So they and their families were on hand to greet us after Papa retired. It was quite a welcoming party!

Mama's Home — Cold Lake, Alberta

If I rise on the wings of the dawn,
  if I settle on the far side of the sea,
Even there your hand will guide me
  your right hand will hold me fast. Psalm 139:9-10 (*NIV*)

Josette Harris

Cold Lake was the bottom of the triangle for the Chipewyan people. The Chipewyan Nation's triangle runs from Churchill down to Cold Lake, up to Fort Chipewyan, and back to Churchill. Within that triangular region most of the Chipewyan people lived. We arrived in Cold Lake in the summer of 1933 and stayed for awhile at my grandpa's farm. Grandpa Noah and Grandma Anzalee Watchapese Janvier were well-to-do with a big farm on the Le Goff Reserve about ten miles from town.

Grandma Anzalee was a skilled fisherwoman, hunter, and she tanned moose hides. She also made baskets of birch bark. Every hole in the birch bark had to be carefully punched with an awl as she decorated her baskets with reeds she cut and dyed. She even made birch bark suitcases that were beautifully decorated. Nozalaze, another little old lady who lived to be over one hundred years old, made baskets too. Not too many of the Indians did that, because it took artistic ability. When we were little, Grandma Anzalee made each one of us a decorated birch bark basket for picking berries. We don't know whatever happened to them, but they would have made special keepsakes to remember our Grandma Anzalee. How wonderful it would have been to carry on her basket making as a family tradition, but we were never in Cold Lake while she was making her baskets to learn that trade.

Mama's people were farmers in the summertime and hunters in the wintertime. They made a pretty good living until the government took away their hunting grounds and gave them a welfare check. Welfare killed their sense of worth and dignity.

During the depression Papa's steady retirement income had more purchasing power, so Papa was considered well-to-do. One day, Papa went to Cold Lake telling people around town he was looking for a home for us. A man in the beer parlor heard him, and said he had a house for sale. Papa said, "I'll meet you tomorrow."

The next day this man brought some whiskey along, and got Papa pretty drunk. The home owner sold Papa a summer cottage along the lakeshore for $1,200. In the years of the depression, $1,200 was a *lot* of money. Papa was too much under the influence to think straight. Before he knew it, that shyster had a bill of sale and the house was ours – the worst house we ever lived in. It was a nice-looking summer cottage on the outside, but it was so cold!

About three weeks after we came to Cold Lake, our furniture from Edmonton arrived in a big van. Oh we had lovely furniture. Papa bought three or four beds, a lovely dining room set, a couch and big stuffed chairs.

We finally got settled into our home at Cold Lake, Alberta, but I hated it, hated it, hated it! I *longed* for the north. The *wilderness* was in my blood. We all wanted to go back, but Papa said, "No, I'm retired now, and we're never going to go back." I cried and cried.

Our house was right beside the lake, also named Cold Lake, which straddles the provinces of Alberta and Saskatchewan. With a depth of about three hundred twenty five feet it is one of the deepest lakes in Alberta. Cold Lake is about forty miles across, and has a surface area of almost one hundred fifty square miles.[66] In the wintertime the cold winds swept across that big lake through the non-insulated clapboard walls right into our house. Even though the house was cold and drafty, we made it work. Mama didn't seem to mind the condition of the house, she was so happy to live close to her mom and dad.

By the time we got the furniture and fixtures nicely arranged and had hung the curtains, we had a beautiful home. As the oldest child left at home, I never let Mama do any of the heavy work. I loved housework and I always liked to keep everything nice and clean. Our family used two of the bedrooms, and kept the third bedroom for company.

My grandpa and grandma stayed with us every weekend, and my aunts and uncles came to visit. Some guests slept on the floor if

---

[66] http://en.wikipedia.org/wiki/Cold_Lake_(Alberta)

there were too many for the guest room. We had nice warm quilts for everyone. My sisters Rachel and Charlotte also visited us with their families, and on Sundays we all went to church together.

Rachel had married Bobby Martineau and they had many children. She raised a big family, took good care of them and was a good mother to her children.

Light-hearted and loving Charlotte made a good home for her family. When she stayed at our house on the weekends, we played cards and other games, and got along with each other really well. Charlotte was married to J. B. Ennow's son, Alec, and they lived on the Le Goff reserve.

J. B. Ennow had been Papa's Indian scout when Papa was in the NWMP, and it was through J. B. that Papa became acquainted with our people near Cold Lake. In the early 1900's J. B. collaborated with a linguist by the name of Goddard. Goddard recorded J. B.'s storytelling as his basis for a detailed study of our Chipewyan' language.

J. B. had never been to school, but he was well-known as a brilliant mechanic. He figured out how to take a car apart and put it back together again without any technical education. All the Indians had a little land to farm after they were done with their winter trapping and hunting. J. B. raised wheat and barley in the summertime on his farm.

Even though Alec's mother had died, his stepmother Phylizine treated Alec and Charlotte's kids like her own. Alec was very nice, but he died of tuberculosis while still a young man after they had two or three children. A few years later when Charlotte married nice-looking Dominic Piche, Phylizine Ennow raised Alec and Charlotte's children.

Dominic and Charlotte lived right on the shore of Cold Lake by the reserve and they had four sons. We loved to visit at Charlotte's house, because she always had some dried fish. In Cold Lake they caught a lot of great big white fish, trout, and so many other varieties of good fish in their nets, and then hung the fish on racks to dry. Sometimes we begged Charlotte to dig carrots and onions for us to eat fresh from the big garden she kept with Phylizine, but we'd eat too much and get sick!

It seemed like we no sooner got settled into our house before the school year was starting. While Nora and I went to the public school right in Cold Lake, my younger sister Rose and my twin brothers

Jack and Bill were sent to a Catholic boarding school on the reserve, which was a better school than the one at Fort Providence.

Nora and I began attending the school right in Cold Lake, when I was fourteen and Nora was twelve. The students and teachers in the public school were all white people: Scottish, Irish, and French. On the first day Nora and I heard the other students whispering, "What are those Indians doing in our school?"

We thought, "Who are the Indians?" We looked around to see who they were talking about; we didn't know they meant us. That was the first touch of prejudice we encountered. Here we were the best-dressed well-to-do people in town, we spoke several languages, our father was a well-known public figure all across western Canada, but that didn't make a bit of difference.

Nora and I came home crying that first day. We ran to Papa who was sitting in his favorite chair reading Shakespeare. We wailed, "Papa, we're never going to school there anymore! We want to go back up north!"

"What happened?" Papa asked.

"Well, they wondered why we Indians were in school," we sobbed.

Papa said, "Just stay home. I'll walk up the hill and talk to the teacher." Later I was told by the girl who befriended me, that Papa was so impressive and dignified. He excused himself for coming unannounced, and asked the teacher if he could have a word or two with the children.

The teacher said, "Oh, yes, Mr. Harris. Go right ahead."

Papa addressed the class from the front of the room. Rolling his "r's" in his Irish burr Papa said, "I underrstand that you don't like the colorr of my children's skin. You see, I am an Irrrishman, and my wife, their motherrr, is a Chipewyan Indian lady. If the colorr of their skin botherrs you children, you will just have to go to anotherr school. For you see, I pay taxes like your folks, and my children are going to attend this school whetherr you like it or not. And if you don't like it, your folks will have to build anotherr school for you to go to." The children just sat in awe!

We were too upset to go to school the rest of that day. When we returned the next day, the other students didn't dare say anything against us. Nora and I never heard that word *Indian* again. Papa nipped their prejudice about us in the bud! We nipped their prejudice about how we lived in the bud, too.

A little English girl named Daisy told me of the wonderful speech Papa gave the previous afternoon. Soon Daisy became my best friend.

I invited Daisy over to my house one day. "Ah," Daisy gasped as she stepped inside. "Linoleum on the floor? Beautiful colors?" The white children thought every Indian was dirty, but they were wrong. Our house was nicely decorated with lovely new furniture, and it was sparkling clean! When I introduced Daisy, I was so proud of my beautiful Mama sitting neatly dressed, sewing her exquisite silk work. Daisy said, "Hello, Mrs. Harris."

Mama replied, "Hello, Daisy."

Daisy she said that she couldn't wait to go home and tell the whole town what a wonderful home we had! From the outside our house looked ordinary, but inside it was beautiful.

I suggested to Daisy, "You can tell the kids from the school they can tour my house from the front to the back, if they are interested."

The next day Daisy asked the other kids, "Do you know that the Harris family has linoleum on their floor?"

The other students all came to see for themselves. I was still upset about them thinking less of us for being Indians, but I smiled and greeted them sweetly, "You may come in."

I gave them a grand tour of our house as if they were going to a museum. Well, they could *not* believe it! They had been ignorant of the improvements the Indian people had been making in our homes.

Nora and I didn't have much of an education in the north, so we were both put in the sixth grade. However, when Nora and I got A's in spelling, grammar, and English, the students soon realized that we were no *dumbshkahs*.

Our teacher, an Englishman by the name of Mr. Finley Reed, was a wonderful teacher, but kind of absent-minded. He kept our attention, because he was really funny, and once in awhile he walked back and forth reminiscing about England.

One day at one o'clock Mr. Reed rang the bell as usual when it was time to come back into the school, but my sister Nora and her friend Grace were missing. They were playing marbles and dibs on the floor in the girl's outhouse. Nervously I kept looking out the window thinking, "Oh, Nora!"

Nora finally came in about fifteen minutes after the bell. As she sat down, all the marbles started rolling out of her pockets to Mr. Reed's feet. As the marbles continued to roll down towards the front, he walked over and stood in front of Nora's desk. Nora hung her head as Mr. Reed looked down at her and said, "You won, eh?"

Pretty soon Grace came in, but of course, she had *lost* all of her marbles. No one said anything as Grace quietly took her seat. Then Mr. Reed walked over to stand in front of her desk and said, "You lost, eh?" That was the end of it. The girls were miserable, because they had been found out. Mr. Reed knew what they had been up to, and being embarrassed in front of the class was punishment enough.

Before Christmas each year, standardized exams from the government determined if students were prepared for diplomas. We Harris kids were very good at grammar, because Papa taught us well. There were questions on the test about the bare predicate, the bare subject, the noun, and the pronoun that stumped some of the other kids. Three of them asked me for help, and although I knew it was wrong, I did coach them. Their scores of 89, 99, and 80, were much higher than normal for them in that subject. When we were back in school after Christmas, naming the three I helped, Mr. Reed said, "You know these three did so well in grammar on their exams, that I'd like them to go up to the board and show the rest of you how they did it."

Mr. Reed wrote the same questions on the board, and then called on them one-by-one. The first student shifted from one foot to the other while looking at the question. The second student just stared at the question on the board, but did not write anything. The last guy approached the board, but he didn't know the answer either, so Mr. Reed had them return to their seats. Then Mr. Reed strode across the room, stood directly in front of my desk, looked me in the eye, and said, "Guilty, eh?" Sheepishly I nodded my head.

One beautiful day in May my friend Daisy and I wandered off during our noon hour to walk in the woods, listen to the birds, and enjoy the warmth and sunshine! We hung around in the woods until it was time to go home. We didn't know that all of the students got the same hankering to be outside on the same day.

At one o' clock that day, Mr. Reed kept pulling the thick rope to ring and ring the big school bell, but not one soul appeared. When he got tired of ringing the bell, he closed the school and went down the street from house to house to tell our parents that we had all played hooky.

When I got home Papa was waiting for me. He looked me right in the eye and said, "Where the heck were you this afternoon?" I noticed the twinkle in his eye was *missing,* and realized I was in trouble.

Thinking fast, I lied, "Well, Papa, I had a terrible nose bleed, so I went home with Daisy. Her mother let me lie down, she put a cold wet cloth on my face, and I took a little rest. That's where I was."

"Huh!" Papa snorted. "Harrumph!" When Papa didn't say any more, I thought he accepted my story and everything was all right.

The next day on his way through town, Mr. Reed stopped to talk with each set of parents to hear the tall tales we told. When Mr. Reed got to our house I overheard him ask Papa, "Well what was Bridget's alibi?"

Papa said, "She claims she had a nose bleed, but I didn't see any blood around." Mr. Reed didn't need to punish us, because he knew our parents would take care of it. After he left, Papa looked me in the eye and gave me the business.

The first year we were in Cold Lake I came down with pneumonia. When my parents put me in the hospital they discovered I also had tuberculosis, and I was put in isolation. Lots of Indians had died back in Fort Good Hope from TB, including a young girl who was our housekeeper, so maybe I had gotten it from her. In the 1930's there were no medications to help you recover from TB. All you could do was rest and hope your body could fight the disease on its own. I was in the hospital for what seemed like a year, and I kept getting thinner and thinner. Finally the doctor told Mama, "You might as well take her home to die."

When Mama brought me home, I started eating good Indian food, and that's what healed me. Mama's moose meat and homemade soup tasted so good!

While I was recovering, I enjoyed watching Mama working around the house. Mama loved to sew on her Singer treadle machine. If she had tanned moose hide on hand she made some moccasins and embroidered them with silk work. The Crees who lived near us decorated with bead work, but our Chipewyan people always decorated with silk work.

Mama started teaching my sisters and me to sew with a needle when we were just little girls making clothing for our dolls. After my left hand had been broken by the nuns, it was difficult for me to sew. As we grew older, Mama taught my sisters how to sew and do silk work to decorate their beautiful leather clothing and other articles. My sisters became almost as skilled as Mama, but I have never been able to do handwork.

Papa's afternoons were kind of long after we kids were in school and Mama was busy sewing or shopping. To pass the time after his nap, Papa would wander over to Mr. Clark's Red and White grocery store a few steps away from our house to play cribbage with Mr. Clark.

When the Indians traded their furs in Cold Lake in the spring, everybody had cash in their pockets. It was in the midst of the depression, but living expenses weren't very high. For recreation in the spring and summertime Mama and I liked to go down the hill to play penny ante poker with the ladies at a little place where the Indian people pitched their tents. The stakes at the men's poker games were higher, but the women just played for fun using pennies.

I gave Mama a whole bunch of pennies so she could play penny ante with her friends. She just loved that game, but Mama was so naïve, she was easily bluffed. When someone said, "I'll raise you three pennies," Mama threw her cards away. Pretty soon she was out of pennies. It was so funny; she never won because she was too kind-hearted. Now and then I checked on Mama and gave her more pennies to help her get back in the game if she was just sitting there broke.

Mama's dad Grandpa Noah was really short and had a little goatee. I was fascinated by him and loved spending time with him when he sat in his teepee. I crawled in there and he rubbed my back and told me stories children loved. His last name, Watchapeze, meant *pointed hat* or something, maybe because our parkas had pointed hoods. Noah wasn't full-blooded Indian, but was part Chipewyan, part Cree, and part French. His Cree grandmother lived with a Frenchman by the name of Janvier.

When Grandpa Noah was ninety-nine years old, I was walking uptown and downtown touring Cold Lake with him. All the white ladies came to pull on his goatee because he was so cute. As the ladies walked away, my grandpa asked me, "Are they trying to date me?"

I said, "Yes, Grandpa. They're trying to date you, but I'm not going to let you go."

One day my sisters and I decided we were going to the dance. We hadn't asked Papa, because we knew Papa hardly ever let us out at night. We told Mama who didn't mind that we went to the dance, but we had a problem. Papa had a hook on the inside of the kitchen door. If we left the house at night, we would be locked out, and Papa would hear us trying to get back in. That day we tried to figure a way to jiggle the hook loose from the outside until we finally mastered it, we thought. That night we pretended we were going to bed, but we were just under our covers already dressed for the dance. When Papa went to bed we waited until we heard him snoring; then we sneaked out.

We had a good time at the dance. Around midnight we followed the crowd for a piece of pie and coffee before going home. Our neighbor, Mr. Sinclair, had some dogs that began barking as we neared our house, "Woo, woo, woo, woo." We thought, "Oh, oh, Papa's going to wake up!"

While we stood shivering in the cold outside our living room window, we watched Papa sitting up having a puff on his Irish twist pipe. After Papa went back to bed, we tried shaking the door, but that hook wouldn't come undone. When we tried to come through the window it squeaked. We pushed it up a little bit, little bit, little bit, little bit, until we could squeeze our bodies through the window, and then tiptoed back to bed. We heard Papa snoring, so we thought we hadn't been detected.

The next morning Papa was up at five o'clock to light the stove as usual. Then Papa called to me, "Bridget, get up! Come and make breakfast!" I got up and made him some porridge, and coffee, and other breakfast fixings. Mama had told him we had gone out dancing, so he asked, "Well, what time did you get home last night?"

"Oh, Papa, around ten or eleven o'clock," I said.

"Ah, the devil you say," he said. "I was awake, and I was up, and you weren't home yet." My lies never worked with Papa; he always found me out.

Papa was so strict we girls didn't invite boys to our house. When I was fifteen I thought I had fallen in love with a Chipewyan youth my age who wanted to be my boyfriend. At that time young people were not using drugs or alcohol; we just had a good clean time. We went skating on Cold Lake, went to the restaurant to have a piece of pie, and normal things like that.

However, while he was walking me home by the lakeshore one dark night, all of a sudden he dragged me down by the lake and raped me. I did not know what was happening and fought with him, but he was stronger and took advantage of me. Then just as suddenly he ran off and left me there like some broken doll he had destroyed and discarded. I had to walk home alone bleeding, so sore, and so hurt, because I had never been touched before.

103

I realized then why Papa was so concerned about his girls, but I was so ashamed, I didn't want to tell Mama or Papa what had happened. I felt like there was *no one* I could tell it to. The horror of that experience was locked up inside of me, and it destroyed part of my heart.

Someone might say that we were just young and these things happen, but rape is a very destructive traumatic act of violence against the victim. I never forgot the terror of being roughly overpowered and violated; I felt so horrible, horrible, horrible, and so betrayed. The innocence of my tender heart was destroyed along with my sense of purity, making me feel dirty and despised.

Although I felt like there was *no one* I could talk to, the boy who raped me bragged to *all* the other boys about it, and destroyed my reputation all over town. Of course he said that I was willing. I couldn't understand how someone I thought I loved could do such an evil thing that hurt me so. My mind and heart were reeling as I realized that all along his goal had been to use me to prove his manhood. He didn't know that true manhood is demonstrated by taking responsibility for his actions, honoring and protecting women, and making a safe place for children to be raised in a loving home. Even in this tragic experience God protected me from becoming pregnant, and somehow I managed to go on with my life.

The first boy I ever brought home was a French boy called Little John who was really in love with me, I guess. When I was sixteen, Little John and I were in plays at church, went skating together, and went out for a cup of coffee now and then. I decided he was nice enough to introduce to Papa. None of my sisters ever brought a boy home, so this was new for Papa.

One Sunday as Papa and Mama left the house for church, I said to Mama, "I want you to bring Little John home with you from church today to have dinner with us. I'll stay home and do the cooking."

"Oh?" she asked, "What will your father say?"

I answered, "We'll see. We'll break him in today!"

Papa and Mama went up the hill to church, and I stayed home to make the dinner. Because he walked so fast, Papa arrived home first, sat down in his favorite chair, smoked his pipe, and read a book while I finished dinner. Pretty soon I looked out the window, and there was Mama with Little John on her arm. When they came in, I brought Little John into the living room to meet Papa. Little John greeted Papa in French, "How are you, Mr. Harris?"

Papa returned the standard greeting in French and asked, "Who are your father and mother?"

"Well, Mr. Harris," Little John said, "my folks are in Montreal. I am here with my brother, and we have a farm."

Papa always asked young people who their parents were, but then he lost interest and went back to reading his book.

When I came in with the dinner, we sat down to eat in silence. Even when we had company Papa always had to be reading a book or something at the table. After dinner Papa wanted a nap, but that day he had to entertain Little John while I cleared the table. I was in the kitchen nervously washing and scrubbing the dishes, because I didn't know what Papa was going to say.

After I finished the dishes Papa came into the kitchen and said, "I've got to take my nap now, so why don't you and John go somewhere." Having excused us, Papa left the room, slammed the bedroom door and went to bed.

I invited Little John, "Come on, let's go." Mama was sitting by the window politely waiting for us to leave before taking her nap, too. Little John and I went skating and had a good time until around four o'clock, when he went to his house and I went home to mine.

I waited for Papa to lower the boom, because I didn't know what he would say! At suppertime I warmed the leftovers and fixed the table in the kitchen where our family ate when we had no guests. Because the Harris family always ate our meals precisely on the hour, it was exactly six o'clock as we sat down for our supper. We were eating quietly as usual with Papa's nose in his book. Finally I could stand the suspense *no more*! Pushing his book down to look him in the eye I broke the silence, "Well, Papa? Aren't you going to say anything?"

With a twinkle in his eye he answered, "Yes. When is the wedding going to be?" Then I knew he wasn't angry. At last I conquered my fear of Papa, because I saw that his bark was worse than his bite.

About that time in my life I figured maybe I could get a job. I was always helping Mama, doing all the housework, and thought it would be good to get out on my own. A crippled woman, whose son was away on a threshing crew for the grain harvest, asked me to milk two cows for her. That sounded pretty easy, so I told my folks that a crippled little old lady wanted to hire me, and I found a ride over to her farm.

When I arrived she explained, "To round up the cows, you need to get on this horse."

I had never lived on a farm, so she limped over to the horse and bridled it for me. She waved her arm toward the pasture and said, "Go around that way, and you'll find the cows."

I got on the horse and found the cows, but those cows paid me no attention. Finally, little-by-little I coaxed them back to the barn. The lady noticed I had trouble removing the horse's bridle, so she had to help me with the bridle again when she brought the pail for milking the cows. After she went back into the house I tried to milk the cows, but I didn't know how. I kept pulling, pulling, and pulling so hard on the first cow's teats, but nothing came out, and the cow tried to kick me. Finally I put my head against the cow and cried, and cried, and cried.

The little old lady wondered, "Where is that girl?" When she came out to the barn she found me in tears with nothing in the pail. She said, "I don't believe you're cut out to be a farm girl!"

I said, "I don't think so, either." She sent me home the next day, and that was the end of my farming career.

After I got back home, news had reached us that my oldest sister Mary had tragically passed away at her home in Fort Simpson. When she delivered her last baby Mary probably had gotten the flu or something. Mama was heartbroken. First we left Jim in Fort Good Hope, and now she had lost her first child, Mary. Papa's retirement in Cold Lake was not turning out to be the happy time Mama had anticipated.

The only one who visited us from the north was kindly old Bishop Breynat. His familiar greeting, "*Ses kenne*," meant, "my people, my children". He spoke our language fluently, and that's one of the things that endeared him to us. My mother loved that old bishop, and was comforted by his visit.

I had finished the eighth grade, and that's as far as my education went. Mama was getting sick by then, so I was needed at home where I did all of the cleaning and the cooking. Mama always said to me, "When I am gone, you take care of your dad. Don't ever leave him. He's getting old now." I promised her I wouldn't leave Papa, and I kept my promise.

Bridget is Left in Charge

O Lord, you have searched me
  and you know me
You know when I sit and when I rise;
  you perceive my thoughts from afar.
Before a word is on my tongue
  you know it completely, O Lord. Psalm 139:1-4 (*NIV*)

Retired T. W. (Flynn) Harris wearing NWMP hat

My sister Nora married Ben Matchatis from Le Goff. When their first child Joyce was born, Grandma Anzalee was the midwife, along with another lady who helped Grandma at times. My aunt also joined us so we could all be together in that little house with Nora on the reserve as she was having contractions. Finally Joyce was born, and they handed her to me right away as soon as they cut the umbilical cord. I gave Joyce her first bath in a basin. It was so wonderful! I know that I bonded with baby Joyce right there. It's as if I had a child, because I have never had the ability to have my own children.

In Cold Lake we hardly ever went anywhere in the winter because of the severe cold. When the lake froze, the winds blew, and the snow came down, down, down. The only way to clear snow back then was backbreaking work with shovels. The men had to brace themselves against the cold to go outside, cut wood, do chores, and then shovel the streets by hand.

One wintry day Mama had gone to the grocery store which was close to our house. Walking home she fell on the slippery icy road and broke her knee cap. There was a hospital, but no doctors in Cold Lake. Without proper treatment Mama's injury turned into something they called *TB of the bone*, but it was probably cancer. After Mama suffered a few months we put her in the hospital where they could at least give her pain medication to help her relax.

While Mama was in the hospital, Papa got lonely and went up the hill to have a few beers with the old fellows who hung out in the beer parlor. When I went up the hill to get Papa, there they all sat in their chairs snoring, sound asleep. I said, "Papa, time to come home and have supper." Then I helped him get up and walked him home.

Papa knew I was lonely and needed breaks from looking after the household. He allowed me to go now and then to visit my best friend Daisy and her family who had moved to Edmonton.

One day I was grocery shopping at Mr. Clark's Red and White store while Papa was playing cribbage with Mr. Clark. While I was at the counter, Mrs. Clark mentioned that she had to go into Edmonton to see the doctor. I asked Mrs. Clark, "Can you take some money out of my Papa's store account so I can ride the train with you to see my girlfriend Daisy?"

Mrs. Clark said, "Sure. We'll work it out." Little by little she took about twenty-five dollars out of Dad's account. I arranged for my sister Charlotte to look after Papa, and Mrs. Clark and I went to Bonneville where we hopped the train to Edmonton. My friend Daisy met me, and we spent three or four nice days together. The train ticket cost about five dollars round trip, which left plenty for spending money in those days. Lunch out at a café and a movie cost about fifty cents in Edmonton, but most of the time we were content to just sit and visit at Daisy's house.

Mama suffered for about two years after she hurt her knee. Mama was born on May 5th, 1886 and she died May 12, 1940 just after her fifty-fourth birthday. Word of Mama's death was brought to my youngest sister Rose who was in school at the convent. Someone from the convent brought Rose and the twins, Jack and Bill, home to see the family. The school year was almost over, so they could just as well have stayed home, but the school officials didn't let them stay overnight. They were hustled back to school without even being allowed to attend Mama's funeral.

I was twenty-one years old when we buried our dear Mama on the Indian reservation where her papa, Noah Watchapese Janvier, was buried in 1935. Grandpa Noah had lived to be one hundred and one years old, so we never thought we would lose our beloved Mama at such a young age. My sisters Charlotte and Rachel lived nearby and were with us during the burial. It was so devastating to lose Mama that when the men dug the grave I wanted to jump in and be covered up, too! None of us could handle it; we were completely shattered. After Mama's burial the whole extended family gathered at my uncle's house. We had a lot of soup and bannock together. Wilhelmina came from Fort Simpson to spend some time helping Papa.

After Mama died, our home was a rather sad house to live in. We lost the peace in our home; the whole family suffered. Rose and our younger brothers thought I was too bossy. The minute they finished lunch or supper, they ran out of the house so I couldn't make them help with the dishes, and then I hollered at them.

Papa seemed to get older overnight. One day I thought Papa would come home for lunch, but I had to go up the hill and fetch him. I let Papa know I was angry, "You promised you'd be home at noon, and I had to go up and get you. Papa, today I'm leaving you and I'm never coming back." After lunch I tucked him into bed for his nap, and then I went out to the little restaurant and had a cup of coffee. When I came home a little later, there was Papa sitting in his chair smoking his pipe.

"Well, you didn't get very far, did you?" he asked me with that old twinkle in his eye.

"Oh, Papa, you know I can't leave you," I said. So we just laughed about that.

It was awfully lonely without Mama. Papa took us to stay south of Cold Lake for the winter near Mama's brother, Sam Watchapeze on the Le Goff Reserve. Uncle Sam had a nice warm house he helped build out of logs.

Uncle Sam and his wife Elise were Rose's godparents. When Rose was growing up she stayed with Uncle Sam once in awhile. Rose learned to be a good hunter from Uncle Sam, so one day Rose decided to go hunting down by the little creek. Rose cleaned the 22 rifle and got it all ready to hunt. She used Aunt Elise's snowshoes to make it over the heavy snow, but Rose didn't know how to walk in them. As she stepped off the creek bank, she tumbled down into the snow with the gun! She had to trudge all the way back to the house again in the snowshoes and clean the gun so the barrel wouldn't rust. When she tried a second time, she fell down the creek bank again, so she decided that was the end of the snowshoes. That didn't stop her from hunting, though. She cleaned the gun, and trudged back through the snow in her boots.

Rose got to be a good shot with the 22 rifle. When hunting snowshoe rabbits in the wintertime, their fur is white against the snow, so all she could see of the rabbit was their eye. Rose would sit out in the field and whistle. A rabbit would come to see what was making the noise and lift its head to listen. When Rose saw the rabbit's little eye, she took aim, held the rifle ever so steady and squeezed the trigger. Rose usually got her rabbit.

The Chipewyan are the only people who make a left and a right snowshoe to fit your feet and make it more comfortable when you walk in them, which was so special. Every other culture makes a generic snowshoe that you can use on either foot.

We stayed until spring and then moved back to Cold Lake, but we were still too lonely to stay in our house without Mama. Uncle Sam had an extra cabin close to the creek. I brought a couple of our beds, and fixed up the cabin really pretty with curtains in the windows. We lived there one whole happy summer.

Sam had never been to school a day in his life. He spoke mostly Chipewyan and very little English, but he was one of the wealthiest Indians on the reserve, and kept lots of his money in suitcases. Because of his wonderful reputation, the banker trusted Uncle Sam. When Uncle Sam needed to buy seed for his crops he told the bank manager, "I'll need a couple of thousand dollars to put the crop in."

The banker said, "It's yours, Sam." My uncle couldn't sign his name, so he put a big X on the signature line, and the banker accepted that as Uncle Sam's signature. In the fall when Uncle Sam sold his grain, the first thing he did was pay back the loan. That's the way he did business.

In the wintertime Uncle Sam went hunting and trapping like the other Indians. Then in the springtime he planted oats, wheat, and barley on his farm. Uncle Sam was a wonderful farmer, and kept horses and cows for livestock. He hired a lot of people to thresh grain in the fall.

It was nice to visit Uncle Sam and his wife Elise, because Elise was a good homemaker who liked to cook. She took care of the horses and milked the cows, too, helping Sam with the farm wherever she could. Sam and Elise always had some good dried moose meat, and Aunt Elise tanned hides to make moccasins and other articles of clothing.

The Ukrainian neighbors in the next little village liked my old uncle and aunt, and always shared whatever they had on the farm. Whenever Sam's mare needed to be bred, he hired the Ukrainians' stallion for stud service. Whenever the Ukrainians had canned food that my people didn't make like pickles and relishes, they brought some over to Elise, and Elise sent some of her food back with them. In the fall when the Ukrainians were done threshing, they put on a great big barn dance. They had lots of good food to eat and lots of homemade beer to drink. People made their own music playing the fiddle and guitar.

Our Uncle Sam was so good to us. I hate to admit it now, but one night we stole his horses. We didn't have Jesus in our hearts at that time, and all we were concerned about was finding a way to have a good time.

Nora and Ben, their little baby Joyce, and my sister Charlotte came to visit. For entertainment I wanted to go to the Ukrainians' Saturday night barn dance. I went over to Uncle Sam's house intending to ask him about using his horses. Instead I got cold feet and just visited with him before returning to the cabin. Three times I tried to work up the courage to ask for the horses, but each time I chickened out. Uncle Sam probably knew we were up to something.

Finally after dark, when my aunt and uncle had gone to bed, I told Nora's husband Ben, "You'd better hitch up the horses and get us ready to go." My sister Charlotte was there to take care of baby Joyce and Papa. Away we went to the dance at the Ukrainians' place. We had so much food and beer; we danced all night until about four in the morning. Then we raced the horses to beat the band to get home before Sam and Elise woke up to do their morning chores. We sneaked into the farmyard ever so quietly, but when Ben put the horses away and threw the blankets over them, their backs were steaming.

Not long after we got to bed Uncle Sam and Aunt Elise got up to milk the cows before church, but we slept late that Sunday morning. Eventually we got up, fed Papa, and just sat around talking about how much fun we had the night before. Around four o'clock in the afternoon, Aunt Elise and Uncle Sam came home from church, took a nap, got up and milked their cows. When Uncle Sam brought us our pail of milk from the barn that evening, he looked at me and all he said was, "The horses were pretty wet this morning." Then he laughed, but, *ooh* – did I feel *guilty*! All God ever had to do to bring conviction to my heart was confront me with the truth of my sin.

Faithful to my promise to Mama, I took care of Papa. As he was getting older, he was very lonely with a broken heart. He often said as he sat looking out at Cold Lake, "When's your mother coming home? When's your mother coming home?"

"Papa, she's not coming home. She's not coming home no more," I told him. Then big tears rolled down his cheeks. It was sad, but I took care of Papa the best I could. With my kid brothers and Rose still in school, I felt so alone. To cover up my hurts, I joined the crowd who drank a lot of beer. When you pick your friends, you pick your future. I didn't realize that I would eventually become an alcoholic.

Papa had a few light strokes, and then in 1943 he fell and broke his hip. I had no way to get him to the hospital in Cold Lake, so Papa had no medical help at all. I put him to bed and looked after him. Papa never left his bed; he died at home in my arms almost three years after Mama's death.

Papa's pension had been $1,200 a year, which was adequate income at that time. Each month he received a one hundred dollar check. Papa died on March 31, 1943, the end of the fiscal year for Indian Affairs which was also the day of his last pension check. I was the oldest child still living at home, but I couldn't inherit the pension. Without a will, his remaining pension would have gone to his widow, and when the widow died, the pension would have been passed on to care for any children who were not yet of age. But Mama died first, and Papa had not made out a will. Therefore his pension just reverted back to the government, and those of us left at home suddenly went from having so much to nothing at all!

I sent someone up the hill to ask the priest and the Justice of the Peace to come to our house. When they arrived, I cried, "The only money we have is Papa's last pension check which is due today, but Papa died before he signed it. What can we do?"

The priest and the Justice of the Peace talked it over, and they told me, "We will take your father's hand and write his name." So they took his dead hand and wrote *T. W. Harris* on the check so it could be cashed, and they both put their initials around it. It was as though he was still breathing and signed the last check. That last one hundred dollar pension check was needed to buy a coffin to bury Papa, and then there was no more money coming in.

The day Papa died was in the middle of a cold, cold winter – so much snow – so far below zero. Snow was over the rooftops, over everything. As the old Indian came by who supplied our house with wood I called to him, "Papa's dead. Please tell my Uncle Sam on the reserve we need him to come with his horse and sleigh, and please tell him that somebody needs to dig a grave for Papa next to Mama's grave."

Rose and the twins, Jack and Bill, were still at the boarding school on the reserve. When Papa died, a priest took Rose, Jack, and Bill out of the school, and told them they had to go home, because their father was very sick. Rose asked, "What about my niece and nephew? That's their grandpa!"

"Oh, I guess they can come, too," the priest said, and brought them along. As they were making their way through the snow the priest said he made a mistake, because Papa was already dead. Rose had figured that out, because she knew the school would not send them home if Papa had only been sick.

We got the coffin, and had Papa embalmed and fixed for his funeral. Uncle Sam finally came the next day with his horse and big sleigh made from a wagon with runners on it. We put Papa's body in the sleigh, and we all rode down to the Le Goff reserve. The ten mile ride in the snow and cold seemed to take forever in the sleigh, but we finally got to my uncle's place close to the mission and had Papa's body displayed nicely for the funeral wake that lasted throughout the night. It was awfully sad and awfully desolate as we gathered together. Most of the Indians were gone for their winter hunting and trapping. Everybody was so poor, but the few Indians who remained on the reserve during the winter brought us fish and potatoes and whatever food they had.

The next day, a handful of Indian people helped us dig the grave. Oh, God, help us! The snow was so high, they didn't know exactly where to dig, but old grandma Anzalee knew in her heart where Mama was buried. She looked at the snow and pointed to a spot saying, "Ja! ja!" meaning *dig here*, and there it was! With no gravestone, no landmark of any kind to guide her under all that snow, God led her right to the exact location. They dug where Grandma Anzalee was pointing, and they were so close to Mama's grave, they even chipped a little corner of her coffin.

The Famous Flynn Harris was laid to rest without ceremony among his wife's people on the Indian reserve where he had served when he first came west with the Northwest Mounted Police. If we had notified the NWMP, they would have sent an honor guard and might even have paid for the casket, but Papa hadn't left instructions for his funeral. None of the officials he worked with, not even Bishop Breynat, knew that he had died. Only Mama's family, the undertaker, and the priest from the mission attended the burial. It was a very, very sad lonely day.

After we buried Papa, my sister Nora, her husband Ben, and their firstborn baby Joyce, came to live with us. It was nice having them with us at that time; I loved baby Joyce as if she were my very own. Taking care of Joyce between little jobs I found in the town helped keep my mind off my sorrows. I had never worked outside of our home before, but people were kind enough to bring me their laundry and their ironing which provided enough money to keep us going for awhile.

At the end of April I went to see Mr. Clark. Our grocery bill must have been over two or three hundred dollars, but I had no money to pay him. I said, "Mr. Clark, I'd like to pay our bill as soon as I can, and I'll try to pay you back at least five dollars a month. I haven't any money on hand, but I am working for people every day."

I went on, and on, and on, telling him how I was trying to keep my family together. While I was talking, he was looking at the store's financial books and marking stuff. When I had cried my way through my sad tale, Mr. Clark closed the books and asked, "What were you saying, Bridget?"

I said, "You didn't listen to me?"

He said, "Your debt has been paid in full!"

He had X-ed out everything! That was a great blessing to us! To me that day it was like Jesus paying for our sins in full on the cross; I had such a sense of relief and of a weight being lifted!

I realized I had to do something about making a living, but I didn't know where to start looking for a job. After completing the eighth grade I had left high school to stay at home to care for Mama and Papa, so I had no job history and not much education. Some of my people brought me some potatoes, fish and other food. I sold some furniture to help with expenses until Rose and the boys came home from school, but it was soon apparent that I needed to find a job, and that would mean moving us to Edmonton.

Edmonton, Alberta

Does he not see my ways
And count my every step? Job 31:4 (*NIV*)

In Edmonton I went to the head of Child Welfare who was well acquainted with T. W. Harris. The director talked with me about my situation and explained that he could not give me enough money for us all to live together. Instead he suggested that I put Jack, Bill, and Ned in a boy's home in Edmonton. It broke my heart, but at least my younger brothers would get three meals a day, their education, and have a roof over their heads. I really needed God's help, but I didn't even know how to talk to God except through recited prayers. My hope was to marry a good man to make a home for my brothers, but as the years went by I was never able to do that.

When I returned to Cold Lake, my brothers were willing to move to the big city. The sale of some more furniture helped us buy train fare to Edmonton. Rather than just abandon our home in Cold Lake with everything in it, I told my older sister Rachel, "Make our house your home for your large family. At least it's paid for." Rachel and her family lived in our home for several years. My sister Rose was eighteen years old, and would be able to find a job and live on her own.

My three brothers went with me to Edmonton where I got them settled into the boy's home. The twins, Jack and Bill, were fifteen and would soon be old enough to leave the home, but Ned was only nine years old. The three of them seemed to be happy, and I promised to spend Sundays with them.

After I got my brothers situated, I needed to find a job. I paid fifty cents a night for a little room for myself, and then I had about two dollars left in my purse. I dreaded living alone, because I still had nightmares of demons, was haunted by the nun's faces, and dreamed of vicious dogs chasing me. I was timid and petrified of everybody, stuttered for many years, and couldn't look anyone in the eye.

Walking through downtown Edmonton I saw a sign in a window, "Dishwasher needed." Nervously pacing back and forth in front of that window about ten times before getting up the courage to walk into the restaurant, I finally sat down, ordered coffee, and smoked a long cigarette. It was a Chinese restaurant with three booths, a little counter, and a nice-looking blond waitress.

After I sipped my coffee for awhile, I asked the waitress, "Does the owner still need a dishwasher?"

She said, "Yes! You want a job?"

I said, "I *have* to find a job; I have no money."

The waitress called to the Chinese man, "I think this lady wants a job."

He asked, "Do you want to start today?"

I replied, "I can start right away!"

He said, "I'd better give you a good lunch first."

The owner fixed a nice lunch for the waitress and me. As we were eating, the waitress introduced herself as Rose Kostashen. I told Rose, "My Mama and Papa are both gone. I had to put my brothers in a home, this is the first job I've ever had away from home, I come from a big family, and I've never lived alone in my life. Do you know of a family I could live with?"

Rose offered, "Well, you could come home with me. I also come from a big family, and we're poor. You don't mind walking, do you? I'm a mile from the bus line."

"I don't mind," I said, relieved at the thought of not having to live alone.

After lunch I checked out the kitchen. Ugh! Pots and pans were all over the place, dirty dishes were just as the last dishwasher left them, with everything else piled on top of that. I encouraged myself, "At least I know how to clean!" By the end of the day that little restaurant had the cleanest kitchen in town.

After work at ten o' clock at night Rose and I took the last bus, and walked the mile from the bus stop to her home. Everybody in Rose's family worked. Her mother washed dishes in a restaurant, too, and Rose's dad worked in a coal mine. Although I was so tired I could hardly keep my eyes open, Rose's mother fed us a little bologna sandwiched between two slices of bread and warmed in the oven. We were all so poor; those were rough times.

Rose's mother said, "Yes, you can live with us. We don't have an extra bed, but you can sleep with Rose."

I said, "Oh that will be fine." The Kostashens accepted me as part of their family. From that time on God has always provided a home for me, so I have never, never, never been alone. On the weekends I kept my promise, and visited my brothers in the orphanage.

While I was washing dishes in that cute little restaurant I didn't want my family in Cold Lake to worry about me. For some reason or other it sounded more glamorous to write to my sister Nora that I was working in a drug store. But one day as I was bringing pots and pans out of the kitchen, I saw my cousin Paul and his friend coming into the restaurant. I thought, "I'd better not let them see me."

As I started to back up Paul said, "Oh, hi!" After I got rid of the pots and pans he said, "I thought you were working in a drug store."

I said, "Paul, if you love me, don't tell anyone I'm washing dishes in a restaurant. Do you promise me that?"

Paul said, "Yes, I promise." Well, he didn't keep it. As soon as he got home he told everyone we knew back home, but that was all right. Eventually my friend Rose Kostashen and I did find work in a drug store where we were both in charge of the little lunch counter.

Even living with Rose's family, in all the hustle and bustle of the crowded city I felt so lonely after Mama and Papa were gone. My brothers were in a home, and I felt I had no purpose. I was in a very vulnerable time of my life.

When Canada and the U.S.A. became involved in WWII, American military came in with their fancy uniforms and all their money to create a first line of air defense for Alaska, in the event of a Japanese attack.[67]

Rose Kostashen and I were pretty good looking. She was blond; I had black hair. We made quite a pair when we went out dancing. I soon met a really dark Latino fellow named Mariano at a few of the dances. Could he ever sing, and could he ever dance!

Mariano fed me the biggest line, and I fell for it head over heels. I thought I loved that no-good, low-down skunk. He grew up in Brooklyn, New York, but his family was from Venezuela, so he spoke both Spanish and English. He told me he fell in love with me, so we went together for a year or two. Then the war ended, and the American soldiers went back home.

In those days it was hard for Canadians to get into the U. S. A. unless you were married to an American. Mariano promised me, "As soon as I get home, I'll send your train ticket, and we'll get married."

---

[67] In 1943 the population in Edmonton increased from 96,725 to 111,745. On the Canadian air force base in Edmonton, air planes were being built and reconditioned for the European front. US. Troops were helping with the war effort, and U.S. civilians were helping build the Alaskan Highway in preparation for a possible Japanese invasion of North America.
http://www.albertasource.ca/homefront/living_with_war/communities/urban/edmonton.html

My sister Rose wasn't in favor of me marrying Mariano and moving to Brooklyn, New York, but she never told me why until years later. Mariano went out with other women when I worked late at night, and he even tried to date my sister Rose, but I didn't know that at the time.

I believed Mariano loved me, and I hung on to him by writing letters back and forth until he finally sent me my train fare to meet him in Montreal. My sister Rose and her friend saw me to the train station, and away I went. Mariano met me in Montreal where he had rented a nice room in a private home that was not too expensive. We spent the night and got married before a Justice of the Peace. We stayed in Montreal just a couple of days, because Mariano didn't have much money and I had nothing. When we were married I was allowed to cross the border into the U.S.A. Mariano and I began our life together in Brooklyn, New York. What a disaster that was!

Brooklyn, New York

Search me, O God, and know my heart;
   test me and know my anxious thoughts.
See if there is any offensive way in me,
   and lead me in the way everlasting. Psalm 139:23-24 (*NIV*)

We lived in an all-Black neighborhood in Brooklyn where Mariano seemed to fit right in with his dark-brown skin. The color of a person's skin had never affected me, but I didn't know whether the black people would accept *me* or not. Mariano worked in a paint factory, so he couldn't afford to pay much for rent. He had rented a room in a lady's apartment on the sixth floor of a building with no elevator. The room was nice enough, but it was in a horrible, horrible, dumpy building. I didn't mind walking the stairs, because I was with the man I thought I loved, so I figured I was happy and could conquer anything.

New York City was different from everything I had ever experienced in my life! I stayed home all day trembling from fear, not daring to go out in the streets while Mariano went to work. We had no television to pass the time, just a little radio. Sometimes when I was all alone during the day, men pounded on the door demanding to see Mariano. I never answered them, but hoped and prayed they wouldn't break down the door. Mariano may have owed them money or something, I didn't know. I knew we needed more money, but I didn't know where to look for a job.

In Canada we were never in crowds, but in New York City the streets were a solid crush of people! You had to *push* your way through the masses to get anywhere. The first time Mariano took me on the subway, I suffered terribly from claustrophobia. It was a modern subway about two stories down into the ground. I clung to Mariano's hand as we kept walking down, down, down those long steep steps into what seemed like the bowels of the earth.

As the train whisked us away into the dark tunnel I was so afraid, I felt like I couldn't breathe. There were too many people packed in like sardines! It seemed like there were a hundred hot sweaty people packed into every car smoking cigarettes and cigars. We got off at our station and walked the two flights back up to the street. I quickly decided I preferred riding the bus on top of the ground.

After awhile I gathered enough courage to venture out of the apartment on my own to look for a job. To begin with the only jobs I could find were in clothing factories. The factories were hot, and the foremen treated people worse than their machinery. These women worked so hard; it's no wonder those places were called sweat factories!

Because I am left-handed I couldn't be a seamstress, the machines were set up backwards for me. My first job was trimming threads after someone finished sewing a garment; later I found a job folding stuff. The jobs were easy enough, but I couldn't stand the stuffy, hot, crowded working conditions!

One of the Italian ladies and I got to know each other during our lunch breaks. She and her husband were buying a house so their apartment would soon be vacant. I told her, "I sure wish I could find a nice little apartment. We live with somebody else, and I don't like it."

She offered, "You might like our apartment."

"Oh?" I asked. "Well, where is it?"

"Just a block away," she said. "If you want to see it, come home with me after work. It's in kind of an old building."

I asked, "How much is the rent?"

She said, "It's fifteen dollars a month."

I said, "I think we can afford that."

So I went home with her after work to see her place. We climbed the stairs, and on the second landing she had a little apartment. I think the building was condemned, but to me it looked just right. There was one bedroom, the bathroom, a little kitchen and a little living room. There was only one problem; it was filled with cockroaches!

I thought, "I can get rid of those cockroaches; I'll clean and I'll scrub." Then the lady introduced me to the slum lord who owned all those buildings that were condemned. I asked him, "When this lady is gone, I would like her apartment. Is that okay?"

"Oh, sure," he said. "As long as you pay me every month, I don't mind."

I told Mariano about the apartment, and said, "We'll have to get some furniture." I found a store where we could buy furniture on time. The friendly sales girl sold us a new fridge, a couch, an easy chair, and a kitchen table and chairs. We paid about five dollars a month, which would take forever to pay off, but at least we had new furniture at payments we could afford. There was just a burner for cooking in the apartment, but a friend from my work place had a nice stove for us.

We were now on a main drag, which was better. A friend I met at work helped Mariano paint the walls so it was cheerful and clean. By continually cleaning, spraying, and scrubbing the floor I kept the apartment spotless, but I couldn't get rid of those cockroaches! That's the way we lived for a couple of years.

I finally found a job I liked at the Pesto Company, a small factory producing tiny light bulbs for sewing machines owned by Mr. Zadar and his partner. The Pesto Company was independent, selling their light bulbs to other companies. In the Pesto factory the work was passed from person-to-person working on machine-to-machine. The process started with a big machine that made the main stem. Then it would go to the next person who put in three dumets – pegs at the base of the light bulb to which the filaments were attached. The last step before packaging was fastening the screw part to the bottom of the bulb. Each bulb had its own little box packed in cases to be sold in case lots.

My job was to pull down two pegs and to see if the filament was okay. It was a simple job I was able to do, and I enjoyed it. The factory was very clean with more space for the workers, and much more pleasant to work in than the clothing factories had been. We worked eight-hour days with morning and afternoon coffee breaks and a break for lunch.

After Mariano and I were married about two years, he started running around on the weekends. At first he told me he was playing pool with the boys on Friday nights. When he was gone I didn't have anyplace to go. There were bars all over but I wasn't drinking in those days, and I didn't dare to venture out alone at night.

As time went on Mariano came home drunk on Friday nights, and I put up with that for awhile. When he started staying out Friday nights *and Saturday nights*, I knew there must be women involved. I was so hurt and so embarrassed at the way he was that I just wanted to get away. I knew that my marriage was not going to last. He was out there cheating all the time, so I never let him touch me, *no more!*

One morning a little old Spanish lady came to tell me in her broken English, "Ricardo no good. Bad. All the time women." She patted my arm and advised, "You go home. Go back to Canada." She was trying to help me.

I thought to myself, "Yes, she's right. I can't put up with this anymore." I decided one night when he was gone I would pack my bag. Once again when I really needed God's help, he heard the desperate cry in my heart, and he looked after me.

One Friday night when Mariano was dressed up like a king and gone, I decided that was it. I was not going to remain there any more; I was going to run away! We were so poor; Mariano's drinking used up any extra money we earned. Except for the radio I carried with me, everything else I owned fit into my one little suitcase. When I had packed, I called my Spanish friend, and asked if her husband could bring his car to help me find a room.

She offered, "Yes, Al will come by to get you around seven o'clock."

When Al arrived I told him, "Al, I'm running away!"

"Good for you!" he said. They all knew Mariano was a cheater. Al put my suitcase into his car, I got in, and Al drove me around to find a place to live. In Brooklyn, ten blocks away I could disappear into the crowd where Mariano would never look for me. Al took me into a Jewish neighborhood close to the El, close to the bus line, and close to the subway. I saw signs in the windows, "Room for Rent", "Room for Rent", "Room for Rent." Finally we got to the end of a block, and I saw a sign that said, "Room for Rent. Girl Only." *That* sounded good. I rang the bell, and a little red-headed Jewish lady at the top of the stairs said, "Yes, yes, yes, what can I do for you?"

I said, "I'm looking for a room!"

She asked, "Are you alone? Are you married? You got a boyfriend?"

"No," I answered. "I'm running away."

She clapped her hands and shouted, "Come right on up!" The lady owned the building, and was renting her daughter's room in her own apartment after her daughter had been married. The room had beautiful curtains, a pretty bedspread, a dresser, and everything I needed. It was also conveniently within walking distance for me to have wonderful transportation anywhere I needed to go.

I liked it right away, so I said, "Oh, that's really nice. How much is it?"

She said, "Ten dollars a month."

"Okay," I said. "I'll take it." Al took pity on me, and paid my first month's rent.

Once again, God provided me a family so I wouldn't live alone. Even though my bedroom could be locked away from her apartment with a little hook, that hook didn't stay hooked very long. My new landlady, Mrs. Feintuk, was the cutest little Jewish woman, and we became good friends. She appreciated my help puttering around, washing dishes that were always piled up, cleaning up her kitchen, or cooking after I came home from work.

I was treated like part of the family right away. In addition to her married daughter, Mrs. Feintuk had a teenage son who had nice friends coming over after school. The son and his friends were well-to-do Jewish kids. They treated me like a mom, hanging out in my room and sitting on my bed while they visited. On Saturday nights we played poker. I liked poker, and they all had money, but they didn't know what a good poker player I was. After we all won and lost money, around ten o'clock someone would say, "Well, let's go and have some pizza!"

Off I'd go with all these teenagers to a pizza parlor. In New York City the pizza crusts were thin and crispy with all kinds of good toppings. If I won their money, I bought the pizza. If someone else won, that person would buy. We shared the outcome of the game that way and had a good time together.

I was so happy to be living at Mrs. Feintuck's apartment! Even though I still worked at the light bulb factory, Mariano never showed up at work looking for me. I was making a new life for myself and never looked back.

Some Puerto Ricans who just arrived in New York were looking for a place to live. The apartment Mariano and I had was available, because he was already living with a girlfriend. I offered the Puerto Rican couple, "You can buy my new appliances and furniture, and I can give you the name of the Jewish man who owns the place." I showed them the apartment and sold all the apartment furnishings in one lump sum clearing about one thousand dollars.

After they paid me, Mrs. Feintuk said, "Let's go put your thousand dollars in the bank." The money in the bank was a nest egg for getting away later on.

Working in Brooklyn

He will call upon me, and I will answer him;
    I will be with him in trouble,
    I will deliver him and honor him.
With long life will I satisfy him
    and show him my salvation. Psalm 91:15-16 (*NIV*)

Monday morning after moving in with Mrs. Feintuk, I went to see my boss, Mr. Zadar. Mr. Zadar was a distinguished elderly Austrian with a kind gentle heart. He hadn't paid any attention to me before, because there were about fifty workers in the factory. Mr. Zadar just knew me as number one-two-three in the factory until he heard my story.

I began, "Mr. Zadar, I'd like to share something with you. I had to leave my husband, because he was not a good man. I'm a Canadian who is half Indian and half Irish, so I blend in with everybody okay; I look like I could be Jewish or Spanish. But I'm not one of these people; my culture is different." He didn't ask any questions but just sat quietly and listened. I cried in his office as my whole tale of woe tumbled out of me. Pretty soon he brought out his big handkerchief and gave it to me.

Mr. Zadar was very interested in my background. He told me that he used to live among the Navajo people a long time ago in Arizona, so he got to know Indian people and our ways. He said, "I had a diamond in the rough, and I never knew it."

I said, "Mr. Zadar, I'm on my own now in a room with a family. I'm not making very much money here, so I don't know if I can pay for my rent, and my food, and everything."

"Well, what are we paying you?" he asked.

"About twenty-five dollars a week," I replied.

"Oh?" he asked. "How long have you been here?"

I said, "About two years."

Mr. Zadar looked at what I made, and he saw I was telling him the truth. He said, "Well, okay, I'll double your salary to fifty dollars a week, but just keep it under your hat."

I said, "Oh, I won't tell a soul."

For the first time since Papa died, I was able to pay my living expenses and have a little to spare for the necessities of life. I started to feel like a human being again.

Mr. Zadar contacted his lawyer friend who helped me through divorce proceedings. The lawyer arranged for Mariano to pay for the divorce, but Mariano never showed up at the hearing. The lawyer's services cost five hundred dollars, which was a lot of money in the late 1940's. Rather than risk seeing Mariano again, I decided to pay the bill myself. The lawyer set up my payments with interest at ten dollars a month spread over several years.

Mr. Zadar took me under his wing as I let him fill the *dad spot* that had been empty in my heart since Papa's death. We had giggled when Papa tried to share his love of Shakespeare with his children, but now that I was an adult Mr. Zadar was able to complete Papa's teaching in that area.

Mr. Zadar was determined to give me an education in the arts. Whenever he got tickets to go to an opera, a really good movie, a Broadway play, or museums where new displays were on loan, he always gave me two tickets.

Down the avenue from my rented room there were two well-educated and high class women whose parents were Russian immigrants. One woman was a clothing designer and her sister was an opera singer. The singer and I became really close friends. She advised me on improving my appearance, "Bridget, don't pluck your eyebrows anymore; just color them." Or she'd say, "Don't wear that color rouge."

One night Mr. Zadar gave me tickets to an opera. I thought, "Opera! I don't like opera music; I don't even want to go!"

I told my Russian friend, "I've got two tickets to the opera."

"What is it called?" she said.

"Aida," I said, "You and I are going."

"Oh yes," she said. "This is the kind of singing I like!" She explained that Aida was one of the best operas in the world, and off we went!

Then another day Mr. Zadar gave us tickets to see the Mona Lisa that was on loan from France to a museum in New York for a year. When I came back to work my boss said, "Did you see the Mona Lisa?"

I said, "Yes. I saw the real Mona Lisa."

Another time he gave me tickets to go to *South Pacific*. Oh, I enjoyed Mary Martin and Ezio Pinza on Broadway. They were the *real McCoy*.

Another time Aphrodite was loaned to a museum. Mr. Zadar told me, "I want you to go to the museum of art and look at Aphrodite, a statue with no arms that is on loan."

I asked, "Why would I want to see an old broken statue with no arms?"

But he encouraged me, "Well, it is one of the most famous statues in the whole world." So off I went again with my Russian friend to develop my appreciation of ancient sculpture.

Mr. Zadar was always amazed that I was not afraid to make my way around New York City to find the museums, theaters, and concert halls. He gave me courage to believe I was capable of doing things that I didn't believe I could do. I had been so insecure and naïve when I came to his factory.

The Pesto Company employed about fifty workers from different races including Puerto Rican, mixed Black, and Latino. The Latinos spoke Spanish among themselves. Quite a few of the Latinos were recent arrivals to the United States, but most of them had been in New York longer than I had. I was mixed blood, but I was the only Indian as far as I could tell. Because I wasn't living in an Indian neighborhood, I felt like I was the only Indian in all of New York City. Liz, my best friend at work, was from northern Alabama and was the only person in the company who was all Black.

Liz was about the homeliest Black girl you could ever meet, but Liz's heart was just simply lovely. I sat at lunch with her and had my little peanut butter sandwich while she had chicken and all the good stuff that she cooked at home. One day I asked, "Liz, when are you going to invite me to your home for chicken dinner?"

Liz said to me in her slow southern drawl, "Oh you wouldn't come to an old black person's house would you?"

I said, "Try me."

She offered, "You want to come over for Sunday dinner this week?"

That Sunday I went faithfully to the Catholic church. Even though the nuns had made me so terrified of God when I was little, I was even more afraid of what God might do to me if I ever dared to stay home from church! After church the subway took about half an hour to get to Liz's stop. It was in the middle of miles and miles of Black neighborhood, but I had not grown up with prejudice, and my love for Liz kept me from being afraid.

All the apartment buildings in her neighborhood were tenement houses with steps out front, but the aroma of Liz's tasty cooking led

126

me right to her door! Liz's place was just spotless! She had invited two couples who were over in the corner playing a little poker, and I was soon in the game.

We had a lovely dinner. At around four o'clock I thought, "Before it gets dark I'd better get home!" On the subway I was so happy after enjoying a wonderful time with my friend Liz!

Monday morning Mr. Zadar asked me, "Well, what did you do this weekend?"

I said, "I went over to Liz's for Sunday dinner."

He shook his head and smiled as he said, "You are amazing!" He was so happy for me.

After I had been working for the Pesto Company for awhile, Mr. Zadar had me help him count the cash on pay days. We made sure the amounts were disbursed correctly for each employee before sealing the envelopes and distributing their pay. Friday night before Christmas, the sealed salary envelopes were completed, when Mr. Zadar noticed his own pay wasn't right, "You know, I'm twenty dollars short, and I don't know what I did with it."

I said, "Mr. Zadar, if Liz has it in her envelope, she will bring it back to you."

I passed the envelopes around, and guess who got the extra money? Liz came into the office, threw the twenty dollar bill over the desk at Mr. Zadar, and demanded, "What? You gave me a raise, and never even told me?"

With a big tear in his eye Mr. Zadar said, "Liz, that's your Christmas present." He was so moved by her honesty, he let her keep the extra money.

As Mr. Zadar began to trust me, he gave me more responsibility. Once a month he sent me over to New Jersey to pick up filaments for the little light bulbs. The filaments came in a small box, about 5 x 4 x 4 inches, but one box contained tens of thousands of filaments so tiny they were like little hairs. That tiny box cost about ten thousand dollars back in the 1950's. Rather than use the postal service, or a courier service for anything that valuable, Mr. Zadar sent me as his faithful employee. As a further precaution, he put me in a taxi.

I felt like a queen riding in a taxi from New York City through the Holland Tunnel. It took about an hour to get to the big General Electric Company in Menlo Park, New Jersey, where all kinds of products were manufactured. I had to go through security before they let me into the building. Once inside I gave them the Pesto Company check from Mr. Zadar, and they gave me the box of filaments. The taxi driver waited for me to complete my business, and then brought me back to the Pesto Company where I delivered my box to Mr. Zadar.

While I was still young and very attractive I dated a lot of good-looking guys in New York City telling myself I was making up for lost time. The Jewish men treated me with the most respect, and took me to the best places in New York: Shangri-La, and oh, such fancy places! I liked that. The Italian men, on the other hand, were hot-blooded and I had to fight them to keep their hands off me sometimes, but I never let anyone take advantage of me. No way!

My heart was hardened against men after Mariano cheated on me and ruined our marriage. Men could love me, but I wouldn't love them back, and sex outside of marriage was unthinkable to me! Anybody who wanted to pick me up in a car wasn't for me. Whenever I went out with a man, we always took the subway or some other form of public transportation.

Once a man fell in love with me, I didn't want anything to do with him. One good-looking Italian in my apartment building was so dreamy-eyed around me I told him, "I can't get serious with anyone, because I'm trying to save enough money to go back to Canada." However, after making payments on my divorce, and paying for room and board, there wasn't much left to set aside for a trip home to Canada.

Without Jesus in my life to help me forgive, the sorrow in my life kept increasing, and the only outlet I knew was alcohol. I was drinking on a regular basis, but I didn't go to bars alone. When I went out on dinner dates, I had a few drinks to enjoy myself. By this time I was also a closet drinker buying liquor and hiding it in my room. I told myself that alcohol didn't control me yet, because I could still decide when I wanted a drink and when I didn't.

A nice-looking man from the factory living near my apartment building, who I'll call George, fell for me, but he was a total alcoholic. One weekend he asked me out for dinner. At seven o' clock he brought me to a place where they had a little music and dancing. After a few drinks and a nice dinner, we had a pretty good time. I went out with him a couple of times. He didn't seem to get drunk when I was with him, so I thought he was okay. I figured, I also had a few drinks, so I couldn't hold his drinking against him.

One night he suggested, "I'd like you to meet my mother."

"Oh?" Things are getting serious, I thought. "Where does she live?"

"Well, she lives across in New Jersey."

One Saturday night we took a long subway ride to New Jersey. Before taking me to his mother's place we stopped and had a few drinks at a very exclusive kind of a bar. I excused myself and found the bathroom. God must have protected me that night, because as I was coming back to our table, I saw George take something out of a little box and throw it into my drink. I thought, "What in the world! I'm not going to drink that drink!"

As soon as I got back to the table, George had to go to the bathroom, so I switched the drinks. When he returned, George didn't realize he was drinking from my glass that he had drugged. Pretty soon he looked like he was crazy; he was acting so strange I was frightened. I thought, "I'm getting out of here!" I wasted no time leaving the bar, hailing a cab, and heading home. George hadn't been taking me to meet his mother. That was just his line to get me to trust him and then take advantage of me.

On the way home I figured, "I'll tell Mr. Zadar what George did, and Mr. Zadar can deduct the money for the cab fare out of George's paycheck."

Taking a cab from Jersey all the way home cost more money than I had in my purse. I told the cabby, "Wait a minute," as I ran up to my room, borrowed the money from Mrs. Feintuk, and hurried back to pay the driver.

Monday George never showed up at work; he may have been too sick. I told Mr. Zadar, "I went out on a date with this George who works here, and I'll never go out with him again. I think he was trying to drug me or something. I was so scared; I left him in a bar in New Jersey. I had to take a cab all the way home, so he owes me the cab fare." When George came to get his paycheck, not only was the cab fare deducted from his pay; Mr. Zadar fired him.

As Mr. Zadar and his partner were getting older, competition for the light bulb market kept increasing and the company's business began to slow down. A work force of fifty dwindled to about twenty. Eventually we weren't making light bulbs anymore. Mr. Zadar and his partner sold the machinery, and gave each of us a check for about a hundred dollars. In the mid-1950's that was a good sum of money to tide us over for awhile.

When the Pesto Company closed, I realized nothing was keeping me in New York. My marriage had failed and now the only job I enjoyed was ending. I wanted to go back home to Cold Lake,

Alberta, but Mrs. Feintuk had other plans and helped me get a sales job at her friend's clothing accessory store.

The shop owner taught me how to sell hats, jewelry, hosiery and other items. We had to write every sale out by hand on sales slips, and then ring up the sales on the register, making change for people. The cash registers were easy to run in those days. With that little bit of sales experience, I was able to get a job in the huge Lerner department store where I worked as a sales girl for a few months.

About that time, Bishop Breynat retired and stopped in New York on his way home to France. There was a story of his fame in the major New York newspapers. Oh how I wanted to see him, but I was too poor to make it to the celebration held in his honor. Just seeing his name in the paper helped me realize how much I missed my friends and family!

Not long after Bishop Breynat was in New York City, I got a call from my sister Rose. She said, "Ward Foote and I got married and we're living in Minneapolis, Minnesota. We have a house with an extra bedroom where you can stay with us, find a job, and look for a place of your own."

Ward was an American fellow who wooed Rose in Edmonton during the war. Rose had moved out to Vancouver with her girlfriend to find work. Ward followed Rose and stayed in Vancouver until Rose married him. Then Ward brought her back to Minneapolis to live near his family in Minnesota. Rose's invitation sounded appealing; I had finished paying for my divorce, so I thought, "I can go out west and have a good life."

I pulled out my one little suitcase, packed my few items of clothing, incidentals, and my radio. I took the nest egg I had set aside out of my savings at the bank and bought a one-way ticket. It took two days to get from New York City to Minneapolis on the train.

I left New York with all its glamour, glitz, and glitter, and never looked back. All I knew was that I had to get away and forget everything that happened there. After I left New York, I didn't try to stay in contact with the friends I made in the Pesto Company, or even with Mrs. Feintuk. It was as if I had vanished. Only Mr. Zadar wrote to me now and then, but when Mr. Zadar died, I finally closed the New York chapter of my life.

Whenever I remember those days, my thoughts are dark and full of fear. Through all my travels, God protected me and provided a way out of my troubles, even though I didn't know him yet.

Making a Home in Minneapolis

Praise the Lord, O my soul,
  and forget not all his benefits —
who forgives all your sins
  and heals all your diseases,
who redeems your life from the pit
  and crowns you with love and compassion,
who satisfies your desires with good things
  so that your youth is renewed like the eagle's.
  Psalm 103: 2-5, *NIV*

Bridget after arrival in Minneapolis

My sister Rose met me at the train station in Minneapolis. I moved into Rose and Ward's house in a small town by the name of Deephaven, which was next to the Twin Cities suburb of Excelsior.

After celebrating my arrival for a few days with Rose and Ward, I went job hunting. The *Back to School* shopping days were in full swing in August, so there were lots of job openings in downtown Minneapolis. My experience at the huge Lerner department store qualified me for a job right away at the large Dayton's department store in the heart of Minneapolis. I was hired in their Town and Country Sports Wear section as a sales person for women's clothing where I worked for over thirty years.

Rose and Ward lived in a beautiful neighborhood, but my work schedule didn't allow me time to enjoy it. In the morning I left early for the hour-long bus ride to Dayton's where I worked until nine o' clock at night. Then it took me an hour to get back to Excelsior where about eleven dogs met me at the bus stop. I was so deathly afraid from my nightmares of dogs chasing me, Rose met my bus each night and then walked me home.

Rose and Ward were very good to me, but I wanted them to have their own space, and I needed to find a more convenient place to live near my job. I wasn't in Minneapolis long before I found a room for rent with the Starkes, a nice family who lived by Lake Calhoun closer to downtown Minneapolis.

I loved my Dayton's job in the midst of the city where I met so many people as they shopped in my department. While waiting on a lady one day, I noticed a small boy about three years old tagging behind her, clinging to a life-size grey rabbit. "What is your name," I asked.

"Craig," he replied.

"And what is that you are carrying, Craig?" I asked.

"A rabbit," he answered. "Feel how soft and cuddly he is."

As I petted his soft furry rabbit, I asked, "What is the rabbit's name?"

"Cornelius, Ma'am," the little boy informed me proudly.

It tugged at my heart strings after he was gone, because of the tender spot in my heart for children. Soon little Craig was back with his big rabbit. He said, "Cornelius is crying, because you forgot to say goodbye to him."

I said, "Goodbye, Cornelius," and as they walked away, I was crying, too.

After living and working a couple of years in Minneapolis, I made friends with two women from Dayton's who accompanied me to a piano bar every night on our way home. It was a nice lounge with a little bar, two booths, and the piano.

My friends from Dayton's were both divorced ladies like me, but unlike me they were Norwegian and they weren't alcoholics like I was becoming. I have always said that the Irish in me made the Indian in me drink. In spite of those differences, we had a lot in common. We were sales girls at Dayton's hurting from our divorce situations with bitterness against our ex-husbands. We were our own little support group, talking over our troubles with two or three drinks, and then taking our buses home.

Both of those women were from Minneapolis; I was the only transplant – the only one cut off from my extended family and from everything that was familiar. One of the women had grown children, the other had young children waiting to see her, but I had only my little pint waiting for me in my bag when I got home. I was getting progressively worse in my drinking, but I hadn't let it affect my job – yet.

The bar tender was a kind interesting Jewish man. We told him, "We do not want to be bothered by any of the fellows." We knew what it might entail if somebody bought us a drink, so we refused all offers.

A young gentleman by the name of Bill Volden also used to come into that little piano lounge after work. Our paths crossed for half an hour each day. He arrived around five thirty in the evening for a beer or two at the bar, and my friends and I would leave around six o' clock. Bill gazed at the corner where I sat with my friends. I hadn't noticed Bill, but one day I heard him tell the bar tender, "Those three girls sit over there all the time. Do you see that dark-haired one? Oh, I'd like to meet her sometime."

I didn't let on that I overheard him.

The bar tender said, "Those three don't talk to anybody in the bar. They just have their drink, and then they go home." So Bill let the matter drop.

A few days later I came to the bar ahead of my two friends. The bar tender came over to me and said, "There's a very nice young man who comes in here, and he wants to meet you."

"Oh, he's probably married with half a dozen kids," I said.

"No he's not," the bar tender replied.

"How do you know?" I asked.

"Well," the bar tender said, "This is the kind of a guy he is. He comes in and has a beer or two, and then he goes home. About eleven o'clock he comes back, has another beer, and waits for the place to close at midnight. He stays on, washes my glasses with me, mops my floor, and just helps me close up the place."

I said, "There can't be a man like that in the whole world!"

The bar tender continued, "Then we stop and have a hamburger with a big onion on it, and I take him home to his little apartment. He's a very nice man."

"Oh," I said, and I started believing him. The bar tender told me a few more good things about Bill, so I said, "Well, we'll see. Maybe."

Another day I came into the bar before my friends again, and there was Bill sitting up at the counter. "He doesn't look bad," I thought. "He looks like he needs me."

Finally one day there was an empty stool at the bar beside Bill. I slipped onto the

Bill and Bridget's Wedding

stool, and Bill just about fell over backward. "Oh, hi!" Bill said to me.

"Hi!" I said.

Bill asked right away, "May I buy you a drink?"

I said, "Only on one condition: that I buy you one right back"

"Oh, that's not necessary," Bill said. So Bill bought me a drink, and I bought him a beer. The bar tender was so happy; at last we were together!

I wanted Bill to think I was a lady, so I said, "Well, I guess I'd better go catch my bus and go home."

Bill followed me out and asked, "Can I take you to a nice place for supper?"

"No," I said. "You don't need to take me anywhere special. I love burgers; let's just go to the hamburger joint next door."

"Okay," Bill said. We had a big hamburger, and then Bill asked, "May I call a cab to take you home?"

"No," I said. "I take a bus for a quarter. If you want to ride with me, it's okay." So he came on the bus with me and rode to where I lived with the Starkes. He walked me home from the bus stop, and then he took the bus back to his apartment. Bill never let me go from then on. We dated, and dated, and dated, and dated, and in two months we were engaged. Four months later, on April 26, 1958, we were married in Bill's Lutheran church.

As a Catholic I had been taught the devil lives in the other churches. When I went to the Lutheran church with Bill I began to learn that God was not way off in heaven, just waiting to beat you whenever you did something wrong. I heard that God loves us, and wants us to get to know Him in a personal way. However, even with Bill's love, and my discovery that God also loved me, I was still battling the demons in my dreams, the memories of my beatings from the nuns, and heartaches from my past.

After Bill and I were married, we were able to share many things about our backgrounds.[68] Bill was also struggling to overcome sorrows. Bill's sister Mildred was eleven years old when Bill was born, so he didn't get to know his sister and older brother John very well. He spent most of his childhood playing alone. Bill loved animals when he was a boy, and became especially attached to his little dog, Ginger. Bill was his mother's youngest, and he enjoyed the

Bill and Ginger

special attention she gave to the baby in her family. Ed Volden was a good father, but he was a stoic Norwegian who did not hug his children. When Bill was about five years old, his beautiful mother Hilda became very sick. Bill was often separated from his mother to give her the rest she needed.

During his mother's illness, Bill's dog Ginger became his primary source of comfort. He was always with his dog, holding on to Ginger, hugging his little dog.

When Bill's mother Hilda died a year later on February 11, 1936, Bill lost the one person in

---

[68] Bill's parents had three children. John Edwin Johnson Volden was born June 8, 1916 in Morris, Minnesota. Mildred Dorothy Johnson Volden was born July 17, 1918 in Hilda's home town of Jewell, Iowa. William (Bill) James Volden was born in Morris on August 10, 1929.

his life who had given him tender love and affection.

After Hilda's death, her nurse, Lily became the person Bill's father Ed leaned on for support during his time of grief. Ed Volden married Lily Wrolson just a few months after Bill's mother died.

Shortly after they were married Ed and Lily sent Bill to visit his aunts and uncles in Canby, Minnesota. Before he left, Bill wondered where Ginger was. Bill looked and looked, but he couldn't find Ginger. All Bill could think of while at his uncle's farm was, "Where is Ginger? What happened to Ginger?"

Ed and Hilda Volden

When Ed and Lily picked Bill up and drove home from Canby, Bill kept asking about Ginger. Finally Lily turned around and said to Bill, "Ginger is dead!"

Bill couldn't believe it! He cried, "What happened?"

Ed said, "A car struck and killed him."

You can imagine how the sad news broke Bill's heart! When they got home, Bill and his father Ed buried the little dog in the back yard. Bill's grief over the loss of his mother seemed magnified with the loss of his little dog Ginger.

Bill's stepmother, Lily, who never had any children of her own, didn't understand the importance of holding Bill close to her to comfort him during his times of grieving.

Bill's life was rather empty and lonely growing up without his mom, and he became a shy person. He did well in school, and went on to college. His special interest was bookkeeping, which he may have acquired from his dad. Bill became an outstanding accountant working for various grain companies where he was always appreciated for his bookkeeping skill.

Bill loved his dad and visited Ed in Morris at every opportunity. In 1952, Bill's dad had a heart attack, but recovered and was able to continue working at the university. Bill's dad retired in 1955, allowing him more time for hunting and fishing.

In 1955, the year Ed retired his students printed a tribute to him in their yearbook: [69]

> Since May, 1915 Prof. E. J. Volden has served the University of Minnesota's West Central School of Agriculture with a degree of efficiency which few attain. Many know of his integrity in seeing that the University receives every cent that is coming to the institution, but few know that he is just as exacting in seeing that every individual gets every cent that is coming to him from the University. Correct in every detail and nothing less is the standard he has lived by. Few indeed ever question any of his many reports.
>
> Not only has Mr. Volden served extremely well in the business office, but he is an exceptionally good teacher. In the classrooms as in the office he respects ambition, honesty and intelligence. His students know their subject matter. They expect to work in his classes and know that the information obtained will be worth the effort. The importance of good credit is taught to all his classes for he has always recognized its value.
>
> While emphatic in impressing on a student the duty of meeting his obligations, few faculty members have been as interested in helping students who are in trouble. When he retires June 30, the University will lose a faithful employee whose outstanding characteristics are efficiency and loyalty. He served under all four superintendents of the West Central School and Experiment Station and to each he gave unquestioning loyal support in the administration of the station business.

After Bill and I were married in 1958, Bill continued making trips to Morris to see his dad as often as he could. On Friday nights Bill would leave for Morris to spend the weekend fishing or hunting with his dad. As a Dayton's employee, I had to work most Saturdays, but I accompanied Bill whenever I could. Bill and Ed took me fishing with them on Pomme de Terre Lake north of Morris.

Just over a year after we were married, on October 21, 1959, when he was seventy-two years old, Bill's dad drove toward Morris after a day of fishing alone at Pomme de Terre Lake. Ed must have realized his heart was in trouble, and he managed to pull over to the side of the highway where his car came to a stop in the roadside ditch. One of the nurses who knew Ed came along and stopped by

---

[69]The Senior Class of 1955, University of Minnesota, Institute of Agriculture, West Central School and Experiment Station, Morris, Minnesota – *The Moccasin*, 42(1955), p. 11.

his parked car where she found Ed slumped over. When she checked his pulse, Ed was already gone from a heart attack.

The story in October 23, 1955 issue of The Morris Tribune[70] included the following account of Ed's life:

> Edwin J. Volden was born at Canby, Minnesota, on March 14, 1887, son of Mr. and Mrs. John Edwin Johnson Volden. He graduated from Canby High School in 1905 and then attended Mankato Business College. He taught for a time in Yellow Medicine County and then engaged in secretarial work in Canby. In 1910 he went to Arlington, S.D. as secretary of the Western Land and Loan Company. He was employed for a time in 1911 in the office of Lidman Steamship Ticket Agency in Winnipeg, Canada, and then for two years was a cost accountant for George H. Archibald Construction Co. in Winnipeg. The following two years he was employed by Butler Brothers Building Co., St. Paul, and the Fred J. Romer Construction Co., St. Paul. He came to Morris from St. Paul in 1915 to join the staff at the West Central School and Experiment Station where he served until his retirement on June 30, 1955.
>
> Mr. Volden was married at Jewell, IA, to Hilda Larson on August 25, 1915. She preceded him in death. To them were born two sons and a daughter. He was married to Lily Wrolson at Morris on December 20, 1936.
>
> Mr. Volden served for many years as chairman of the board of audit of the Morris Building and Loan Association, now the First Federal Savings and Loan Association of Morris. He was retained as an auditor by the City of Morris for a number of years, and was an auditor for a number of cooperative organizations in this area for many years.
>
> He was a member of First Lutheran church and was very active and helpful in its work. He had served as a member of the church board and as church treasurer. He gave generously of his time and abilities as a member of various church finance committees over the years.
>
> He had been a member of the Morris Civic and Commerce Association, forerunner of the Chamber of Commerce, and of the Chamber of Commerce, and in other ways had demonstrated an interest and helpfulness in civic and community affairs.

The loss of Bill's dad was another deep, deep heartbreak for Bill. It took him a long time to get over his father's death. After Ed's death, when I had a Saturday off, Bill and I went to Morris to spend

---

[70] "E. J. Volden Rites Will Be Friday", *The Morris Tribune* (Morris, MN) 85: 43, pp. 1-2.

some time with Lily. We also visited some of Bill's uncles or Lily's Wrolson relatives who did their best to be cheerful around us. We had some good times visiting them.

When Lily died, Ed and Lily's home was sold to Bill and Jean Myers who still live there. The proceeds from the house were split among my husband Bill, his brother John, and his sister Mildred as their inheritance from their dad. Later when Bill and I bought our first home in Richfield, Minnesota, we used Bill's inheritance from his father toward the purchase of our home. I always told Bill that Ed had bought that house for us, and that helped Bill feel closer to his dad.

Coming from a large family, I knew the importance of hugging and cuddling, and I gave Bill all the love I could to help him get over the emotional pain from his grieving. The deepest pain, though, seemed to be the loss of Ginger so close after his mother's death. Hardly a day went by that Bill didn't talk about losing his little dog Ginger.

Although we were enjoying our marriage, and getting to know each other better, I had a hidden problem that continued to grow. In the early years of our marriage I was getting more and more addicted to alcohol. Bill didn't realize how addicted I was, because I did most of my drinking in secret.

One More Drink Will Kill You

> I waited patiently for the Lord;
>   he turned to me and heard my cry.
> He lifted me out of the slimy pit,
>   out of the mud and mire;
> he set my feet on a rock
>   and gave me a firm place to stand.
> He put a new song in my mouth,
>   a hymn of praise to our God.
> Many will see and fear
>   and put their trust in the Lord. Psalm 40:1-3 *(NIV)*

In 1965 when Bill's grain company moved us to Cedar Rapids, Iowa, not everything was coming up roses. No matter how much Bill tried to help me overcome my drinking, I kept getting worse. Then on August 10, 1965 I really hit bottom.

When I woke up to get ready for work, Bill was already gone. Pulling out the bottle I always saved for the next day, I wondered, "How would it taste to have a little shot of whiskey in my coffee?" I made coffee, fixed my hair, took a shower, and poured a cup with some of the whiskey. Oh, did that taste good! Whoa! That hit the spot! Then as I added the rest of the whiskey to another cup of coffee, I said to myself, "You know something? I think I'll quit my job today. Then I'll buy myself a pint of whiskey every day, turn on my TV, put up my feet, and just enjoy the rest of my life."

Just then the thought appealed to me, but today when I look back on it I can say, "Isn't that crazy?"

I went to work on time, but when my boss came to relieve me at noon I said to her, "Gloria, I don't believe I'll be coming back this afternoon."

"Oh?" she said.

"I'm not feeling too good," I lied. I wasn't sick; I was just making an excuse to slip down to the liquor store, pick up my pint of whiskey, and go home. I didn't bother calling Bill. I just went home, opened my bottle, and started drinking, little by little, drinking it down. By three o'clock, like I always did after I had been drinking, I took a nap to sleep it off.

As Bill always did, he went to my workplace, reading the paper while he waited for me to come out of my shop. As they were locking the door, Bill asked, "Where's Bridget?"

"Oh, she went home at noon," was the offhanded reply.

It was like an arrow pierced his soul. When he got home about six thirty and found me sleeping, the tattling odor of the whiskey told the rest of the story. Bill sat on the bed sobbing, sobbing, sobbing, and shaking the bed so hard that I woke up. Hearing him cry was the turning point in my life; I felt so terrible! I really loved Bill, he was always so kind and thoughtful to me, and he had never done anything to hurt me.

"Bridget, I can't take it anymore," Bill cried. "You're drunk every night. I'm going to send you back home to Canada. I don't want you anymore! I can't take it anymore! You walked out of your job today, and you never even called me. We were supposed to go out for dinner tonight. It's my birthday!"

I had *forgotten* his *birthday!* Oh, that was bad, *so* bad. I said, "I'm sorry. I really don't want to be this way, but . . .."

"You've said that before, but I can't believe you anymore."

There was deep sadness in his voice, but fire in his eyes as Bill said, "I'm going out for supper alone. You're going to sleep on the couch tonight! I don't want you ever sleeping in the bedroom again!" He slammed the door and left.

I may have forgotten his birthday, but I would never forget this day for the rest of my life! As I fixed the bed on the studio couch in the living room, and crawled between the covers, I felt so terrible and so alone. I heard Bill come home later, but he didn't say a word to me. He slammed the bedroom door and went to bed.

Then I started praying the most earnest heartfelt prayer I had ever prayed in my life, "Oh, dear God! *Dear, dear*, God! I don't know what to *do!* I *want* to quit drinking, but I *can't* by myself. *Please*, Lord, *help* me," I cried.

It seemed like God said, "You have to give it all up – every bit of it!" So, I prayed, "All right, God, I won't ever drink this again, and I won't ever drink that again." I named all the whiskeys and beers that I ever drank. My conversation went on all night long as I tried bargaining with God to hang on to drink after drink, but God insisted that I had to give each one up. Wringing wet with sweat, I wrestled with God and the devil at the same time. Even the covers were soaked with my perspiration. Back and forth I was tossing and praying the best way I knew how. At four o' clock in the morning, I was still tossing and turning.

I said, "Dear God, I can't give up my favorite drink." As I held up the imaginary dry martini to God in my hands, it was very real to me.

141

God said, "You have to give it all up. If you keep drinking you will die. One more drink will kill you."

I asked, "All of it, God?"

"Yes, all of it," God answered.

Finally I surrendered, "Okay, Lord. Take it all away." I fell back onto the pillow in an exhausted sleep.

At six thirty in the morning, I heard Bill get up to take his shower. When I woke up, I was different. God had touched me; my craving was gone. I got up, opened the blinds, and let the sunlight stream in. Bill never drank coffee, but I made coffee, set the table, and set out the Rice Crispi's – just so! When he came out of the shower, he brushed past the breakfast, went into the bedroom, and got dressed for work.

As he was heading to work, I followed him toward the door pleading, "Bill, Bill, Bill . . .." I wanted to tell him about the wonderful thing that happened to me during the night.

"Nope." He said, "I'll buy your one-way train ticket back to Cold Lake, Alberta, as soon as I get to the office!"

"Bill, Bill, Bill, Bill, Bill . . .." He slammed the door, and away he went. Oh, boy! That was the end of the world for me. I cried, "Dear, dear God, what do I do now? I don't know what to do. I don't know what to do now."

It seemed like God said, "Go to the telephone, open the phone book and call Alcoholics Anonymous." By now it was seven o' clock in the morning. I went to the telephone, but I didn't even know where to look. As I opened the Cedar Rapids phone book, there on the first page, almost the first number was Alcoholics Anonymous! I was afraid to place the call, so I prayed the Lord's Prayer. I said the Lord's Prayer again. I said every prayer I ever knew, and then I dialed that number.

A gruff old male voice rasped into the phone, "Alcoholics Anonymous. Can I help you?"

I didn't know what Alcoholics Anonymous was. I didn't know what to say, so I said, "Hi. Is there a lady there I could talk to?"

He said, "No, but I can get you a lady, if you give me your name and phone number. You don't even have to give me your whole name; we're anonymous."

I was so desperate I gave him my full name and phone number.

He called a lady, and she called me right back. "Hi! My name is Carol and I'm an alcoholic. Can I help you?"

I didn't understand their lingo; I thought she meant she was still drinking. "Well, if you're an alcoholic," I said, "I guess you can't help me." Something prompted me to ask, "When did you have your last drink?"

She said, "Just a minute now . . . ten years, eight months, five days, fourteen hours, and twenty minutes ago."

I objected, "Why do you say you're still an alcoholic?"

She stated flatly, "Once an alcoholic, always an alcoholic." In other words, she was saying, that's the way the alcohol addiction works.

"Oh, I didn't understand," I explained. "Can you come over right away and talk to me?"

She said, "Sure, but I have a little girl. I'll have to get her dressed first, and then bring her over."

She told me what color her car was, and I gave her my address. In the meantime I took a nice shower, and fixed myself up pretty. In Cedar Rapids we lived in a beautiful brand new building above some doctors' offices. The six apartments were rented to five widows and then Bill and I. I didn't worry about the appearance of our apartment which I always kept clean and neat.

I waited for Carol at the bottom of the stairs. I expected a toothless old woman, with a broken nose and cauliflower ears. Soon a lovely car drove up, and a stunning blonde stepped out with a little girl. I couldn't believe it! Completely astonished, I involuntarily gaped at her; she was gorgeous!

When she saw me, Carol asked, "Are you Bridget?"

I said, "Yes. Are you Carol?"

She and her little girl climbed the stairs ahead of me and found the door to my apartment was open. As they walked in and looked around all she could say was, "Wow!"

"Is there something wrong?" I worried.

"No," she replied, "but this is the best twelfth step call I ever made! Usually they're in some dumpy old motel with bottles and stuff all over the place, and filthy!"

"No, that isn't me," I said. Then pointing to my heart I explained, "It's inside. It isn't my present situation that is bad; it is the hurts I carry with me."

After I invited Carol and her daughter to sit down, I gave the little girl the Rice Crispi's I had set out for Bill, and turned on the TV to entertain her while Carol and I visited. We talked, and talked, and talked. I described the old ache from painful memories that tormented me. Then she told me her wild tale of woe, and I began to think there must be hope for me.

She suggested, "Well, here's what we'll do. Tonight you'll come with me to a meeting. I'll pick you up around seven this evening."

Then I remembered, "We must call Bill at the office! He's so mad at me, he's ready to throw me out and ship me back to the reserve."

When I dialed Bill's work number, he hung up on me several times. Finally he answered, and I pleaded, "Bill, don't hang up. I called the Triple A!"

He said, "Huh? What? What?" Then he said, "I'm busy with a client. I'll call you right back." Pretty soon the phone rang. Bill asked, "What did you say, Bridget?"

My words tumbled out one on top of the other in rapid succession, "I called that number you always wanted me to call. There's a nice lady here talking to me. The way I feel, I'm never going to drink again. God touched my life last night, and I just know that I'm never going to drink again, and I'm going to a meeting with her tonight." All out of breath I handed the phone to Carol, "Say hello to my husband, so he'll believe me."

Carol took the phone and said, "Hi, Bill! How are you?"

Then he knew I was telling the truth. Oh, he was so happy! Carol stayed with me until about two o' clock in the afternoon. I fixed a really nice dinner for Bill who got home a little after five o' clock. He took me in his arms, and held me close. We both knelt down and said the Lord's Prayer together. Then Bill made a vow. "Bridget, as long as I live, I'll never have another can of beer, either, and I'll never go into a bar again." He kept his promise until the day he died.

That night I attended my first AA meeting. The meeting was way up above a shoe store in a big, big room! There was a long table with a cake over in one corner, and coffee going galore. Everybody seemed so happy as they were talking and laughing.

I knew nothing about AA; I thought they would give me a little whiskey to wean me off or something. I whispered to Carol, "Which ones are the alcoholics?"

She laughed, "All of them."

Young and old! Rich and poor! There were a couple of kids who were ten years old. Old timers were sitting over by the wall. With all the visiting beforehand, it was about eight o' clock before the meeting started. First everyone stood to say the *Serenity Prayer*. Then we sat down, and someone read the *Preamble of AA* with the twelve steps for overcoming alcoholism.

That was my introduction to AA. It was wonderful! I thought I was the only one in the *whole world* who ever felt this way or drank that much. It was so good to realize I was not alone with my drinking problem.

Those first years we went to meetings every night, every night, every day, every night, and every day. I got on that *pink cloud*! I was so excited I couldn't believe that I'd been sober all these days and months and hours. That went on for six months; then we returned to Minnesota.

I decided I didn't just want to get over my drinking; I wanted to be healed of the hurts that caused my drinking. As time went by, God kept working on my heart to forgive the people who had hurt me over the years, especially the nuns in the boarding school in Fort Providence. I read in the Bible that unless you forgive others, God won't forgive you.[71] When I read that Jesus said we need to forgive our brother not seven times, but seventy times seven times, [72] I was really impacted.

It was difficult to forgive at first. I wanted to feel sorry for myself, and to hang on to bitterness, but that only meant I lived with the pain for a longer time. Eventually I learned that God brings healing to my heart and to my memories as I forgive those who hurt me. As time went by I wasn't thinking about the painful memories anymore. I began to enjoy the freedom that comes with living life in the present.

Soon after Bill and I returned to Minneapolis we were back at work. I was given my old job at Dayton's, and Bill was hired to work for the Bungee grain corporation as one of their senior accountants. Now that Bill and I were back in Minneapolis, Minnesota, we wanted to get as close to Jesus as we possibly could. We both had experienced changed lives when I gave up my drinking. In addition to attending Augustana Lutheran Church in downtown Minneapolis, we heard about a Christian community in Bloomington called Bethany Fellowship. Although we continued to attend Augustana Lutheran Church faithfully, Pastor Haas and his family at Bethany Fellowship became our special friends and they really encouraged Bill and me in our faith.

---

[71] Matthew 6:15
[72] Matthew 18:22

145

God began to show me the emptiness in the words of Shakespeare's soliloquy that Papa used to recite to us:

> To-morrow, and to-morrow, and to-morrow,
> Creeps in this petty pace from day to day,
> To the last syllable of recorded time;
> And all our yesterdays have lighted fools
> The way to dusty death. Out, out, brief candle!
> Life's but a walking shadow, a poor player
> That struts and frets his hour upon the stage
> And then is heard no more. It is a tale
> Told by an idiot, full of sound and fury
> Signifying nothing.[73]

God had something significant in mind for our lives when he created us. I discovered hope as I read the following passages in the eighth chapter of the book of Romans:

> I consider that our present sufferings are not worth comparing with the glory that will be revealed in us.
>
> In the same way, the Spirit helps us in our weakness. We do not know what we out to pray for, but the Spirit himself intercedes for us with groans that words cannot express. And he who searches our hearts knows the mind of the Spirit, because the Spirit intercedes for the saints in accordance with God's will.
>
> And we know that in all things God works for the good of those who love him, who have been called according to his purpose.
>
> What, then shall we say in response to this? If God is for us, who can be against us? He who did not spare his own Son, but gave him up for us all—how will he not also, along with him, graciously give us all things? Who will bring any charge against those whom God has chosen? It is God who justifies. Who is he that condemns? Christ Jesus, who died—more than that, who was raised to life—is at the right hand of God and is also interceding for us. Who shall separate us from the love of Christ? Shall trouble or hardship or persecution or famine or nakedness or sword?
>
> No, in all these things we are more than conquerors through him who loved us. For I am convinced that neither death nor life, neither angels nor demons, neither the present nor the future, nor any powers, neither height nor depth, nor anything else in all

---

[73] Shakespeare's *Macbeth* (Act 5, Scene 5, lines 17-28).

creation, will be able to separate us from the love of God that is in Christ Jesus our Lord. Romans 8:18, 26-28, 31-35, 37-39, *NIV*

How quickly God began to take all my yesterdays, both good and bad, and put them together into something that He could use for His good purpose! I was no longer moving on a "petty pace from day to day". My life soon became filled with hope and purpose as I saw the Holy Spirit begin to open doors for me to offer His forgiveness, new life, and hope to my people.

The American Indian Bible Fellowship

Fear not, little flock, for it is your Father's good pleasure to give you the kingdom. Luke 12:32-34 (KJV)[74]

After we had been in Minneapolis for awhile, I began to have migraine headaches. Although the doctors knew I was addicted to alcohol, they put me on Percodan and Valium. Valium and the oxycodone contained in Percodan are both habit forming. Soon I was addicted to those medications, but this time I knew I needed help. I asked Bill to check me into a hospital where I stayed for a whole month. While I was in the hospital, I couldn't just sit in my room, but found ways to volunteer. Helping others took my mind off my own troubles.

While at the hospital, a pastor from Emmaus Lutheran Church in Bloomington visited me. I told him about a letter I wrote to my mother as part of my treatment. He invited me to share it with him. The pastor liked it so well, he asked if it would be okay if he copied my letter and made a sermon out of it. I said that if my letter to Mama would help somebody, I would be happy to share it with others. This is the letter I wrote to Mama:

Dear Mama,

I am writing today to let you know that I still miss you, and I have never been able to resolve my grief about your death. In my heart I never let you rest in peace.

When you died I wanted to die too, because I still *needed* you. I was so young and immature I didn't know how to cope with reality. Without you, life in Cold Lake was tough, because I had no one to talk to.

Mama, I remember when I was five or six years old, we were all so close to you. I remember best of all coming downstairs to crawl into your bed after Papa left for work. There were always five or six of us at a time cuddling up to you. You were so warm and affectionate. You loved us so much we clung on to you like chicks to a mother hen.

How I have missed you all these years, but I didn't want to face the fact that you would never return!

When I was really little I could tell you what I felt, and you comforted me. When I told you the nuns at school beat us up for no reason, you believed me. You were strong enough in your gentle

---

[74] The King James Version of the Bible is public domain.

way to ask Papa to check it out and he took care of the problem, because Nora and I were telling the truth.

Mama, I had something awful happen when I was fifteen years old. A young boy raped me and left me to find my way home in the dark. I was bleeding, too, and if I could have run away then I would have. I was so scared. I was so ashamed, and never told anyone until now. If I could have shared that with you, then I know my life would have been different. The guilt and shame I carried all my life until now had a traumatic effect on my womanhood. Everybody knew each other in Cold Lake. That boy told all the other boys about me. Oh, Mama, I don't know how I survived! I could never have a date with a decent guy, without that other boy bragging about his conquest over me. Again I thought it was because I was so bad. Now as I have grown older, I feel ashamed of things that I wouldn't share with you.

When I first menstruated I thought it was awful, but you watched me silently and lovingly. Then you discovered my stained clothes under the mattress. Oh, how I wanted to die, but you held me close even though I was sixteen years old. You told me that I had become a woman, it was a natural thing, and not to be ashamed. Thank you, Mama, for your kind, gentle, and caring ways.

I knew you depended on me in Cold Lake as the eldest daughter in our home. I'm glad you gave me that responsibility. I was so young to be your helper and to take care of everyone at home including Papa when you got so sick. You suffered so long before you died. I did keep my promise to you to take care of Papa and the rest of the family the best I could after you died, but my life had no meaning without you.

Mama, I started to drink quite a bit, trying to forget my hurts, but drinking only made it worse. I am writing you all this to get rid of my guilt and shame, because I have found a new way of life.

Unable to face reality I became an alcoholic. At last I couldn't help myself, so I decided to do something about it. I want to begin to live and face the truth about myself even if it hurts. I remembered all the good qualities you gave me, and I also believe in God like you did.

I know now that you were filled with the Holy Spirit, because you loved everyone, even me your bad daughter, and you were at peace with yourself.

Mama, I want to grow up now and let you rest in peace. Thanks for listening and helping me bury the past forever. God is giving me the tools to work through past hurts in the AA program. I am meeting new friends and we are all helping each other, because we have all suffered from chemical abuse. We are learning to be honest for the first time. We are taking a good look at ourselves. No matter how terrible we were, we are not alone. There is hope for us as we find forgiveness in Jesus.

I am a patient and also volunteer in a hospital where I have come to know many people. Instead of hiding at a treatment center, I chose to come here. I think God wants me here so I can be an example for others who need help, and not to be ashamed about this disease.

I will not be ashamed from this day on, Mama, because God loves me, my husband loves me, and all our family back home plus the friends along the way love me. Bye-bye for now. I look forward to the day we will all be together in heaven where you are. God bless your memory. Rest in peace.

Your loving daughter,
Bridget

Another difficult thing in my life was my inability to have children. I wrote letters to many of the newborn babies in our family. I wrote the following story to a grand-niece for her mother's baby shower expressing the miracle of love, marriage, and birth:

I Am a Secret
By Bridget Volden

I am tucked away in the coziest spot in the whole world. It's warm and safe here very near to mommy's heart. This is my own secret world before I make my debut into the open world.

How did I come to be?

Well, when my very handsome daddy saw my beautiful mommy's hair, nose, eyes, legs, and mouth, he suddenly had very *weak knees*, his *heart pounded* like mad, and daddy almost *fainted* – men are like that, you know.

Well anyway, in a great rush of passion and emotion Daddy just *fell* real hard on the floor, I believe, and proposed to Mommy so fast that Mommy has not been able to catch her breath yet.

Anyway, when he asked her a simple question like, "Will you marry me, and live with me for a lifetime?" which is only about ten thousand years, Mommy said simply, "Yes!" And do you know they were so much in love that no one could ever come between them, so they thought.

But I, *just a mere secret*, sneaked into their lives, and now I live right with them wherever they go – especially Mommy. It's hard to understand why I can't go to work with Daddy.

Do you know, in the *open world* they have names like Marion, Inky, John, Mark, and Sue? And do you know I'm glad that my mommy's name is Sue, because it's so soft and easy to say, and it rhymes with, "I love you".

Then there are other funny things like ringing of phones all day, and tap-tap-tap on machines, and numbers like, *1-2-3-4-5-6-7-8-9-10*, and words like *Southdale, Brookdale, St. Paul,* and *Rochester*? I hear a lot about a place called *Minneapolis*. I think that is where we all live, 'cause I hear it every day.

Yes, here I am so warm and cozy, so close to Mommy's heart, and how did I really come to be?

It started long ago with the beginning of time when the *open world* was just an idea, and our great God, whose name is *Love* created our great world by saying, "Let there be" and all living things upon it.

God created many beautiful things like flowers, trees, animals, birds and lastly *man* after His very own image. He chose me, *a mere secret* to be part of that image. When God's love intertwined with Daddy's and Mommy's love, I came into being, filled with this special *love*.

I can't stay hidden for too long here, 'cause soon I need to be spreading more love around to make lots of people happy like Mommy, Daddy, Grandma, and Grandma, and Grandpa, and Grandpa, and cousins, aunts, friends, and mostly people you know!

I told you about how I feel for now. I'm so glad God chose me to be part of the human race. God once chose to also be part of our own human race. When he was born, they called him Jesus, and he was full of love like I feel now, because he truly is Love come to earth.

When I make my debut, I will no longer be *a mere secret*, but I will be a baby. I mustn't even tell if I'm a boy or a girl, but you'll just have to wait, 'cause I have to be in this warm cozy place for a whole nine months.

And now I am sooo sleepy. I'm just going to nap for now. "Brrrp – Mommy just ate some pickles and whatever she eats, I have to help her *burp*. So please forgive my manners, and see you all very soon.

My sense of humor never left me. Laughter seemed easier as I was getting stronger in my spiritual life. I even wrote playful little poems. Here is one I wrote for Bill:

Poem for My "Bill"
By Bridget Volden

"Bill" is the name of my husband,
who changed my name to his in the

twinkling of an eye.

Now it was "Bill" who did all that
   proposing and said
   "I will take you to the moon if you like."

But now that I am his,
   Bill never takes me even as far
   As the country store!!

Now "bill" is also the name for the things
   That I charge on my Dayton account.

So Bill, please take this to heart:
   "Bill" will be "billed"
   Till death do us part!!

After the bout with addiction to pain medications, I realized that I needed to cling as closely as I could to Jesus as my hope for recovery and freedom from the demons that haunted my memories. When we returned to Minneapolis in the mid-1960's I helped begin The American Indian Bible Fellowship. I knew that if I was experiencing a new life of freedom, my people could also. In addition to the hope of eternal life in heaven, Jesus would free them from addictions to drugs and alcoholism. As I prayed for my people, I met some of them who shared my love for Jesus. We formed the advisory committee which included Maurice (Al) Wensman, Rose Foss, Cecelia Huntington, Eldon Lawrence and me. A friend helped me make little invitations:

You Are Invited to The American Indian Bible Fellowship

A group of concerned Indian people have organized a Bible fellowship. This group is non-denominational – everyone is welcome! The meetings are informal with a hymn sing and guitar music. There is also a class for children with Bible stories and pictures.

We meet every Sunday afternoon at 2:30 p.m. in the Assembly Room at 24th Street & Chicago Avenue in Our Savior's Church. Then stay for coffee and goodies and meet the crowd. Come for fellowship and make new friends! The teacher is Art Holmes and the pianist is Vivian Wynde.

Our theme: "Fear not, little flock, for it is your Father's good pleasure to give you the kingdom." Luke 12:32.

My friend and I handed out our invitations in the Indian neighborhoods of north Minneapolis by knocking on doors, visiting bars, and greeting people on the sidewalks. If they had a beer in their hand, they would put it down long enough to listen to us and accept our invitation.

The first week over a hundred Indian people showed up. We served them coffee and donuts at that first meeting, but I was determined to raise money to provide them with at least one good meal a week. I saw how starved they were for good news, and how hungry they were for good food as well. Soon we became known as simply as The Fellowship.

Bill and I attended Augustana Lutheran Church in downtown Minneapolis. One day in 1968 I spoke with Pastor William Berg about The Fellowship. Pastor Berg offered to let me use our church kitchen and fellowship hall on a weekly basis. John Bohnsack, a leader from our church, opened up the building for me every Sunday afternoon, and closed the church after our meeting at night. He watched over us as we held The American Indian Bible Fellowship meetings, and was on hand if we needed anything.

When I helped organize The Fellowship, Bill set up a bank account to deposit the money we received. Bill's accounting skill was put to good use taking care of the financial records for us. He deposited the money in the bank right away after my speaking engagements, and every penny that was donated was well accounted for in the financial books.

Whenever the account dipped below five or six hundred dollars, I scheduled more speaking engagements. A friend drove me around to visit women's groups in churches and other women's organizations in the Twin Cities of Minneapolis and St. Paul, telling my story, and inviting women to donate money so I could buy more food for my people.

The women's groups suggested a topic they wanted me to cover. After teaching on their requested topic, I explained how the Lord was saving native people out of drug addiction and out of alcoholism, and how many of them were dedicating their lives to Jesus. Eventually I traveled further into the towns surrounding the Twin Cities in outstate Minnesota.

After my talks I told the ladies, "Do *not* write the checks out to *Bridget Volden*. Checks are to be written to the *American Indian Bible Fellowship*, because that's where all the money goes. We use that to provide meals for our people at The Fellowship."

The ladies were kind and generous, and the money began to come in. They collected the money at the end of each meeting in a brown bag for me to bring home.

I've heard people say you can't out-give the Lord. One week Bill came across a check written to my name for fifty dollars. I looked at it for a minute, and I teased Bill, "Oh, boy! I can go shopping now. That's written to me!"

Bill said, "Oh no, you won't. It goes right into The Fellowship money!"

Of course I wanted all of the money to go to The Fellowship; I had just been joking, but how God multiplies! That very week Bill was paid an extra five hundred dollars. The Bungee grain company where Bill worked had sold so much grain to the Russians that their CEO gave all the employees a bonus.

The Fellowship quickly grew until over two hundred native people were attending the meetings every week. At special holiday meetings up to three hundred people packed the meeting room with about fifty of them standing around the sides and back of the room. After our gatherings grew to an impressive size, there were white preachers who asked if they could speak at The Fellowship meetings, but it seemed that some of them just wanted to add another accomplishment to their resume'. I explained that for too long the white people have been talking down to the Indian people. Furthermore, native people would receive Jesus more easily if the gospel was brought through native pastors and speakers. I told the white ministers that if they wanted to help, they could pitch in with the work in the kitchen where I always needed more workers. Some of them really cared for our people and did come to help.

When the native people saw that The Fellowship truly was a ministry to Indians that was provided by the Indian people, they soon took ownership of the meetings. Each week I would be busy in the kitchen along with any volunteers who showed up. As the crowd gathered, I would step out of the kitchen with the invitation, "Has Jesus done anything for you this week? Who would like to tell us your story?"

Maybe a woman would stand and offer, "I haven't had a drink for two days," or a man would say, "I haven't smoked a cigarette today." They were taking baby steps, and Jesus was helping them. I would begin clapping and telling them how wonderful that was, and soon the crowd would break into applause. After people were given

154

a chance to share their victories for the week, the native pastor or speaker would encourage us from God's word.

I was still working full-time at Dayton's, but somehow God helped me manage my time to continue leading The Fellowship for ten years. I hadn't been trained in Christian ministry or leadership; God merely showed me the practical things to do each week to feed people in spirit, soul, and body. Bill and I were determined not to scrimp and save on the food, but rather to buy quality food for my people and trust God to provide the finances.

Every Friday night Bill and I shopped at Lund's or Byerly's. My Saturdays were spent at the church kitchen cooking hot dishes for the Sunday afternoon meetings. Sunday afternoons I had the food ready to go in the church fellowship hall at four o' clock in the afternoon.

I led the meetings from the kitchen, poking my head out now and then, encouraging people to share, and introducing the worship team or the speaker. Although my name was on the program, I kept a pretty low profile. After the meetings I scrubbed the fellowship hall, the kitchen, and the bathrooms until they were spotless so The Fellowship wouldn't be a burden on our church.

Unless people could match my name with my face, they never knew that I was the one in charge. As far as they were concerned I was an unusually cheerful and talkative kitchen helper, which is the way I wanted it to be. There was always plenty of food. I brought empty cottage cheese cartons to send extra food home with my people. As time went by some of the native people began to contribute food for the weekly meals. Most of them were very poor. They knew it was just me and my husband who brought the food from what we were paid from my speaking engagements. We bought the best of everything, and every Sunday I brought in two huge casseroles made with wild rice. Some of the women began to ask me after the meetings, "Could I bring something next Sunday for The Fellowship meal?"

I knew they didn't have much income so I would say, "Sure, if you would like to bring some salad or some Jell-O that would be good, because a lot of these fellows have no teeth."

So the women began contributing little hot dishes, salads, or whatever they could afford.

Four native pastors in the Twin Cities area were each willing to take one Sunday a month to speak to The Fellowship. They had overcome drugs, alcohol, or both. Pastor Mackety and Pastor Art

155

Holmes were especially effective in ministry. They didn't talk down to us or make us feel dirty or sinful. They could speak to us through the language of the heart from their shared experiences, and through shared culture and native languages. The pastors knew that unless hearts were touched by the love of God, native people wouldn't give their lives to Jesus. Pastors invited those who wanted to give their lives to Jesus to say a simple prayer that went something like this:

> Lord, I know my life has been heading down the wrong road that has led to pain and suffering for me and my family. I confess all of my wrongdoing to you as sin. I am giving you my whole life just as I am, because I trust you as my Savior and Lord. I want you to be my God. You already paid for my sin with Jesus' blood that he shed on the cross. I accept that gift. Now use my life in the way that you have planned for me. Thank you, Lord. From now on I belong to you. Amen.

After people began giving their lives to God, Jesus' blood shed on the cross cleansed their hearts, and the Holy Spirit began to fill them up so they could respond to God in love and obedience. It gave me so much joy to see my people becoming new through Jesus' love, just as I had. Jesus did not take away our Indian-ness; he helped us become confident that we as Indian people can also truly become God's children when we give our lives to him.

It was my responsibility in The Fellowship to raise the funds to feed the people. A lot of the people were down-and-outers, and those were the people we wanted to come, and we did reach them. We passed a little basket around for an offering each week, and I picked out two guys who looked like they were most in need to take the offering. As the basket went around, I noticed how each person had a quarter in his hand. Probably they had been bumming money all week for their drinks, but on Sunday they kept a whole quarter to put into the offering basket. I cried many times when I saw that.

The Lord really blessed our times together. I would invite people, "If someone plays a guitar, you're sure welcome to come up and play for the people. There were seven Indian guitarists who began playing for our hymn singing and praise and worship at The Fellowship. After The Fellowship had been going for awhile, John Bobolink began taking his turn as a preacher. John was a preacher who could play and sing, too.

Some of the people from my church joined me in serving the meals as time went by. Walter Johnson, a college professor who attended our church, would address my people when pouring coffee, "Gentleman?"

All these down-and-outers looked up questioningly as if to ask, "Who, me?"

Walter smiling reassuringly, overlooked their amazement as he offered, "May I pour you a cup of coffee?" They had never been called a gentleman before, especially by a white person. I got tears in my eyes whenever he served my people so lovingly.

An Ojibwa man began helping with cleanup. After he had lunch, he went into the kitchen to wash all my pots and pans and clean up the stove while I was in the front talking to different people. He left as soon as he was done cleaning before I could even get to know his name. Finally one day I ran after him saying, "Thank you for always helping with everything in the kitchen, but I don't even know your name, because you always run out so fast after The Fellowship is over."

He told me his name and said, "I leave so soon, because I have to stand in line for a job for Monday."

I asked, "Isn't it cold to work outside in the wintertime?"

"Yes it's cold," he said, "but what else can I do?" So he left to stand in line to find work.

At that time I was helping in the food service at the hospital bringing in food trays for patients. At the hospital I went to the director of human resources and asked if there might be jobs in maintenance. The director said, "Yes, we have an opening for someone to clean up the operating rooms, washing all the machinery after they perform an operation."

I told the director, "I know a young man who would be the cleanest man you could find."

The next Sunday before that young man ran away again, I said, "How would you like to work inside the hospital?"

He said, "That would be so wonderful!"

I encouraged him, "Tomorrow I go to work about 7:00 a.m., and I'm done about 10:00 in the morning. Meet me in the lobby of the hospital."

He was there to meet me on time. Together we went to see the human relations director. I asked, "Is there still an opening for that person you needed to wash down the machines in the operating rooms?"

The director said the job was still open, so I asked my young friend if he thought he could do that type of work. He said, "Oh yes,

157

I could." So the director hired him on the spot and had the young man fill out all the paperwork. He loved that job and did well, working faithfully until the day he retired.

Pastor Berg had a good friend, Mr. Lund, who owned the Lund grocery stores. They used to talk about things that were going on in the church. Pastor Berg happened to mention The Fellowship to Mr. Lund. He explained how we operated as Native people bringing the gospel to our own people.

Mr. Lund asked, "I wonder if Bridget would let me contribute to The Fellowship?"

The next time Pastor Berg saw me he asked me if it would be okay for Mr. Lund to contribute. At first I refused, because I knew if the Indian people learned that white people were providing money, it would feel like just another handout. I told Mr. Lund that I couldn't accept his money. He kept offering to contribute, though, because he could see how much food I was buying each week, and he knew it was so expensive for me. Finally I allowed him to contribute turkeys or hams for the Thanksgiving, Christmas, or Easter celebrations.

Our Fellowship continued growing by leaps and bounds. As Christmas approached we needed gifts. I called a friend who worked for Tonka Toys, and asked if his company could donate toys for the boys and girls for Christmas. He said he would see what he could do. One Saturday afternoon early in December my friend drove into our driveway with a truckload *full* of Tonka Toys. It was just wonderful! I invited a lot of Indian ladies to come and help me wrap and label the packages, **FOR BOYS** or **FOR GIRLS**. We had been given so many toys that every child who came to the Christmas program could have one or two toys. I called people who sold Avon and things like that, asking if they could contribute gifts for the ladies. I asked a man who owned a men's store if he could afford to write off men's gifts to The Fellowship for taxes. He gave us nice socks and warm gloves. Everyone in The Fellowship who came to the Christmas program had a gift. That's the way God provided for us.

We were planning a Christmas pageant with all native children, to present the story of the Baby Jesus. Pastor Mackety's wife, trained in vocal music, taught the children little songs. Mrs. Mackety translated the Christmas carol, *We Three Kings of Orient Are*, to make the words in our Indian tongue sound like the song was from the heart of the native people:

158

"We three chiefs of the Indian nations:
Athabascan, Algonquin, Iroquoian, Confederacy
Came far for a Baby to see."

Three of the Indian ministers each wore a headdress that was handed down from their ancestors. They paraded in, dressed in native clothing as if they were the three kings of the Orient. The first one sang, "To my Jesus I bring a blanket."

The second one sang "To my Jesus I bring moccasins."

The third one sang, "To my Jesus I bring moose meat."

It was so beautiful! We had standing room only that night. I'll never forget the looks of awe on the faces of the people! The story of Christmas had become their story. It was so wonderful! One of my friends even made Indian fry bread as part of our holiday meal.

In 1978, I turned The Fellowship over to John Bobolink and his lovely wife. My ten years with The Fellowship was a fruitful time of ministry giving back to my people the freedom that I had found in Jesus Christ from shame and condemnation. We were able to leave The Fellowship with around a thousand dollars in their bank account, so they had something to work with after I stepped down as the leader.

I thank every person who came along to help us, whether it was in food ministry, singing, preaching, or donating money when I spoke to women's groups. Special thanks go to Pastor Berg and our Augustana Lutheran Church for allowing us to hold our meetings in their fellowship hall. Each one who helped in whatever way, worked together to make The Fellowship an effective ministry for the Indian people in the Minneapolis area.

John Bohnsack informs me that the meetings continued at Augustana Lutheran Church for awhile and then moved to the Augustana Church Crossroad and Community Emergency Service Center where John Bohnsack worked at 1900 11th Avenue South in late 1978. Meetings continued there until about the midsummer of 2003. At that point the Native American attendance had diminished, because Bible studies became available elsewhere, especially at Anishinabe Wakigan. Some of the Native Americans also began attending a neighborhood worship service at the nearby Marie Sandvik Center where a meal was also included.

John Bohnsack wrote, "Over the years, many of the men and women made their way off the street into faith and into a local church because of the tremendous bridge The Fellowship provided.

The Spirit Filled genius of The Fellowship was that street folks who would never have considered going to a traditional church service came, feeling a welcome and a belonging, heard the Gospel, responded over time, and gave their lives to Christ. Truly, The Fellowship was a BRIDGE between the streets and the congregations where those new in Christ ended up finding a spiritual home. But, not all who came to faith found their way to victory over chemical dependency. That number will never be known, except to the Lord, because we did not see the results outwardly."

In a recent conversation, John Bobolink told me of several people from The Fellowship who completed Bible training. I am thankful for their faithfulness and dedication to bring Jesus' true message of love and forgiveness to native people not only in Minnesota, but in other places as well.

Visitors from the North Country

God sets the lonely in families . . .. Psalm 68:6a, (*NIV*)

Thad as Guide at Great Bear Lake, NWT

About the time I was helping start The Fellowship in the mid-1960's, my oldest brother Thad decided to pay us a visit. Thad was a trapper and hunter in the winters. In the summer he was a fishing guide on Great Bear Lake in the Northwest Territories. Two of Thad's regular customers from Minneapolis were the president of Northwest Airlines and a judge from Excelsior. They liked my brother and brought Thad all kinds of gifts like radios, televisions, and other modern gadgets. The president of Northwest Airlines told Thad, "If you ever want to come to the states, I would be glad to give you a ticket to wherever you want to go."

Thad told the Northwest Airlines president, "Well, I would like to go to Minneapolis where you come from. I have two sisters there."

So the Northwest Airlines CEO said, "Anytime you want to go, just give me a call."

After the summer guiding season ended, Thad went to the airport in Edmonton. He told the clerk behind the desk that he wanted a free ticket to go to Minneapolis, because he knew the head of Northwest Airlines.

The woman stared at him incredulously. Thad was dressed in his native attire so she didn't believe him. Thad said, "Give him a call. He said to call him anytime I wanted to go."

Reluctantly the woman at the reservations desk placed the call, "There's an Indian man here at the desk claiming that he can get a free ticket to Minneapolis anytime. His name is Thad Harris."

"Oh yes," the Northwest Airlines CEO said, "book him in a first class seat." Was she ever surprised! She wrote out the ticket without another word.

So Thad landed in Minneapolis. Rose's husband Ward met Thad's plane and brought Thad out to their home on Lake Minnetonka. Thad liked Minneapolis. Bill and I came out to visit Thad while he was staying with Rose and Ward.

After awhile Thad got bored doing nothing, so he decided to go to work. First he got a job planting trees and landscaping through his friend the judge who knew someone who owned a nursery. Thad loved working outdoors until about October when it started to get cold.

He thought, "Maybe the guy at the airport could give me a job." So he rode with Ward to the Minneapolis St. Paul International Airport to see the big shot at Northwest Airlines. When he was invited into his office Thad said, "Say, I'd like to go to work for you."

The CEO said, "What would you like to do?"

Thad said, "Well, I don't know. I like working with my hands."

The CEO checked their job openings, and then offered, "Well, you could work in the food department. When the planes come, you take out the containers of used trays and food that wasn't eaten, and you load them up with fresh food and supplies for their next flight."

That sounded good to Thad, so the CEO hired him right there. Thad worked for Northwest Airlines for a couple of years. As an airline employee he could go on vacations wherever he wanted as part of his benefits package. He went all over Alaska and everywhere. He took advantage of all the Northwest Airlines employee perks.

Once in awhile Thad would stop by Dayton's where I worked. The girls always surrounded him, because he was handsome and had so many stories to tell about the North. They were fascinated by him. One day when I came back from lunch there was Thad again, but this time he was waiting for me.

162

Thad said, "I've got a very bad cold, and I need some medicine." He wanted some cough medicine, and some Vicks, and stuff to rub on his chest. He gave me an order to pick up some cold remedies, because he was going to go home and go to bed. After work, I picked up the things on Thad's list, and Bill dropped me off at Thad's apartment. I knew Thad was pretty sick with a cold, so I told Bill to go ahead and go home and have supper, and come get me in about an hour. I would take care of Thad and straighten up his apartment. So Bill left me there. I gave Thad his cough medicine and Tylenol. I rubbed his chest and back with Ben Gay, covered him up and let him sleep.

While Thad was resting I decided to clean up his apartment. He was not a dirty housekeeper, but he was awfully messy, and had papers all over. I did a good job of cleaning up his bathroom and his kitchen. Then I picked up everything in the living room, and kept busy until Bill came to take me home. It was Friday night so Thad rested Saturday and Sunday. By Sunday he was feeling much better, so he gave our sister Rose a call.

Thad told Rose, "Oh, that Bridget. She came over to my apartment the other day." He didn't tell about the good things I did, but he said he couldn't find his glasses, he couldn't find this, and he couldn't find that. So Rose called me and we laughed about that.

A couple of days later when I was out for lunch Thad came by Dayton's. I found him sitting in the midst of the girls in my department again telling stories. I said, "What kind of a brother are you anyway? For all the good stuff I did for you, and then you called Rose and told her that I messed up your apartment and everything!" Then Thad laughed and slapped himself on his thigh as if he had pulled a fast one on me.

Thad liked to play the violin, or fiddle as it was called in the old days. Thad found an old violin in a secondhand store in Minneapolis. The only thing wrong with the violin was that it had become unglued. One day when Bill picked me up after my work at Dayton's, we walked over to Thad's apartment. When we knocked on the door, we heard really good fiddle music. While he was still playing, he opened the door and kept on playing. You would have died laughing at that old violin all patched together with Band-Aids, yet Thad made good music come out of it. After awhile Thad decided to head back to the north country.

Some time later Bill and I got a phone call from my sister Nora in Cold Lake, Alberta about another brother. The Edmonton hospital had notified Nora that our brother Jim had been in a plane crash with two other people up in the north and that eighty percent of Jim's body was badly burned. The medical staff didn't think Jim would live. Our sister Rachel couldn't go with Nora to Edmonton, because Rachel had small children to care for. I traveled with Rose from Minneapolis and met my sisters Nora and Charlotte in Cold Lake. The four of us took the train to Edmonton and went to see Jim in the hospital. It was really sad. Jim was bandaged from burns all up and down his body. His face was good, but his arms and everything else were terribly burned.

Jim was under a canopy. Nothing could touch him. We had to wear gowns and masks to come in to see him. Only two could go in at a time, so the other two would stand at the door where we could see him looking at us. It was the first time we had seen Jim since we left him at Fort Good Hope when he was sixteen. He had been so good-looking. It was a heart-wrenching meeting; we were so sad to see him that way.

We encouraged him and he was so happy to see us again after all those years! I said to him, "Jim, if you get better, I'll send you a ticket to come and visit me in Minneapolis," which I did later on.

Jim was in the hospital for quite awhile, but eventually he healed slowly, slowly, slowly. It was quite an ordeal he went through. The surgeons had to take skin grafts from his legs and put on his arms leaving him all scarred. He finally got better and could leave the hospital. His foot never completely healed, it was burned too severely.

When Jim was finally feeling better and could travel, Bill and I sent Jim a ticket to come to Minneapolis on the train. There was a train at that time that went from Edmonton to Winnipeg, and from Winnipeg down to Minneapolis. Jim stayed with Rose for awhile and then he stayed with me. Bill and I lived by a little park in Minneapolis. Jim enjoyed sitting out in the park while we both went to work. He fed the squirrels and visited with people around him. When his visit ended Jim took the train back to Edmonton where he lived with his family for the rest of his life.

When Nora's first child Joyce was going to graduate from high school, she wanted to live with Bill and me so she could graduate in Minneapolis. I was happy to send her a train ticket and sponsor her for her final year of high school. Joyce graduated with flying colors as a straight-A student. She also got a job at Dayton's working in the stockroom, so she could afford to buy her necessities. Nora and Ben came down for Joyce's Commencement celebration and they all traveled back to Cold Lake, Alberta together. What a gift to spend a whole year with Joyce, who seemed so much like a daughter to me!

It had been so wonderful to be able to reconnect with my brothers and my niece Joyce. How I had missed my family! But I was beginning to allow Jesus to fill those lonely places in my heart. As the years passed I learned to love Jesus more and more as my dearest Brother.

In busy downtown Minneapolis in 1974, I discovered a quiet place for meditation in a small chapel on the eighth floor of a huge bank building. I usually allowed an hour to pray on my way to work each day. I savored my time alone in that little chapel, my special quiet place for just God and me. That summer, when I was away on a long vacation, others discovered the chapel. The atmosphere became alive, filled with such richness of God's blessings as we read the Word of God together and grew spiritually stronger day by day.

We even had a cheerful chaplain to share our needs who was filled with the warmth of God's love. Pastor Hanson was on duty in the chapel from eight in the morning until five in the afternoon. You could tell that Pastor Hanson had known the Lord for a long time, because he was full of the light of Jesus.

At eight o' clock, either Pastor Hanson or I started the coffee brewing, whichever of us arrived first. With our coffee the two of us prayed in that upper room. About eight-thirty, we heard footsteps that soon became familiar as Jerry brought a fresh yellow rose to the chapel every morning in memory of his dear mother. After prayer we enjoyed wonderful fellowship together in Pastor Hanson's office before heading off to work.

I wrote the following poem while I was meditating in the little chapel the morning of September 20, 1974 on my way to work in downtown Minneapolis:

Autumn Theme
By Bridget Volden

Who said, "There is no God?"
What a sad state of affairs
If we all thought that way.
Waking to a new dawn,
Just being alive is a miracle.
We drive out in the countryside
Taking in the breathless beauty of autumn.

In the warmth of the sun –
Yellow, bright, and shiny new –
We see the smile of God
Melting the icy sky blue.

In the white clouds up in the sky
God sculpts fantastic figures and forms
The face of mother, so gentle and kind,
Smiling from God's beautiful heaven.

God's puffs of white etch Papa's face
Strict, God-fearing, upright.
Then God blows the two clouds into one.

Now I know for sure
When God took Dad away
Two years after Mother
They met in that beautiful
Blue yonder called heaven.

My gaze returns to mother earth
To the sudden burst of autumn colors.
We wind our way among trees of many species.

The golden hues, orange shades,
Bright reds and dusty pinks, next to
Green trees still clinging --not letting go
Of the last breath of summer.

In good time, God still master
Paints them, too,
As He changes us, when we hang on
To things a little longer.

Autumn speaks, "Humans created in God's image
Are many colors blended in harmony."
Like richly colored leaves let go and flutter to earth,
Let us release things in His time.

Reflected upon the cool and placid lakes
Are hues of trees in autumn gowns –
The reds and yellows, greens and blues,
And sometimes earthy brown.

Yes, I'm glad there is a God who gave me
This soft shade of earthy clay.
For although Dad was white, you see,
My native mother was autumn beige.

While I was leading The Fellowship in Minneapolis, my heart ached for my own brothers and sisters and their families. I often prayed for them and longed to have peace in my heart that we would all be together in heaven someday with Mama and Papa. One day when I was living in Minneapolis I got a call from Cold Lake, Alberta. I heard a lot of giggling going on. Two women were squeezed into a phone booth together, trying to share the telephone receiver – my sisters Charlotte and Nora.

Charlotte said to me, "Bridget, your prayers have been answered! Dominick and I quit drinking! We came home from the bar with a great big jug of wine as usual. We were feeling so bad; we had become such drunks! We had nothing in the house to eat, but it never used to be like that. All my cups in the house had no handles on them anymore. My plates were all cracked. Everything I had was broken."

Charlotte continued, "We didn't know how to pray in our own words, so we just knelt down and said the Lord's Prayer together. Then Dominick took that big jug of wine and smashed it against a tree. It looked like fire came out of the bottle!"

They could actually *see* the fire! That was the last time they drank; they didn't *want* to drink anymore.

When they got up in the morning, they were like new people. They took out their fishing nets that had gotten all moldy in the basement. Charlotte said, "We started mending and cleaning our nets. We put the nets in the lake that same evening."

There are such good fish in Cold Lake. The next morning when they got up, that net was so full they could hardly pull it in. It was like Jesus telling the disciples to let their nets down on the other side of the boat. When Charlotte and Dominick tried Jesus' way of life, their nets were bursting with fish. They pulled up the fish and kept what they could. They took the rest of their catch to the fish plant in Cold Lake, and got a lot of money for it. They started buying food, new cups, new dishes, and threw away the broken dishes. Pretty soon everything in the house was becoming like new again. Oh, I was so happy for her!

About the time that Charlotte and Dominick quit drinking, Leon (Bud) Elford and his wife Marjorie (Marge) came to work as missionaries close to our people. Bud was born in Ontario in 1924. Having placed a personal faith in Jesus Christ at the age of 16, Bud committed his life to God for missionary service. When Bud was

Bud and Marge Elford with Bridget

seventeen, he enlisted to serve in the military in WWII. After the war Bud worked for a year in Canada and married Marjorie. Bud and Marge went to England where Bud earned his Bachelor of Theology degree in Missions from the London Bible Institute and Theological Seminary. His linguistic training included three summers with the Summer Institute of Linguistics and a summer workshop at the University of Oklahoma.

They applied to be sent by New Tribes Missions to Papua, New Guinea, but no one was going to Papua, New Guinea at that time. Instead of sitting around and waiting for a door to open, they decided to go north to work among the Indian people in Canada.

In 1952 when Bud was 28 years old, he and his wife Marjorie joined the Northern Canada Evangelical Mission (NCEM) and served fifteen years as field missionaries. In Churchill, Manitoba Bud was introduced to Chipewyan where he translated a few hymns with the help of Tommy Fortin. Tommy was a French and Chipewyan boy. When the Elfords moved to Brochet, Manitoba, Bud became comfortable speaking Chipewyan. In Brochet an Indian man living behind Bud could speak English, but never let on to Bud, forcing Bud to learn Chipewyan until Bud could speak it fluently.

After working in Brochet, Bud and Marge went back to Churchill for a year, and then up to Fort McPherson, further north on the Mackenzie than Fort Good Hope. Before arriving in Cold Lake, Bud had spent twenty years doing work in the Chipewyan language. By that time he had put together a grammar book and written several hymns and some tracts in the Chipewyan language.

When the Elford's moved to Cold Lake, they translated the Gospel of Mark from English into Chipewyan. Bud hired my sister Charlotte and her daughter Sara to help him develop new words in Chipewyan that were in the Bible, but not in our language. While in Cold Lake, Bud and Marge were also working on the *Chipewyan Dictionar*. The dictionary was designed for use in schools to preserve the language, and by missionaries to reach the hearts of the people. Bud and Marge completed the dictionary, and their son Kit printed it for them in NCEM's Northern Canada Mission Press publishing house. When Bud completed the translation of the Gospel of Mark, he began the translation of the Book of Acts.

In one of Bud's tracts called *My Little Lost Canoe*, he told of a little old Indian man who made a birch bark canoe, and fixed it fine. He loved that little canoe and had it on the shore. One day a storm came up and the canoe drifted away. He searched and searched until he found his canoe, but someone else had it. He loved that canoe so much, that he bought it back from the person who had it. He told his canoe, "Little canoe, you're mine twice." The story is compared to what God has done for us. He made us, but let us go free. When we followed our own sinful ways and drifted away from God, he bought us back. God's son Jesus made full payment for our sins with his own precious blood when he was sacrificed for us on the cross.

Bud Elford did his best to reach my people, but not too many responded at first. My people had become Catholics, but Bud and Marge were Protestants. My people were afraid to step away from Catholicism. The way Bud and Marge endeared themselves to the people was showing they cared about them by learning their ways and by learning their language as my Papa had done.

I heard there was a minister interested in our people who had learned our language with my sister Charlotte's and her daughter Sara's help. I was anxious to meet him, but for some reason or other when I went to Cold Lake our paths didn't cross.

One day Bud went to Charlotte's house to ask about the correct pronunciation of a certain word. After Charlotte helped him she asked, "Bud, you're always going somewhere. Where are you going this time?"

Bud said that he was going to Minneapolis, Minnesota to visit his son, Kit, who was attending Bethany Fellowship's Bible school. Charlotte said, "Well, you might as well look up my sister Bridget. She's always preaching just like you. Ever since she quit drinking, she's preaching to us." Charlotte gave him my phone number, and Bud began looking forward to meeting me.

On a beautiful Saturday morning I was busy in my kitchen when the phone rang. In my language a man's voice said, "Hello, my sister. How are you?"

Thinking it was one of my brothers I said, "Which one are you?"

He said, "I'm Bud Elford!"

He sent some students from Bethany Fellowship to pick me up, because he wanted me to make a cassette for his radio program. I was so excited to finally meet him!

Bud recorded my testimony about God saving me from my addiction to alcohol in my language and also in English. Bud used that little tape on his radio show and on their missionary travels throughout the north. For about eight years Bud preached in Chipewyan, and the hymns translated into Chipewyan were sung on his radio program *The Chipewyan Gospel Broadcast* that lasted fifteen minutes every Sunday morning. People loved hearing a service in their own language so much that the priests in the Catholic churches would stop mass early for their people to make it home in time to hear the broadcast.

A few years later, Bud phoned to ask me if I would give my testimony on television. Their program *Tribal Trails*, produced in Prince Albert, Saskatchewan, is broadcast every Sunday morning via satellite all across Canada. It is also broadcast on community cable and local television stations. The program features a native host and native guests who have given their lives to Jesus, some who are also good singers. Bud's greatest effect in sharing the gospel was through radio and television ministries. Kit's greatest effect has been in the printing and publishing ministry producing books, tracts, and CD duplication. Kit ran NCEM's Northern Canada Mission Press printing and publishing division for thirty years.

Since 1967, Bud was involved in mission administration. During these years he completed the Chipewyan alphabet, did the phonology, translated and published a song book in Chipewyan, the Book of Mark, *The Chipewyan Dictionary*, as well as other publications. He wrote several poems and pamphlets. His articles appeared in *Advance, Good News Broadcaster, Message of the Cross, Northern Lights,* and *Christian Life* magazines. The *Chipewyan Gospel Broadcast* was founded and directed by him. Bud was the main voice on the radio program from 1967 to 1977. A number of Native language literacy seminars were conducted by Bud in the Northwest Territories for the Canadian government.

Bud served as Assistant Western Field Director for NCEM from 1967-68, Assistant General Director from 1968-78, Western Field Director from 1978-80, and General Director from 1980-89. He lectured at the Key-Way-Tin Bible Institute, Northern Missionary Training Camp, Candidate Orientation Program and Evaluation, and at mission and Bible conferences.

Bud became so assimilated into the Chipewyan culture, that when native Chipewyan[75] people go to minister in the villages, they are given access to the community if they give Bud Elford's name.

Bud and Marge Elford's translation work is still being carried on in Prince Albert. Right now the Book of Genesis is being translated from English into Dene by Tim Gradin, Bobby Maberly, and Gilbert Bekkatla. When Gilbert goes to the North now to work among his own people, he says, "I'm a good friend of Bud Elford." As soon as people hear Bud's name, Gilbert's own people accept his work as trustworthy.

Bud and Marge's two sons, Roan and Kit, with their spouses all serve with NCEM. Their daughter Terry and spouse serve on the staff of Briercrest College.

Roan Elford, Bud and Marge's other son, was the business manager of Key-Way-Tin Bible Institute in Lac La Biche, another arm of NCEM. He worked with many different tribes, but mostly Dene. Now Roan is the chief financial officer of NCEM. There are several arms in the mission of NCEM: NCEM aviation, Northern Canada Mission Press, Northern Canada Mission Distributers, Key-Way-Tin Bible Institute, Timber Bay Bible Center, and several Bible camps.

Roan is fluent in Dene as well, and has taught Dene in the Northern Teacher Education Program (NORTEP). NORTEP developed methods for Dene teachers to teach their students the Dene language. The only written material in the Dene language for

---

[75] The name of the Chipewyan tribe and language has been changed to Dene, which means "the people".

teachers to use in the schools was the Gospel of Mark, the Book of Acts, tracts, hymns and Christian books that had come through the NCEM print shop. No one else had been publishing written material in the Dene language.

Kit now lives in Billings, Montana, heading up the United States headquarters for NCEM. When Kit calls me up, he always says, "How's my sister?" in my language.

It is sad to say that in September of 2008 Bud Elford became quite ill, and passed away just a few days short of his 84th birthday. Bud Elford was so loving and faithful to our people working among them right up until he died. He left a legacy of good work and good memories. He traveled and preached, teaching the gospel all over the north. Some of his Dene friends were at his funeral. I really thank Jesus for having Bud and Marge Elford and their family in my life.

Bud recorded a prophecy he called The Chieftain's Song that is similar to some other prophetic words God has spoken to Indian tribes. I have kept a copy of this prophecy for many years, because it has been so full of meaning for me.

The Chieftain's Song[76]
By Leon W. Elford

On an ancient night, in the fire-light
An old Chief sang this score,
"From the rising sun will a new race come
To bring LIGHT to our shore;

"With the Book of God, they'll show His love,[77]
So prepare the tribes to wait . . .,"
But the ones who came had a lust for gain,
And exalted crime and hate.

A few who came knew the Savior's name,
Had a Book of Heaven too.
But the Good News song was hurt by wrong
And failed to make it through.

---

[76] Used by permission from Kit Elford, The Northern Canada Evangelical Mission, Inc., Box 3030, Prince Albert, Saskatchewan.

[77] This prophecy has been found in several different tribes and in various forms over the past 200 years. It is recorded by McLean of the Blackfeet, Blood and Flathead tribes.

So the old Chief died and the council tried
To find a reason why
That the prophecy of the elderly
Seemed lost and doomed to die.

Then the small ones grew and their mothers knew
The spirits ruled the day.
So they tied their wrists as the demons wished[78]
Since there was no other way.

And the hunter brave as a spirit slave
Burnt bones in the sweetgrass smell.
He found his meat, when he took his seat
In the sweatlodge in the dell.

Then the soap-stone pipe came to lose its light
For the calumet[79] had failed.
For it brought no rest to the troubled breast
Or balm to the heart that wailed.

"We cannot see, and it's growing dark,"
Is the cry ten thousand strong,
"We've walked in fright in this starless night,
And we're tired of doing wrong."

The race that came seemed to bring more pain
And was dark in heart and plan.
They brought no love from the God above
And neglected the forest man.

So the seer's tale seemed bound to fail
And the council fire is cold.
The hopes are still and a passive will
Says, "The prophecy is old."

Was the ancient song misread or wrong?
Is there no great Book of God?
Did the Lamb not come for the native son?
Is their only hope the sod?

---

[78] A practice of some northern tribes to protect new born infants from spirit powers, usually a thong of caribou hide is used.
[79] A peace pipe.

NO! The Chief was right and his message Bright
Was sent from heaven and true.
But the task still waits and it's growing late,
And it hangs like an unpaid due.

Now if hope was meant for the discontent
And LIGHT sent on its way
Will He say, "Well done" to the faithless ones
At the dawn of the Judgement Day?

Though the time was long and the demon throng
Had caught and held them fast,
For each tribe that comes from the Bering Sun
Has redemption sprung at last.

Through the Son's own blood is the way to God
And the door is open wide.
Let the sinning cease and hearts find peace
All washed in the crimson tide.

Time is nearly full and the grave sleds pull[80]
But the Book of Light is here.
Old age and youth hear the Way of Truth
And the Harvest time is near.

Now the native church bursts forth in birth.
Its ranks are growing fast,
And the Chieftain's song that was stayed by wrong
Is to be fulfilled at last.

Let the forests sing and the drumbeats ring.
Telegraph the news abroad.
Let the clans emerge with a joyous surge,
And return the tribes to God.

I was grief stricken when my dear sister Charlotte died from a
stroke in 1981. Years later Charlotte's daughter Sara died of cancer.
After Charlotte's daughter Sara died, I poured out my heart in a

---

[80] A practice of the Carrier tribe. With the coffin on a sled, three clans pull toward the grave
while the clan of the deceased pulls back. The grave pullers always win.

letter to her. It helped ease the pain that weighed so heavy on my heart:

This is your aunt Bridget gathering together a few remembrances of you. First of all, you were born into a very special family. Your mother was our beloved sister Charlotte, and your dad was Alec Ennow, a wonderful dad who died much too young.

You had two famous grandpas. On your dad's side, you had J. B. Ennow, and on your mom's side you had my dad Flynn Harris. J. B. was a good hunter, trapper, and mechanic. He was self-taught as a mechanic and could fix any piece of machinery or car. When Flynn Harris was a Mountie, J. B. Ennow was his scout. Many fond stories have been told about them. Flynn loved J. B. very much and nicknamed him *ni wool tchoo*. Your grandpa Flynn Harris became a legend in the Northwest Territories of Canada. He was Indian Agent of several tribes, and spoke many languages including many Indian languages. Flynn was very well beloved. You were the apple of his eye. You were the only one who inherited Papa's crooked eye, and that made you special.

You had many talents. One was music. You could play any tune on the organ at church. One day you burst into a dance tune, "In The Mood," just as the priest walked in. You sure got a scolding.

Your grandma Philizine Ennow was a wonderful lady. She adopted all of you kids in her heart and raised you after your mom remarried. So you see, you were surrounded by a lot of love. Philizine had such a good sense of humor and loved to laugh. I can still hear her when I think of her. One day when I was visiting you at Le Goff, your mom ran out of ingredients for making bannock (Indian biscuits). After finishing a pair of moccasins, she sent us to Josvanger's store at Beaver Crossing. Philizine drove her horse and buggy, and of course, you and I had to tag along. As she started to buy some lard and flour, we knew that dollar was going fast. We were afraid there wouldn't be enough for candy. Every time I saw you in later years, we had a good chuckle about that incident. I always greeted you with *ttles lan.* [81]

Your aunt Rose told this story about you. While in school at Onion Lake, you often told old Father Teston it was your birthday when you went to confession. He would then invite you and your gang up to his room for a little treat. The gang was Adeline, Mary Nest, Rose and you. After spanking your hand for your age, he would give you a piece of good candy from Belgium.

---

[81] There's enough lard. We were saying there was enough lard at home.

175

Another talent you had was language acquisition. God used that in a mighty way. You and your family helped Bud and Marge Elford, Missionaries to the Chipewyan, to translate the Bible and many hymns. The Elfords loved you very much and were with you in your last days. They helped you to give your life to Jesus just before you died, so now we know you will be with Jesus forever in heaven.

Life in Montana

In my Father's house are many rooms; if it were not so, I would have told you. I am going there to prepare a place for you. And if I go and prepare a place for you, I will come back and take you to be with me that you also may be where I am. You know the way to the place where I am going. John 14: 2-4 (*NIV*).

Bridget and Bill the day he retired

Every year Bill and I spent our vacations traveling. We went all over: Colorado, San Francisco, Los Angeles, The Grand Canyon, and many other places of interest. We were on the road for a couple of weeks each year. In 1967 we made our first trip together to Cold Lake, Alberta to see my family. We often drove through Montana on our way to visit my sister Rose and her husband Ward. In 1975 when Ward retired from Northwest Airlines they had moved from Minnesota to the tiny town of Waterloo, Montana near Dillon. Every time we were in Montana visiting Rose and Ward, we said we would also retire in Montana.

By 1993 Bill had developed heart disease, drugs and crime were increasing in Minneapolis, and we didn't want to remain there any longer. Bill was sixty-four years old; I had already retired from Dayton's back in the 1980's, so it seemed like a good time for Bill also to retire. Bill asked me, "Where would you like to move?"

Having become used to living in big cities my response was, "I'd like to go to Seattle." Bill compared many factors including taxes. When he discovered that Montana had no sales tax, he asked, "How about Montana?"

I said, "Sure, let's go." I packed our bags, and we left the next day to check out Montana. We drove to Great Falls, Montana where we rented a room in a motel to look the town over. We liked the town, so we looked for an apartment. The lady who helped us said, "Well, better than an apartment, there's a place where you can buy a mobile home and move it to Highwoods Mobile Home Park where I live."

God intervened. She brought us to see the place, and there was only one lot open in that beautiful park. We rented the lot, and then drove to Missoula to buy a mobile home. There we found a nice affordable double-wide mobile home. We ordered it, and told the dealers we were coming back to Montana in a month.

We drove back to Minnesota and made preparations to move to Montana. We packed all of our things and had them shipped to our new home. When we left Minnesota, we went west to Great Falls, Montana in Big Sky Country where we lived for eight years. Our mobile home was a double-wide with two bedrooms, two bathrooms, a dining room, a kitchen, and an office. It was just right for two people.

After we got settled into our home in Great Falls our top priority was finding a good church. We tried this church, that church, the other church. One day we went to a Bible church that we liked. When we were leaving, a lovely little dark-haired lady followed us out asking, "Are you visiting us from somewhere?"

We said, "Yes, we just moved here from Minneapolis, and we're looking for a church. We went to two or three others, and we thought we'd come here today."

"Welcome to Montana," she said. "What are you folks doing for lunch?"

"We were going to a restaurant," we said.

"Why don't you come home with us?" she invited. "I've fried up a whole bunch of chicken, and I've got all kinds of food. My family was supposed to join us, but they can't make it. So come home with us."

I asked, "Where do you live?"

She said, "In Highwoods Mobile Home Park."

I said, "So do we!" That's how we met Pastor Joe's parents. Pastor Joe was starting the new Bible church in Ulm, a suburb of Great Falls about ten miles from our mobile park. That Sunday we became friends, and began attending the church in Ulm to encourage that family. Pastor Joe's mom and dad have died now, but Pastor Joe and his wife Colleen became our very dearest friends in Montana. We remained friends even after we moved from Great Falls to Helena.

Not long after moving to Great Falls, I came home from my annual checkup with serious news. My mammogram showed the beginnings of breast cancer, just a little dot. Bill was so concerned, but I never got depressed about it. I kept telling Bill, "It's going to be all right; it will heal with God's help. "

My doctor recommended removing the breast. After surgery I told Bill and the doctor, "If I don't need any chemo, I don't want it; God will heal the rest of it."

Then a few years later the cancer showed up in the other breast. If I had known the cancer would come back, I would have told my doctor the first time, "Take them both off!" But I had been voluptuous, and didn't want to have them both removed at once. After the second one was removed, my doctor put me on tamoxifen to help prevent further recurrence of cancer in my body.

Bill's loving, quiet, gentle ways, and his good Norwegian humor helped me heal. By this time Bill knew the expression my papa used when he saw a homely woman, "Ah, there's a face that would stop a clock."

To cheer me up when my face was all crunchy from being cranky or stressed, Bill would look at me and say, "Oh my God, Bridget! Your face could stop ten clocks!" Then we would laugh, and it would break the tension.

We moved to Helena, because we liked the mountains surrounding the city. The sale of our home in Great Falls paid for a new home in Helena. We searched for a mobile home park in Helena, and once again found the last available lot in the best park in town. When we first moved to Helena, Bill wanted to visit the

Lutheran church. We visited a couple of Lutheran churches, but we didn't feel like we fit in the Lutheran churches anymore. Then we found Hannaford Bible Church, a sister church to Pastor Joe's church in Ulm. We felt right at home there.

Bill had been having heart trouble for a long time, but it kept getting worse. One day when Bill saw our doctor who was a dear friend, the doctor said, "Bill, your heart is getting to be so bad now, I don't think you should drive anymore." We all cried including the doctor.

Bill couldn't believe it, and asked, "No more ever again?"

The doctor explained, "I mean never again."

When we came home it was quite an ordeal for Bill to give up his car. All of his things were leaving him, his life and everything. I kept him at home, but he started getting really weak. His legs got so weak he needed a walker, but he kept falling out of bed. When he'd get up to go to the bathroom, he'd fall. Finally I couldn't pick him up anymore. I wanted to keep him at home, but I couldn't do it.

We tried to make the most of our time together. One Sunday in 2003 Mary Lou Potts from the Hannaford Church paid us a visit. My sister Rose from Dillon, Montana, was there to help celebrate Bill's birthday. I remember that Mary Lou happened to have her camera with her, so we asked her to take a picture of the three of us.

Shortly after that, Bill decided to put our business papers in order. Bill called Hannaford Church to ask for advice in locating someone who would be able to serve as power of attorney for me after Bill was gone so I wouldn't have to worry about financial matters. The church recommended Mary Lou Potts, so Mary Lou made another visit to our house. Bill worked with Mary Lou on the legal and financial papers. Bill was so worried about me, because figures and details had always been difficult for me. Mary Lou told Bill not to worry about that, she would take care of me after Bill was gone.

Then Mary Lou began visiting us more often to help out in whatever practical ways she could. When I felt like I needed to get away for a few days to visit friends in Great Falls, Mary Lou offered to take care of Bill.

The day I checked him into a nursing home was terrible. I looked over all the homes, and settled on one that looked like a good home. I didn't realize it, but most of the patients had Alzheimer's. They treated Bill as if he also had the disease, but his mind was as clear as mine. At that home no one talked to him. I was there every day to make sure they treated him right. So many things happened. Sometimes his oxygen would be out of his nose. Sometimes he was left sitting in his little chair and no one had put him back to bed.

I tried to come at the same time every day. One day I came and breakfast was over, all the tables had been cleaned, the lights were turned off, and there was Bill sitting at a table by himself in the dark. I was so angry.

"Bill," I asked, "why are you sitting here by yourself?"

"Well, I couldn't finish my prune juice." Oh, did you ever see an angry Indian or an angry Irishman? I just stomped in to the office! I told them how angry I was that he was left alone sitting there all by himself!

Then one night I got the call at three o' clock in the morning, "Bill fell down in the bathroom, and he can't get up. We believe he broke his hip, so we called the ambulance."

I called my girlfriend, who brought me to the hospital to wait for the ambulance. It took so long before the ambulance got there. When he was checked over, sure enough his hip was broken. The bone specialist who belonged to our church examined Bill. At first he thought that he could set Bill's hip, but Bill was too ill. Bill lasted only two days, and then he was gone.

In the meantime I called my sister Nora and her daughter Joyce and told them Bill was dying. They made the long trip from Cold Lake, Alberta, to Helena. They had to stay overnight somewhere, and they had a little trouble at the border crossing, but they kept calling me to see if Bill was still breathing. I would reassure them that he was, but I didn't know if Bill would be alive when they got there. I kept praying with Bill and our two pastor friends.

May 14, 2004 was the last day of Bill's life. Bill had lost consciousness, but I kept telling him, "Bill hang on. Nora and Joyce are coming to see you. Hang on a little longer." You could see his eyes quiver like he heard me, and he hung on. They finally arrived and said, "Bill, we're here," and half an hour later Bill died.

Mary Lou Potts described those days,

> When Bill died, Bridget had Pastor Joe from the Bible church in Ulm officiate at the funeral. Bridget was a pretty lost girl when Bill died, but the thing that really sustained her was her faith in God. Bridget let me know when she was grieving, and then Bridget and I cried together. Bridget did a lot of crying when nobody was around, but she was very solid in her faith. There was never a time that Bridget didn't get up, dress up, put on her wig, look nice and

presentable, and get around. She might cry at the drop of a hat, but she was still a testimony of God's love. No matter how much she hurt, Bridget went on blessing people around her and staying active. When Bridget dies, Pastor Joe will be in charge of Bridget's funeral as well.

After Bill died, I was afraid to be alone at night. Oh, God, help me it was terrible! I had to call all my friends and say, "Pray for me. I'm so afraid of every little noise I hear at night."

I couldn't live in our home by myself. I went to Vancouver, to Edmonton, to Cold Lake, stayed a week, came back, and cried some more. One morning after running away on all those travels I said, "Dear God, what am I to do?"

It seemed like God said, "You have a beautiful home here. Try to enjoy your lovely home. Settle down and just stay here for awhile."

I surprised myself by staying in the house two years after Bill died. I did not like being alone, but little by little I found ways to cope. I kept my TV on all night just to have other voices in the room. The expenses in my home were only two hundred dollars a month, but I was so lonely. I moved into Hunter's Point, a large retirement complex with lots of people. While I was at Hunter's Point, my friend Tom Furlong, who was in Real Estate, sold my mobile home for me. I was happy to get my money back out of the home.

Hunter's Point was beautiful, but it was more expensive than I could afford. Near Hunter's Point I found a lovely apartment at East Park Villa for about double what my expenses in my house had been. I try not to be sad and filled with tears, but that feeling of losing your partner of a lifetime stays with you forever. I try not to think all the time about being alone, and that helps me be more cheerful. Staying active in church, volunteer activities and AA helped my life remain filled with purpose.

Back in Minneapolis, when I was active in The Fellowship, I didn't have as much time to attend all the AA meetings, but after Bill retired and we moved to Montana, I became more active in AA again. In Helena I attend a group that meets every day at noon. Sometimes people I haven't met, call me on the phone wanting to get free of alcoholism or drug addiction. Just as Carol did for me, I always go and talk to people. I tell them my story about how Jesus freed me from alcohol, and I encourage them to join AA. Many of them have given their lives to Jesus.

After I gave my life to Jesus the use of bad language made me feel like I had been violated. I told other AA members, "I came here to *forget* how to swear, not to learn how. When I drank I probably used bad language, too, but when God cleaned me up, he cleaned me all the way including my mouth. So I would rather that these words were not used in the program."

One of the lawyers said, "What? Are we going to have new rules around here now? How many more rules are we going to have in AA?"

I said, "Yes. This is another rule, and it's going to be kept, too." Oh, he was so angry at first, but he honored my request. Once in awhile he let a bad word slip, but rarely when I was present.

After I spoke up, the AA members began to clean up their language. Many of them are well-educated people. They all say, "Oh, Grandma Bridget is here. We can't use those words."

"That's good," I would say, "but don't do it for me. Do it for yourselves."

Sometimes Discouraged, Never Defeated

The Lord is close to the brokenhearted
   and saves those who are crushed in spirit.
A righteous man may have many troubles,
   but the Lord delivers him from them all;
he protects all his bones,
   not one of them will be broken. Psalm 34:18-20 (*NIV*)

This is the chapter of my life I have not wanted to write, but is the most important for me to share. When I have gone through times of sickness or sorrows, I have had difficulty fighting alcoholism. After I first joined AA I was fine. Things were wonderful in my life for a long time. When I joined The Fellowship things got even better. I still went to AA when I could, and I even went to a Christ-centered group called Alcoholics Victorious that met in Minneapolis.

When I was first learning to fight temptations to drink, I heard a voice in my head, "No one will know if I go buy a bottle and drink it all."

But then I heard the voice of God say, "I will know and so will Bill." When the Holy Spirit encouraged me in that way, I would forget about drinking. People told me to call on the name of Jesus when I was tempted, but in those times I never remembered to do that. I suppose that would have helped me, also, but I did the best I could to just cope with each day.

We can never get complacent in our thinking. It is in our thoughts where the battles with Satan begin. If we let our guard down, that is when we get attacked and are apt to fall. Becoming a Christian does not put an end to difficulties in this life. Giving our life to Jesus is only the beginning. Jesus is not like a pill we take, and then we no longer sin. We need to continue to resist the devil in order for the devil to flee from us, and then we need to draw near to God to be strengthened again during our times of weakness.[82]

As we study the Bible we can learn to recognize Satan's schemes. If we know how he tempts us, and when he is most likely to attack us, we will be prepared to resist him. Satan has no authority over a Christian. After someone has given their life to Jesus, they belong to Jesus alone. Christians do not need to obey Satan.

---

[82] Paraphrase of James 4:7.

Satan never plays fair. He waits until we are tired, discouraged, sick, afraid, or until something terrible is happening in our lives. Then when we are down and weak, he will attack most often with thoughts in our minds. Sometimes we can feel the attack physically with a gripping fear, or an overwhelming feeling that comes over us. Sometimes the attack is through another person who yells at us, accuses us falsely, steals from us, or physically beats us. Sometimes Satan attacks us with sickness or a traumatic event.

There are times when bad things happen that we have the strength to hold ourselves together. When I found out that I had cancer, I refused that cancer. I didn't want it in my body. God gave me courage and faith to believe that he would heal me. I trusted my Father in heaven to take the cancer away, and He did. The cancer has never returned. I didn't want the cancer to kill me. Attitude can make a great difference in anything we struggle against. By the time I got cancer I had already fought against Satan in my thoughts against alcoholism in the same way for a long, long time, whenever Satan wanted me to just give up.

However, after we retired and came out west, I could see Bill was not so strong anymore. Bill had a weak valve in his heart and was on a lot of pills. When Bill's heart condition just kept getting worse and worse, I was petrified of being alone again. In those times it would cross my mind to have a drink, but then I realized that a drink would not bring Bill back to health. In that way I argued against the thoughts Satan put in my head.

But eventually these thoughts would overcome me. It was when I couldn't face reality that Satan filled my thoughts with how discouraged I was, how my whole life would fall apart if Bill died, how our dreams for travel in our retirement years were lost, how I would be so lonely if Bill should die, and how afraid I was of being alone. These thoughts plagued me.

Twice in Great Falls I crumbled in the face of discouragement. I allowed myself to meditate on those dark thoughts, rather than grabbing my Bible to find the encouragement and strength I needed in God's word. The first time I bought a pint and drank all of it in one night. First Satan overwhelmed me with despair, he tempted me until I gave in and drank, and then right away Satan accused me with shame and failure. I felt worse after I drank the pint than before. I felt so guilty for having those secret sins in my life. I felt like I had let Bill down, I let my friends in AA down, I let my friends in the church down, and worst of all I let myself down.

After the first slip in Great Falls I told myself that would be it, and no one would need to know. I tried to keep my drinking hidden. Those were the secrets I kept inside. I didn't even talk to my friends at AA. But when I gave in and drank a second time, I knew I needed help and called Pastor Joe. He came to talk to me and pray with me. Then I felt like I wasn't facing the battle alone anymore.

Bill and I moved to Helena, because we thought the city was so pretty. It is surrounded by mountains. It was also closer to the hospital where Bill could get medical help for his heart condition. After we moved to Helena, Bill kept getting worse and worse, and I just kept getting more and more discouraged. When Bill died, I didn't know how I could go on without him. I did not want to live after Bill died. I wanted to just go to sleep and sleep forever. I hated being alone, and I missed Bill so badly. Feelings of loneliness would overwhelm me. I began to travel quite a bit to try to take my mind off my situation, but I still felt so terribly alone. Then when I returned home, I could hardly stand to be in our house all by myself.

My AA group has always been so supportive, and I have had a wonderful church in Helena as well as Great Falls, but I found it difficult to share the struggles I was having with my urges to drink again. There have been just a few times when I couldn't face reality, and have bought a pint to drink by myself. Again I tried to keep it hidden. I thought I could control the liquor now and no one else had to know. A few times since Bill's death in 2004 loneliness has overwhelmed me like a flood, and I couldn't fight off the feelings of despair. I didn't realize that each time I turned to liquor for my comfort, I was taking another step away from my true strength that I have in Jesus. With the help of God, he let it come to a head where I had to face it.

One Saturday in February of 2009 my loneliness was getting to be more than I could bear, and a feeling that I needed a drink overwhelmed me. I thought I just had to go and buy some whiskey, get drunk, and sleep it off. I have been able to just let those thoughts go when they come, pray against it, and then the thought is gone and it has no power over me. In AA they tell us to dismiss the thought for having a drink, and to say the Serenity Prayer. I've done that in the past. "God grant me the serenity to accept the things I cannot change, the courage to change the things that I can, and the wisdom to know the difference." When I have taken the time to do that, the feeling that I need a drink goes away.

But that day I just stayed on the thought. I meditated on that thought until it was so strong in me that I grabbed a cab and went down to the liquor store. In the old days when I was drinking I could only handle one pint, and that was enough to get me drunk. For some reason or other I bought two pints.

When I got to my apartment I put on a nice big pot of coffee and opened one bottle and started sipping it with my coffee. Saturday night I drank the first pint without eating a thing. I did a pretty good job of finishing that little bottle and crawled into bed to sleep it off.

I woke up about five in the morning. I didn't have a hangover, and was ready to open the other bottle on Sunday morning. At about seven o' clock I called Mary Lou, "I don't think I'll go to church today. I'm not feeling very good." Mary Lou thanked me for calling. Then I went ahead with my drinking, without eating any breakfast or anything. I opened the second bottle and began sipping on that.

About two o' clock in the afternoon I decided I was hungry. As I began to open my refrigerator and get some food, I passed out. I fell down hitting the table, hitting the kitchen chair with my arm, and landed on the floor. My neighbors heard the crash when I fell. I tried and tried to get up, but was so drunk I couldn't.

All of a sudden I looked up, and there were people all around me. My neighbors had gotten the man who has the key to open all our doors. They came in, but they didn't know what to do.

I said, "Oh, I can't get up. I'm not feeling good."

My neighbors called the ambulance. Then they called Mary Lou Potts who is listed as my emergency contact. Mary Lou happened to be right next door. She and I always visited people in the nursing home next door to my apartment building every Sunday. When my neighbors called Mary Lou, she was visiting next door as usual and came right away.

I looked an awful mess. You would never have known me – no wig, hair flying all over, and wearing just a raggedy old shirt. The ambulance came, and the first thing you knew, I was in the hospital! Mary Lou came with me. They took all sorts of x-rays, and nothing was broken! When they were done checking me over, I fell asleep.

About two in the morning the thought hit me, "What have I done?" I felt so ashamed I started to cry! I didn't know what to do! I really felt like jumping out the window – make it the end. They had me tied down so I couldn't even get out of bed, but I had to go to the bathroom. I pressed the call button.

The nurse came in and asked, "What can I do for you?"

I said, "Oh, I'm so hungry. Can I take a shower? I smell so bad."

The nurse assured me they could get me a bite to eat. Then she helped me shower before the food came, helped me put on a clean gown, and I went back to bed. The nurse brought me some cheese, crackers, and milk and stuff. I ate that, and then fell back asleep.

At breakfast time about six o' clock, I woke up again. I called the nurse and apologized, "I'm so sorry; I don't even know what happened to me. I drank too much, and that's all I remember."

The nurse was really nice, and the aide brought me breakfast. A little later Mary Lou came to see me. I was sobbing and feeling so bad. Then the hospital sent in a lovely young woman who is a social worker. She said, "It's apparent that you're an alcoholic."

I agreed, "Yes, I am. I haven't had a drink for many years, but I fell off the wagon yesterday."

The social worker asked, "What are you going to do about it?"

I said, "I don't know. I just want to go home, and crawl into bed."

She said, "Are you going to go back to your group and tell them what happened?"

Well, that was pretty big to say to me right at that moment. I had intended on doing that, but in my time. So I said, "Well, I'll do that after I get home."

She said, "No, you have to do it right now."

I told the social worker I would call someone from my group and tell that person what happened, and then she left me.

So there I was; I had to make the call. I have a good buddy at AA who I figured would understand. Well, he fell out of the chair when I called him and told him. He fell right out! He fell down. He was shocked, because I had been sober for so long! I've been so faithful to attend AA.

I said, "I need you. Can you come over as soon as you can?"

He assured me he would be right over.

In the meantime I asked Mary Lou, "Call my friend Pastor Joe Haney in Great Falls. Ask him if he'll come to see me."

It happened that he was coming to Helena that morning. How God works so wonderfully! Mary Lou's call reached him as he was coming out the door of his home! Mary Lou said, "Bridget needs you."

Pastor Joe asked, "Oh, what's the matter?"

Mary Lou explained, "Well, she got drunk yesterday, she fell, and she's in the hospital. She wants you to come."

Pastor Joe said, "I was coming to Helena anyway." He had to pick up something. He assured us, "I'll be there pretty soon."

So I was sitting there with my two friends, telling them what happened. I was sobbing and felt so terrible. I asked Pastor Joe to pray for me, so we all prayed together.

I told my friend from AA, "I want to come back and face the group. It's going to be very difficult for me, but I have to do it. You'll have to wait until about Tuesday or Wednesday, because my arm is so bruised and painful."

Monday afternoon about four o' clock I was discharged from the hospital. Nothing was broken. Nothing was broken! I thought, "How wonderful God is! Even there he took care of me."

I went home and rested until Wednesday when I called my friend from AA, "Pick me up and we'll go to the meeting."

I prayed so hard, "Oh, dear God, how am I going to meet all these people?" It was like I was climbing a big mountain! When I arrived I asked the woman who was leading the AA meeting, "I wonder if I could speak for a few moments longer than our usual three or four minutes? I have a lot to say."

She said that would be okay, so I started telling them my story. There wasn't one dry-eyed person in the group. They loved me, and I love these people! I've worked with them! I felt so ashamed to tell them what I had done.

I began, "God saw me when I went to the liquor store. He knew what I was going to do. He knew I was going to buy two pints. He knew I was going to fall, but I wasn't going to break a bone. He knew all that. God allowed me to get that second pint, so things could come to a head and I'd be able to face reality."

My story took about twenty minutes. When I sat down I was worn out, but also relieved that I had gotten rid of those awful secrets and surrendered them to God. The lady sitting next to me was sobbing, sobbing, sobbing, "Oh Bridget, I'm so glad you paved the way for me. I was drunk this weekend, too, and I was *never* going to say a word to *anybody* about it! After I heard your story, I'm going to tell them that I got drunk, too."

Another person in AA said, "I've been keeping some secrets in my life, too. I don't tell every time I take a slip."

So right there, I thought, God is using me in this bad situation, turning it into good in someone else's life when I trust him. Right away, that's what he's using me for! It took courage to share my failure with my friends in AA, but it has opened up the way for them to be more honest with each other.

After the meeting everybody came and hugged me. As difficult as it was to face them, they thought it was wonderful that I had shared my struggles and even my failure. They realized I was a real person, and it took so much courage to be honest with them. I began to see that my openness about my struggles gave them hope. They were thinking, if God has restored her life, there might be hope for me, or for my family, or for my friends.

When I got back to my apartment, I thought of how God had touched my life again. I rededicated my life to God, "With your help, I know I never want to go through this again! Thank you for saving me, not letting me break anything, and I will get better from this." Then I decided I would also go to my church and tell them what I had done.

When Mary Lou picked me up the next Sunday for church, I told her, "Mary Lou, I'm going to get up in front of church and tell them my testimony."

The pastor allowed me to come up front and make my confession. Mary Lou held the mic for me while I was speaking so I wouldn't be distracted. Having her with me gave me some moral support as well. After I got done, more people than I ever thought knew me came up to me, surrounded me, and a lot of them were sobbing. They shared things with me that they have never shared with another person. "We have a son who is dying of drug addiction. We haven't seen him for a long time." "My mother has been lying in bed drinking for two years. She can hardly even get up, but she drinks every day." "My brother died in a car accident." All these people were coming to me and telling me their stories.

The devil meant it for evil, but God turned it around for good. Joseph, speaking about being sold into slavery in Egypt by his brothers said, "You intended to harm me, but God intended it for good to accomplish what is now being done, the saving of many lives."[83] Paul the apostle when encouraging New Testament believers in Rome not to become slaves again to sin, wrote, "And we know that in all things God works for the good of those who love him, who have been called according to his purpose."[84]

---

[83] Genesis 50:20, *NIV*
[84] Romans 8:28, *NIV*

Another Bible verse that has encouraged me to confess my sin publicly is, "Then you will know the truth, and the truth will set you free."[85] It has been so hard for me to tell about my struggles with alcohol, but by bringing the facts out, I feel like I have come from darkness where I was trying to hide my sin, into God's light where I can be free. God forgave me and gave me another chance. He gave me a brand new life again after I brought my sin into the open and he forgave me. God will always forgive us. That is why he sent his Son Jesus to die for us.

A lot of the reason why I gave in to drinking had to do with my grieving. I have grieved for so long. Grieving is a process that you have to live through. It has been hard for me, like going through a fire.

Ruth Thielke came to Helena in March of 2009 to help me work on the final touches for the book. We rented a car and drove to Billings to visit with Kit Elford, who ran the publishing arm of the mission in Canada for NCEM.

When I told about stumbling with my drinking to Kit and his wife Debbie, Kit said, "The grieving process is a lot like getting out of alcoholism. You've got to make a determination, 'I have done it long enough. I'm not going to do it anymore. Satan, I stand against you. This grieving is not normal anymore.' After so many years it does become *not normal*. You have to stand against the enemy. That's what it says in James 4:7-8: 'Resist the devil and he will flee from you. Come near to God, and he will come near to you.'

"Mom's going through the same thing you are after Dad passed away last fall," Kit said, "She's fine, but she needs the help and support around her as well. We all grieve differently. Before I produced the video of Dad's funeral, boy, I had three months before I could even look at it! I wouldn't even go look at him in his coffin. I wanted to remember him the way he was, not have my last picture of him lying in a coffin. But grieving comes to a point where it is not normal anymore. It becomes something that Satan has you bound up with that you have to be set free from."

Kit's wife Debbie agreed, "Especially when grief caused you to drink again. Grief depresses a person and affects how you react to things, to people, and your spiritual life. I have found that out from circumstances in our life that have affected me over the years. My

---

[85] John 8:32, *NIV*

worries and concerns will color everything I do, my relationship to the Lord, to my husband, and to other people. Worries are always in the back of my mind. If I allow myself to think of my worries, my thoughts go wild. Kit has been so good. He encourages me that he just wants me to be free in my thoughts. That clicked, and I have been better when I don't allow myself to dwell on destructive thinking. My spirit lifted, because my worries were a burden I was putting on myself. It helped when I decided to make a stand against the enemy."

Kit added, "God has given you a brand new life in everything. It isn't just overcoming the alcoholism. God has given you a brand new life in overcoming the grieving as well."

I agreed, "It has been a lot easier recently after I faced my grief. I know Bill is never coming back. I wanted him to come back. Every night I looked for him. Every little noise I would hear, I would think, 'Oh, there's Bill.' "

Debbie said, "You have that hope, though, that you will see Bill again in heaven."

"Oh, I know I will," I said.

Kit shared, "Kids grieve in much the same way, although not so much as a partner. Before Dad died, I talked to him every night on the phone for eight years. We discussed *everything*! After Dad died, I would pick up the phone in the evening to call Dad, and I would ask myself, 'What am I doing? I'm not going to get to heaven by phone.' That desire to talk to Dad every night is still there, but over time I began to realize, 'No, he's gone. We'll see him again.' "

"But it's hard; it's not easy," I told Kit. "It has never been easy for me to get over grief in my whole life. For my mother I cried for ten years."

Kit cautioned, "Well, don't do that again. Remember this passage:"

> Brothers, we do not want you to be ignorant about those who fall asleep, or to grieve like the rest of men, who have no hope. We believe that Jesus died and rose again and so we believe that God will bring with Jesus those who have fallen asleep in him. – 1 Thessalonians 4:13-14.

"That is true," I told Kit. "I didn't know Jesus when my mother died. No one cared about us after our parents died. It is one of the lies of the enemy that I would grieve like that again after Bill died.

I'm not going to grieve again like I did for my mother. It's much better now, but there was a time when I couldn't even talk about it. I have Bill's pictures all over in my house of him alive and well."

Debbie tried to understand, "You have been all by yourself. If you are reaching out to others, you forget about yourself."

"That's what I aim to do the rest of my life," I reassured her.

Then to get me on to a different track, Kit teased, "Maybe I should send home some books to help you learn some more Chipewyan."

"Oh, that Kit," I laughed. "I'm going to wring his neck one of these days." We all started laughing.

When we left Kit's house, Ruth and I drove to the little town of Dillon to visit my sister Rose. While we were in Dillon we attended the Baptist church on Sunday morning. The pastor's message was all about truth. He talked about Jesus saying he is the way the truth and the life. The sermon was filled with scriptures about truth and how truth sets us free. Ruth believes that God hand-picked that sermon for me that morning.

Back in Helena that week, Ruth encouraged me to share my fall in this book, because she said it would help people who are feeling weak in their struggle against alcoholism and other strongholds in their lives. In order for God to turn the things Satan meant for evil into good in our lives, we need to give even our failures to God and allow him to use our stories of how God was with us in the midst of our struggles. God was with me, and he brought me through this a stronger person. He surrounded me with the love and support of my friends when I confessed my sin and asked people to forgive me.

God isn't up in heaven wringing his hands wondering, "Oh, oh. What do I do now? Look what this person did; look what that person just did." God has figured out how to take care of us. Our sins are already paid for on the cross. We aren't just forgiven for our sins when we give our lives to Jesus. Jesus' blood also covered our sins that we commit after we belong to him. His forgiveness goes beyond understanding.

Satan wants us to believe that if we sin we can't go back to God, but I know that is a lie. Many people don't dare come back to God after they sin, because they think he is angry and will punish them. But the first place I go for strength is to God. I know he loves me and will wash away what I have done and help me feel free again. My testimony has been very difficult for me to go through. There are a lot of things I have had to try to forget – different things I did, the feelings of the abuse I had to get rid of. Now that I rededicated my life to the Lord, I want him to forgive me for all my past sins, and whatever slips I might have had even in thoughts. Even if you don't do it, it's already a sin if you are thinking about it. All these things I wanted God to erase from me, and forgive me for anything I have done wrong. If this part of my life can help anyone, I want to let you know that I have been there and have felt some of the feelings you have felt. When you feel there is no place else to go, turn up to the Lord. He will help you go on with life.

God has given me another chance. I decided to go forward with my life. I hope my book can touch a lot of people and give you courage and hope.

Bridget's Sisters and Brothers

"Be still, and know that I am God;
  I will be exalted among the nations,
  I will be exalted in the earth." Psalm 46:10 (*NIV*).

Wilhelmina Weams Campbell (Harris) McGurran – 1901-1986

After Papa retired and most of the family had left the north, in 1937 Lord Tweedsmuir, Governor General of Canada, came down the river. There was a large celebration for Lord Tweedsmuir in Fort Simpson as the people warmly received him and his traveling entourage to their little village. After the speeches had been made, in the midst of the festivities before the whole company, my sisters Wilhelmina and Mary presented Lord Tweedsmuir with a large white deerskin on which they had embroidered the whole map of Canada in silk work. It was an extraordinary work of art and a credit to the artistic skill in silk work Mama had patiently and lovingly passed on to her children.

Mary Owen (Harris) Villenueve – 1905-1939

My oldest sister Mary married and stayed at Fort Simpson. Mary was so thoughtful. She never forgot a birthday when we moved away. She remembered all the anniversaries. She made beautiful leather gloves and moccasins with silk work. We loved getting little letters from her, too. She was good like that.

We never saw Mary after we left the north.

Rachel Fowler (Harris) Martineau – 1907-1956

Mama's second oldest child was our sister Rachel, a very good cook. Rachel could make a meal out of practically nothing. God gave her the gift of cooking, because she had over ten children, and she raised her children the best way she could. Later on she even went out to clean houses, scrub floors, and iron for people to raise money to help make ends meet. They were poor, because times were tough when they were raising their children. Rachel raised a beautiful family, and somehow or other everybody survived with the help of God.

Charlotte Tremain (Harris) (Ennow) Piche – 1909-1981

My older sister Charlotte and her husband Dominick met each other in Cold Lake, Alberta, and they lived their whole life there. One of their sons got burned in a fire and died.

Charlotte and Dominick both drank whiskey trying to drown their sorrows, and in time they became alcoholics. I had been delivered from alcohol, so I began praying for my family, especially for Charlotte and Dominick. I prayed, and prayed, and prayed for them for many years.

I was so happy the day Charlotte called to tell me that she and Dominick had quit drinking. They never drank again. A miracle happened there.

Thaddeus Richmond Harris – 1912-1968

After Thad was in Minneapolis, he went back to the Northwest Territories where he worked in Fort Nelson with some of our relatives who owned barges. In 1968 as they were traveling along, he fell when he jumped from one barge to another. The two barges came together and crushed him. Thad died from that accident. How we missed our brother Thad! He had an adventurous, light-hearted, playful spirit.

James DeLapp Harris – 1916-2004

Jim was a good hunter and trapper, and made a living as a guide part of the time. When he wasn't guiding he found jobs as a skilled construction worker and did pretty well for himself, but Jim lived a sad and lonely life.

Eventually he married an Indian girl who was a Hare Indian from Fort Good Hope, and they had lots of kids. Later they moved to Inuvik, which is another village further north on the Mackenzie. Jim helped build a round church there that is shaped like an igloo.

Jim relocated to Edmonton after his recovery from the burns received from the plane accident. After Jim's wife died, his children still visited him. We enjoyed some good times together with Jim and his children in Edmonton. Jim died on April 13, 2004. I was unable to make it to Jim's funeral, because he died just one month before my husband Bill.

Nora (Harris) Matchatis – 1921 –

Nora, who had attended the boarding school with me at Fort Providence, lived on the reserve near Cold Lake all of her adult life. Nora had to carry on after her husband Ben got sick and passed away. Nora learned to sew and do silk work from our mother. Nora makes the most beautiful moccasins, vests, and beadwork for sale. I always love buying things from her to give as gifts. She also made a lot of the clothes for her family.

196

Nora had ten children in Cold Lake, and they all went to the Blue Quills Catholic School in St. Paul, Alberta run by the nuns. It was a pretty good school compared to the school at Fort Providence.

Joyce Metchewais, Nora's first child, is a registered nurse and served as chief. Nora's other children are Shirley Cardinal, Marlene Matchatis, Cecilia Matchatis, Bridget Matchatis, Kenneth Matchatis, Valerie Wood, Wayne Matchatis, Dale, Matchatis, Conrad Matchatis, and Connie Santos. Shirley earned her diploma in Management Studies. Cecilia earned both a Bachelor of Administration and a Bachelor of Arts with a diploma in Child Care. Valerie earned her Bachelor of Arts in Linguistics and Anthropology with a Diploma in Child Care. Connie Santos earned her Bachelor of Arts in Psychology and Sociology and also completed a diploma in hair dressing.

The second to the youngest, Connie Santos, was the first to earn the Bachelor of Arts degree. Among her many accomplishments she is the Supervisor for the Alberta Children's Services. She is a published co-author in a professional journal.

Valerie Wood, the youngest is currently employed as the Director of Child and Family Services in Saddle Lake. Valerie has published works in linguistics and teaches the Dene language.

Nora also adopted Joan McVay in her heart. Joan was the child of a Caucasian family in Cold Lake. Nora loved Joan as if she was Nora's own daughter.

Nora's sons Kenny and Wayne are still living. The youngest son, Conrad, died suddenly. A documentary film featuring Nora and her family was produced by public television in California depicting the life of the Indians on the reserves in Canada. In the film they showed the funeral procession of our family making their way to the grave in the falling snow, with Nora's son Wayne leading Conrad's riderless horse. After Conrad died, I wrote him a letter to pour out on paper what I was feeling in my heart.

In Memory of Conrad

> He heals the broken-hearted and binds up their wounds.
> He counts the number of the stars and calls them each by name.
> -- Psalm 147:3-4 (*NIV*).

Since you were a little boy, you loved horses. You rode to your heart's content until you became a man. You were very close to your mama Nora and lived with her to help her out. Your health was not so good, and yet you worked so well and so hard every day.

Your sisters loved you. You were the very best babysitter they ever had, and they could trust you with their little ones. You never said, "No", to anyone. You were always willing to help. Many a night you stayed over at your sister's house when you babysat.

You never failed to let your mama Nora know where you were. One morning when you didn't call or come home, after many phone calls to you from your mama Nora, she went to your sister's house and found the door open. It looked like you had left in a hurry. There was no trace of you at all.

The Mounties came with dogs and searched for you many times and could not find you. For seven months you were gone. Many prayed for you daily, not knowing where you were. Your brother Kenny searched for you every day without fail. One day, he discovered part of your clothing. Immediately the Royal Canadian Mounted Police were sent for, and they discovered your remains in the area where your clothes were found. Needless to say, it was very sad; they concluded that you had a heart attack.

Conrad, Jesus called you that day to come to the beautiful place in Heaven prepared for you. You are sadly missed by all, but never forgotten. Many times when Mama Nora and all your family get together they remember you with a lot of fondness and love. Mama Nora remembers you with a song in her heart that says, "You are Mine, All Mine," and now Jesus says to you, "You are Mine, All Mine!"

The day you were buried, you had a beautiful service and your brother Wayne led your favorite horse ahead to the cemetery. Many a tear was shed that memorable day when you were laid to rest. Only then could healing take place in our hearts. So, Conrad dear, this is Auntie Bridget's way of saying I loved you, too. Just a short story filled with love to remember you by.

In Jesus' Name, Your Aunt Bridget

Nora's Daughter Joyce

After completing high school with honors, Joyce wanted to continue with her schooling, but she came down with tuberculosis. She was sick for quite awhile. After she recuperated, she married Maynard Metchewais. They had three sons and they adopted one of her sister's babies, a little girl who she raised as her very own.

When her children grew up, Joyce was able to finish college in Edmonton with her daughter. In Edmonton Joyce graduated from college as a full-fledged Registered Nurse. She did good work as a nurse, and the people loved her, because she could speak our language. She had been a nurse for a few years at Cold Lake and on our reserve at Onion Lake when they elected her to be a chief for a couple of terms on our reserve.

198

Bridget and Joyce in Joyce's office as chief

Joyce was a wonderful chief, building roads, cleaning up all the debts that had been left by the previous chiefs, helping the elderly by building homes for them, and making sure their utilities were paid. As chief Joyce employed quite a few good, honest, hard-working people on her staff.

Joyce attends church faithfully; she has given her life to Jesus, and has lived a very good life. Joyce and her husband built a beautiful home. Inside the front door is a big dining area with a big kitchen. It has a master bedroom, guest bedroom, an office, a large living room, and a nice big porch. The floors are beautiful hardwood. There are great big windows in the house. The land she is on is about a mile from where she was born. The land is so fertile. There have never been chemicals or anything used on it. Her family all live around her. Her son lives half a block away in a nice home.

Rose Marie (Harris) Foote - 1924-

Rose now lives in Dillon, Montana, close enough for me to visit her now and then. When Rose and Ward first moved to Montana, they made friends with a woman by the name of Georgine. Ward is gone now, but Georgine remained Rose's close friend and also became a good friend of mine. When I visited Rose in Dillon, Georgine let me stay with her sometimes in her mobile home. We were sad to lose Georgine in the winter of 2008. Rose and I call each other and stay in touch.

I am so thankful for Rose inviting me to come to Minneapolis when I was living in New York. If it hadn't been for that phone call, I would never have met Bill. Through my relationship to Bill, I gave my life to Jesus and was set free from alcohol. Bill and I had many good visits with Rose and Ward over the years. She helped me feel connected to my family, who are so important to me.

John (Jack) Patrick Harris - one of the twins - 1928-1996

One of my deepest regrets when I was in New York was that I had not been able to take my brothers out of the orphanage. The orphanage only kept them until they were sixteen, so the twins, Jack and Bill, went into the world, and did the best they could. They both worked very hard. Jack went to the west coast in British Columbia where he became a lumber jack and married a really nice Indian girl. They had about three children, and he was doing well to begin with. Jack never came to visit us in Minneapolis, but I visited him in Vancouver. When he got older, he moved away from Vancouver and the family lost track of him.

It was a sad day when I got a call from his daughter that she found out Jack had died. I had to comfort Jack's children. I told them they could remember their dad by having a service for him at their church. Then perhaps they could plant a tree in his name and beautiful rose bushes in their mother's garden. I had heard other people say that was a way to remember their loved one. That's what they did, and it helped ease their grief.

Thomas William (Bill) Harris - one of the twins - 1928-2000

When Bill left the orphanage, he studied how to build homes to became a contractor. He married a woman in Edmonton, they had a couple of children, and he did really well with his building trade.

After a few years, Bill went to British Columbia to be close to Jack. He found work, but when his wife wasn't willing to join him they eventually divorced. Bill married another lady in British Columbia, and they had quite a few children.

After Bill's divorce, his first wife didn't let their children know what happened to Bill. Their oldest daughter Barbara began searching for Bill. Barbara worked in Edmonton in a jewelry store. One day Nora happened to go to that jewelry store with a couple of her daughters from Cold Lake to have a piece of jewelry fixed. When Barbara saw Nora's address on the check, she said, "My dad, Bill Harris, was from Cold Lake. Maybe you have heard of him."

Nora began to cry as she told Barbara, "Bill Harris is my brother!" Pretty soon they were all crying and hugging each other. Our family had also lost track of Bill, but Barbara began visiting Nora's family on the reserve who she had never known.

Barbara kept searching for her dad until in her late twenties she found him in a hospital in Vancouver, British Columbia. He had been having strokes. Barbara was so happy to find her dad, that she relocated to Vancouver, and went to school there. Every day she visited Bill at the hospital. He lived for about a year after she found him, allowing enough time for Barbara to get acquainted with Bill. Barbara also got to know Bill's second family when they came to visit him in the hospital.

I happened to be visiting Bill in Vancouver at the time of Bill's death, so I was able to be with his family at his death and at his funeral in Cold Lake on September 16, 2000. They had his body brought back to be buried on the reserve right next to our mother.

Barbara had also been involved in drugs, so she understood Bill and accepted her dad for who he was. Barbara had given her life to Jesus, who gave her strength to overcome her life in drugs and alcohol. After she finished college, she became a counselor to help people who struggle with addictions.

Charles Edward (Ned) Harris – 1933 –

My youngest brother Ned was also in the boys' home in Edmonton until he was sixteen. Then they sent him out of the home to learn a trade. He worked on a farm. He began drinking and spent many of his years in and out of jail due to alcohol.

Ned married a woman from Cold Lake and they had a beautiful daughter, but he couldn't support his family. He lived a sad life in Edmonton. Whenever I traveled to Cold Lake I spent a day in Edmonton going down the avenue where a lot of people would be drinking wondering if Ned might be there. I wasn't afraid as I walked along trying to find Ned, but I didn't know where he hung out.

God has his ways of bringing people to us in His time. Ned was on a drunk a couple of years ago on the LeGoff Reserve, and he fell down, because he had such a bad leg. Someone picked him up on the road and took him to the hospital in Cold Lake. The hospital got in touch with Nora, and she phoned to tell me. We were glad that he got to Cold Lake and that he was being cared for. When he was

Ned Harris

released from the hospital, Joyce was able to get Ned a place to live in the lodge, and she still looks after Ned's finances.

Ned has a very tender heart, and he inherited Papa's good sense of Irish humor. He laughs at himself. It has been a joy to visit him and tell him various aspects of our home life. Ned was only nine years old when Papa died.

Returning Home

For as high as the heavens are above the earth,
   so great is his love for those who fear him;
As far as the east is from the west,
   so far has he removed our transgressions from us.
   Psalm 103:11-12 (*NIV*)

Nora, Rose, and Me visiting Fort Simpson

"Letting Go"
By Bridget Volden

All of life seems to say
   Let go of yesterday
      Hang onto life, which is today.
         Be what you are no matter what *They* say.

I come from a place
   Where they always say *ay*.
      Which rhymes with gray
      A color I hate,
         But what can I say,
         It's here to stay.

Our beautiful home in Fort Simpson had gotten old and had been removed to make way for newer construction. The house should never have been torn down, but during the demolition an old trapper by the name of Faille saw that the house was in very good

203

condition. Faille was sort of a bush man. He was a white trapper, hunter and guide who had spent most of his life in the wilds. When he was old, he wanted to retire on the Mackenzie River. He hadn't found a place to live, so he asked the people tearing down our house to save the kitchen for him. He bought that one little piece of the big house and had it moved down by the river bank.

Years later my sisters Nora and Rose decided we should all make a trip back to Fort Simpson to visit the home of our childhood. Rose met me in Helena, Montana, and we traveled together to visit our relatives in Fort Nelson. Nora who still lives in Cold Lake, Alberta, met us in Fort Nelson, and the three of us traveled together the rest of the way along the Mackenzie River to Fort Simpson. We have a lot of relatives in Fort Simpson.

A man who was in charge of the newspaper heard that T. W. Harris's daughters were visiting, so he offered to drive us all over town. As he drove us around, he said, "I've got to show you a little museum right on the river."

They made a museum out of Albert Faille's house. They left his house just as it was the day he died. His tea pot was still half full. His moccasins were on the floor by the bed. The bed was unmade. When we walked into his little house at the museum, we didn't recognize it from the outside. But when we stepped inside, we had a sense of, "We've been here before!"

"Ah!" I said to Nora and Rose, "Look! It's our kitchen!" Even the same light red paint was on the ceiling just as it had been when we lived there.

Our host was so happy! He said, "I wondered if you would recognize it."

As we looked around we said, "Yes, this was our kitchen." Mama's stove was there in the same spot, and a little old table and chairs were just the same. The old trapper certainly wasn't as good a housekeeper as Mama, but it was fun to see at least part of our house again.

I visit my people in Cold Lake every year at treaty time. When the treaties were first made, only full-blooded Indians were entitled to treaty payments. But our papa, the Famous Flynn Harris, worked hard to convince the government that the Métis, or Indians who were half-blooded, needed to be included in the treaty payments. The government treated Papa as their best expert in Indian affairs, so he was able to convince enough members of Parliament to have the law changed way back in the 1920's.

When I am in Cold Lake I stay with my niece Joyce Metchewais (sounds like Met-chew-as). Now that Joyce has completed her terms as chief she is resting from those responsibilities, but she is still an active member of her community.

The place where our home in Cold Lake once stood down by the lake was bought by a developer. There are million dollar houses on that piece of property.

Treaty 11 that Papa worked so hard to protect is still in effect. For as long as the Indians live and as long as the land shall last, the Indian people can hunt, trap, and fish on their reserves and receive their five dollar treaty payment each year. By now treaty payments are more of a ceremony, a cause for celebrating together once a year. At treaty time there are all kinds of festivities with games and a big pavilion where they can dance. There are no drugs, and no alcohol of any kind is allowed. It's really nice right by the lake where they pitch their tents, and some bring their travel trailers.

My siblings and I still collect our five dollars each year. I fly from Helena to Edmonton. Rose (Kostashen) Kokotovich and her mother are still alive and to this day they are still my friends. Rose is filled with cancer now, but whenever I go to Edmonton, I usually go stay with her. Her mother is over one hundred years old and is in an assisted living home, but still flits around. Even though she was only a few years older than me, I called her "Ma".

My niece Joyce and my sister Nora pick me up with their car in Edmonton and we drive the three hours to Cold Lake. When family members see me, they cry, "Oh, you bring back so many memories – my relatives!" One fellow always cries with the tears just rolling down his face when he sees me. It feels wonderful to be so loved by my people!

But the cry of my heart is that my people, all the native born in Canada and the U.S., will experience the joy and freedom I have found in a living relationship with Jesus Christ. Some people think Jesus is the white man's God, but it is not so. *He Who Made the Earth* through the miraculous work of the Holy Spirit is Jesus' father and Jesus' mother Mary was a descendent of Abraham from Israel. Her people living in the Middle East are Asian, not Caucasian. My people came to America through Alaska from Asia. In that sense Jesus is more the God of the Indian than the God of the white man, but it doesn't work that way.

Jesus' mother Mary represented all mankind. In the New Testament it is written that Abraham is the Father of all who believe in Jesus, whether Jew or Gentile. Whether we are Catholic or Protestant, non-denominational or no religion, Jesus loved each one of us enough to die in our place so that we could live with him in heaven forever. There is forgiveness for each one of us, and wonderful peace as Jesus washes away our sins with his precious blood that he shed freely on the cross for us all. Our part is to recognize our sin, and accept his death in full payment for our sin as we give our life to him.

As I near the end of my days, my dearest prayer and hope is that I will see each of you with me in heaven some day. Some of my family called me preachy, and some called me bossy, but I want you to know what is in my heart. I was left with the responsibility of caring for my brothers and sisters who were still at home when Mama and Papa died. I never had children of my own, but all of my life I have wanted to make a home for others. This is also in Jesus' heart. He has prepared a home and is waiting for us in heaven. If we will just give him our hearts and our lives, we can be with him and with each other in heaven forever.

If you would like to pray that prayer we prayed in The Fellowship, I have reprinted it here to help you to find it again:

> Lord, I know my life has been heading down the wrong road that has led to pain and suffering for me and my family. I confess all of my wrongdoing to you as sin. I am giving you my whole life just as I am, because I trust you as my Savior and Lord. I want you to be my God. You already paid for my sin with Jesus' blood that he shed on the cross. I accept that gift. Now use my life in the way that you have planned for me. Thank you, Lord. From now on I belong to you. Amen.

Appendix 1

Prime Minister Stephen Harper's Apology on behalf of Canada for Indian Residential Schools – House of Commons, June 11, 2008

Mr. Speaker, I stand before you today to offer an apology to former students of residential schools. The treatment of children in Indian Residential Schools[86] is a sad chapter in our history.

For more than a century, Indian Residential Schools separated over 150,000 Aboriginal children from their families and communities. In the 1870's, the federal government, partly in order to meet its obligation to educate Aboriginal children, began to play a role in the development and administration of these schools. Two primary objectives of the Residential Schools system were to remove and isolate children from the influence of their homes, families, traditions and cultures, and to assimilate them into the dominant culture. These objectives were based on the assumption that Aboriginal cultures and spiritual beliefs were inferior and unequal. Indeed, some sought, as it was infamously said, "to kill the Indian in the child". Today, we recognize that this policy of assimilation was wrong, has caused great harm, and has no place in our country.

One hundred and thirty-two federally-supported schools were located in every province and territory, except Newfoundland, New Brunswick and Prince Edward Island. Most schools were operated as "joint ventures" with Anglican, Catholic, Presbyterian or United Churches. The Government of Canada built an educational system in which very young children were often forcibly removed from their homes, often taken far from their communities. Many were inadequately fed, clothed and housed. All were deprived of the care and nurturing of their parents, grandparents and communities. First Nations, Inuit and Métis languages and cultural practices were prohibited in these schools. Tragically, some of these children died while attending residential schools and others never returned home.

The government now recognizes that the consequences of the Indian Residential Schools policy were profoundly negative and that this policy has had a lasting and damaging impact on Aboriginal culture, heritage and language. While some former students have spoken positively about their experiences at residential schools, these

---

[86] Used by permission. Also part of Public Domain.

stories are far overshadowed by tragic accounts of the emotional, physical and sexual abuse and neglect of helpless children, and their separation from powerless families and communities.

The legacy of Indian Residential Schools has contributed to social problems that continue to exist in many communities today.

It has taken extraordinary courage for the thousands of survivors that have come forward to speak publicly about the abuse they suffered. It is a testament to their resilience as individuals and to the strengths of their cultures. Regrettably, many former students are not with us today and died never having received a full apology from the Government of Canada.

The government recognizes that the absence of an apology has been an impediment to healing and reconciliation. Therefore, on behalf of the Government of Canada and all Canadians, I stand before you, in this Chamber so central to our life as a country, to apologize to Aboriginal peoples for Canada's role in the Indian Residential Schools system.

To the approximately 80,000 living former students, and all family members and communities, the Government of Canada now recognizes that it was wrong to forcibly remove children from their homes and we apologize for having done this. We now recognize that it was wrong to separate children from rich and vibrant cultures and traditions, that it created a void in many lives and communities, and we apologize for having done this. We now recognize that, in separating children from their families, we undermined the ability of many to adequately parent their own children and sowed the seeds for generations to follow, and we apologize for having done this. We now recognize that, far too often, these institutions gave rise to abuse or neglect and were inadequately controlled, and we apologize for failing to protect you. Not only did you suffer these abuses as children, but as you became parents, you were powerless to protect your own children from suffering the same experience, and for this we are sorry.

The burden of this experience has been on your shoulders for far too long. The burden is properly ours as a Government, and as a country. There is no place in Canada for the attitudes that inspired the Indian Residential Schools system to ever prevail again. You have been working on recovering from this experience for a long time and in a very real sense, we are now joining you on this journey. The Government of Canada sincerely apologizes and asks the forgiveness of the Aboriginal peoples of this country for failing them so profoundly.

Nous le regrettons
We are sorry
Nimitataynan
Niminchinowesamin
Mamiattugut

In moving towards healing, reconciliation and resolution of the sad legacy of Indian Residential Schools, the implementation of the Indian Residential Schools Settlement Agreement began on September 19, 2007. Years of work by survivors, communities, and Aboriginal organizations culminated in an agreement that gives us a new beginning and an opportunity to move forward together in partnership.

A cornerstone of the Settlement Agreement is the Indian Residential Schools Truth and Reconciliation Commission. This Commission presents a unique opportunity to educate all Canadians on the Indian Residential Schools system. It will be a positive step in forging a new relationship between Aboriginal peoples and other Canadians, a relationship based on the knowledge of our shared history, a respect for each other and a desire to move forward together with a renewed understanding that strong families, strong communities and vibrant cultures and traditions will contribute to a stronger Canada for all of us. God bless all of you. God bless our land.

National Chief of the Assembly of First Nations Phil Fontaine's response to the apology:

Prime Minister, Chief Justice, members of this house, elders, survivors, Canadians: For our parents, our grandparents, and great-grandparents – indeed for all of the generations that have preceded us – this day testifies to nothing less than the achievement of the impossible. This morning our elders held a condolence ceremony for those who never heard an apology, never received compensation, yet courageously fought assimilation so that we could witness this day. Together we remember and honor them, for it was they who suffered the most as they witnessed generation after generation of their children taken from their family's love and guidance. For the generations that will follow us we bear witness today in this house that our survival as First Nations peoples in this land is affirmed forever. Therefore the significance of this day is not just about what has been, but equally important, what is to come. Never again will this house consider us "the Indian problem" just for being who we are. We heard the government of Canada take full responsibility for this dreadful chapter in our shared history. We heard the Prime Minister declare that this will never happen again. *Finally* we heard Canada say it is sorry. Brave survivors through the telling of their painful stories have stripped white supremacy of its authority and legitimacy. The irresistibility of speaking truth to power is real. Today is not the result of a political game. Instead it is something that shows the righteousness and importance of our struggle. We know we have many difficult issues to handle. There are many fights still to be fought. What happened today signifies a new dawn in the relationship between us and the rest of Canada. We are and always have been an indispensible part of the Canadian identity. Our peoples, our history, and our present being are the essence of Canada. The attempts to erase our identities hurt us deeply, but it also hurt all Canadians and impoverished the character of this nation. We must not falter in our duty now. Emboldened by this spectacle of history it is possible to end our racial nightmare together. The memories of residential schools sometimes cut like merciless knives at our souls. This day will help us to put that pain behind us. But it signifies something even more important: a respectful and therefore liberating relationship between us and the rest of Canada. Together we can achieve the greatness our country deserves. The apology today is founded upon more than anything else the recognition that we all own our own lives and destinies, the only true foundation for a society where peoples can flourish. We must now capture a new spirit and vision to meet the challenges of the future. As a great statesman once said, "We are all part of one garment of destiny. The differences between us are not blood or color, and the ties that bind us are deeper than those that separate us." The common root of hope will bring us to reconciliation more than any words, laws, or legal claims ever could. We still have to struggle, but now we are in this together. I reach out to all Canadians today in this spirit of reconciliation. *Me gwet.*[87]

---

[87] "Thank you" in Cree.

Appendix 2: The Harris Family[88]

Generation 1

Lieutenant James Harris, born April 4, 1673 in Boston, Massachusetts and died in Connecticut in February, 1757 at age 83. Lt. Harris served as an officer in the British army in the American Colonies.

Generation 2

Lebbeus Harris, seventh child of Lt. James Harris, moved from Connecticut to Horton (now Kentville) Nova Scotia in 1761 as part of the loyalist repopulation of the area. Lebbeus was given an officer's commission in a company of militia in Kings County upon his arrival in 1761. From 1761 to 1765, Lebbeus Harris represented Horton [Kentville] in the provincial Legislature. He also served as a Justice of the Peace in 1768 and again in 1783. Lebbeus Harris was appointed Judge of the Inferior Court of Common Pleas for Kings County in 1783 and again in 1788. In addition to managing large tracts of highly productive farm land, Lebbeus owned one of the large mercantile stores in Horton.

Generation 3

Thaddeus Harris was the fifth child of Lebbeus and Alice Harris. When his father's mercantile burned, several important records stored there including records for the township of Horton [Kentville] and the records for his church that he kept as clerk of the vestry were destroyed in the fire. The store was rebuilt and became one of the major stores in Kentville, remaining in the family for several generations.

Generation 4

The Hon. James Delap Harris, long one of the leading merchants in Kentville, and his wife Wilhelmina, a woman of lovely character, were for many years considered among the most important people in Kings County, and indeed in the province of Nova Scotia. He was one of the two early successful Kentville merchants along with Caleb Handley Rand. His wife, Wilhelmina Wemyss Campbell, was the daughter of Col. William Campbell of Cornwallis, Nova Scotia. Col.

---

[88] Most of this information is taken from *The History of Kings County*, by Arthur Wentworth Hamilton Eaton, M. A., D. C. L. (The Salem Press Co., Salem, Mass.: 1918) Facsimile edition printed by Mika Studio, ISBN 0-919302-49-1, Belleville, Ontario, 1972. Also available on the web.

Campbell from Scotland was Judge of the Superior Court of Nova Scotia and Judge of Probate for Kings County for many years.

The Hon. James Delap Harris was appointed Judge of the Inferior Court of Common Pleas for Kings County in 1840. He was appointed Justice of the Peace in 1825 and again in 1843. In 1843 he was also appointed a Commissioner in Kings County for taking special bail. Judge Harris lived in one of the four most conspicuous houses in Kings County, built in the style of an Italian villa. His family attended St. John's, an Anglican Church in Cornwallis.

Generation 5

Rachel Ana Harris, second daughter of the Hon. James Delap Harris, a gentle, cultivated, charitable woman, and a devoted, unselfish friend, was deeply loved by citizens of Kings County.

Thomas William Harris, Barrister and Attorney, Q. C., was the fourth child of the Hon. James Delap Harris. Flynn's father was appointed Barrister in Kings County in 1860, 1867, and 1876. Thomas William Harris, Sr. married Marie Sophia Fowler. Their eight children included: John Inglis Harris, Thaddeus Harris, Frances Harris, Wilhelmina Wemyss Harris, James Harris, Mary Owen Harris, Thomas William (Flynn) Harris, and a child who died young.

Generation 6

Wilhelmina Wemyss Harris and her sister, Mary Owen Harris, left home to became cloistered nuns.

T. W. (Flynn) Harris, born in Kentville, Nova Scotia, February 12, 1861. Flynn Harris left home at the age of 13 to join a monastery in Montreal where he was educated to become a priest, but not ordained. Flynn headed west to Alberta where he married Judith Scani on October 18, 1892. Flynn and Judith had two daughters, Francoise Sara Harris, September 18, 1895, and Wilhelmina Weams Campbell Harris, February 18, 1901, both born in Cold Lake, Alberta. Judith died of TB on January 18, 1902. Flynn married Josette Enedzhiy Janvier on September 27, 1902. Flynn and Josette had four children in Fort Chippewyan: Mary Owen Harris, April 12, 1905; Rachel Fowler Harris, May 31, 1907; Charlotte Tremain Harris, August 18, 1909; and Thaddeus Richmond Harris, July 11, 1912. Their next three children were born in Fort Simpson: James DeLapp Harris, December 21, 1916; Bridget Angela Harris, April 16, 1919, and Nora Harris, May 31, 1921. Rose Marie Harris was born in LeGoff at Josette's family home near Cold Lake on December 28,

1924. A set of twin boys were also born in Fort Simpson: John (Jack) Patrick Harris and Thomas William (Bill) Harris, June 10, 1928. Their last child, Charles Edward (Ned) Harris was born after Flynn retired in Cold Lake on December 11, 1933.